T0297779

RDF Database Systems
TRIPLES STORAGE AND SPARQL QUERY PROCESSING

RDF Database Systems
TRIPLES STORAGE AND SPARQL QUERY PROCESSING

Edited by

OLIVIER CURÉ
Associate Professor of Computer Science,
Université Paris Est Marne la Vallée and
Université Pierre et Marie Curie, France

GUILLAUME BLIN
Professor of Computer Science,
Université de Bordeaux, France

ELSEVIER

Amsterdam • Boston • Heidelberg • London
New York • Oxford • Paris • San Diego
San Francisco • Singapore • Sydney • Tokyo
Morgan Kaufmann is an Imprint of Elsevier

Executive Editor: Steve Elliot
Editorial Project Manager: Kaitlin Herbert
Project Manager: Anusha Sambamoorthy
Designer: Mark Rogers

Morgan Kaufmann is an imprint of Elsevier
225 Wyman Street, Waltham, MA 02451, USA

First edition 2015

Copyright © 2015 Elsevier Inc. All rights reserved.

No part of this publication may be reproduced, stored in a retrieval system
or transmitted in any form or by any means electronic, mechanical, photocopying,
recording or otherwise without the prior written permission of the publisher

Permissions may be sought directly from Elsevier's Science & Technology Rights
Department in Oxford, UK: phone (+44) (0) 1865 843830; fax (+44) (0) 1865 853333;
email: permissions@elsevier.com. Alternatively you can submit your request online by
visiting the Elsevier web site at http://elsevier.com/locate/permissions, and selecting
Obtaining permission to use Elsevier material.

Notice
No responsibility is assumed by the publisher for any injury and/or damage to persons
or property as a matter of products liability, negligence or otherwise, or from any use
or operation of any methods, products, instructions or ideas contained in the material
herein. Because of rapid advances in the medical sciences, in particular, independent
verification of diagnoses and drug dosages should be made.

Library of Congress Cataloging-in-Publication Data
Curé, Olivier.
  RDF database systems : triples storage and SPARQL query processing / by Olivier Curé,
Guillaume Blin. — First edition.
    pages cm
  Includes index.
  ISBN 978-0-12-799957-9 (paperback)
  1. Database management. 2. RDF (Document markup language) 3. Query languages (Computer
science) 4. Querying (Computer science) I. Blin, Guillaume. II. Title.
  QA76.9.D3C858 2015
  005.74 — dc23
                                                                          2014034632

British Library Cataloguing in Publication Data
A catalogue record for this book is available from the British Library

For information on all Morgan Kaufmann publications
visit our website at http://store.elsevier.com/

This book has been manufactured using Print On Demand technology. Each copy is produced to order
and is limited to black ink. The online version of this book will show color figures where appropriate.

ISBN: 978-0-12-799957-9

Working together
to grow libraries in
developing countries

www.elsevier.com • www.bookaid.org

CONTENTS

LIST OF FIGURES AND TABLES

PREFACE

In 1999, the *World Wide Web Consortium* (W3C) published a first recommendation on the *Resource Description Framework* (RDF) language. Since its inception, this technology is considered the cornerstone of the *Semantic Web* and *Web of Data* movements. Its goal is to enable the description of resources that are uniquely identified by *uniform resource identifiers* (URIs), for example, `http://booksite.mkp.com`. Recently, RDF has gained a lot of attention, and as a result an increasing number of data sets are now being represented with this language. With this popularity came the need to efficiently store, query and reason over large amounts of RDF data. This has obviously motivated some research work on the design of adapted and efficient data management systems. These systems, frequently referred to as *RDF stores*, *triple stores*, or *RDF data management systems*, must handle a data model that takes the form of a directed labeled graph where nodes are URIs or literals (e.g., character strings) and edges are URIs. This data model is quite different from the currently popular relational model encountered in a *relational database management system* (RDBMS). But RDF stores have other features that make their design a challenging task. In the following, we present four major features that differentiate RDF stores with other data management systems.

The first feature is related to the data model of RDF, which is composed of triples corresponding to a subject, a property, and an object, where the subject takes an object as a value for a property. A set of triples is characterized by the omnipresence of URIs at the three positions of RDF statements, although over forms can also be used, e.g., literals at the object position. The fact that a given URI can be repeated multiple times in a data set and that URIs are generally long strings of characters raises some memory footprint issues. Therefore, the use of efficient dictionaries—encoding URIs with identifiers that are used for the representation of triples—is crucial in triple stores, while in relational models a suitable database schema minimizes such data redundancy.

The second feature is that a data management system requires a language to query the data it contains. For this purpose, the Semantic Web group at the W3C has published the *SPARQL Protocol and RDF Query Language* (SPARQL) recommendation; one of its main aspects is to support a query language. Although some clauses such as SELECT and WHERE make it look like the popular *Structured Query Language* (SQL) language of RDBMS, SPARQL is based on the notion of triples and not on relations. Answering a SPARQL query implies some pattern-matching mechanisms between the triples of the query and the data set. This requires research in the field of query processing and optimization that goes beyond the state of the art of the relational model.

The third feature concerns vocabularies associated to RDF data sets. The most predominant ones are *RDF Schema* (RDFS) and *Web Ontology Language* (OWL), both of which enable the ability to reason over RDF data—that is, they enable the discovery of implicit data from explicitly represented ones.

The final feature is that RDF data is concerned with the *Big Data* phenomenon, which induces the distribution of data sets over clusters of machines. The graph nature of the RDF data model makes the distribution a challenging task that has to be understood in an inference-enabled context.

This book aims at presenting the fundamentals on all these features by introducing both the main concepts and techniques, as well as the principal research problems that emerge in the ecosystem of RDF database management systems. The presentations are based on the study of a large number of academic and commercial products. It is important to understand that the fulfillment of the Semantic Web vision largely depends on the emergence of robust, efficient, and feature-complete RDF stores.

WHO SHOULD READ THIS BOOK

The book targets a wide range of readers. We consider that technology practitioners, including developers, project leaders, and database professionals, will find a comprehensive survey of existing commercial and open-source systems that will help them to select a system in a given application implementation context. We also consider that students and teachers could use this book for lectures in Semantic Web and knowledge representation, as well as for advanced database courses. In fact, the idea of providing a textbook for our master's students at the University of Paris Est was one of the motivations for starting this work. Finally, researchers in both the Semantic Web and database fields will find in this book a comprehensive and comparative overview of an active research domain. Indeed, we were in need for such an overview when we started our work on the **roStore** and **WaterFowl** RDF stores.

ORGANIZATION OF THE BOOK

This book is organized in two parts composed of short chapters to support an efficient and easy reading. The first part defines the scope of the book but also motivates and introduces the importance of efficiently handling RDF data. To make the book self-contained, it also provides background knowledge on both database management systems and Semantic Web technologies.

With these notions understood, readers can delve into the second part of the book, which investigates an important number of existing systems based on the criteria we have defined: the definition of an RDF dictionary, backend storage of RDF triples, indexation, query processing, reasoning, distribution of workloads, and query federation. We dedicate one chapter per criteria for easier reading of the book. With this structure, for example, a reader can learn about a given aspect of RDF stores in Chapter 4 on RDF dictionaries without searching through the complete book. This approach imposes that the different components of important systems are detailed in different chapters—for example, the *RDF-3X* system is discussed in Chapters 4–6. At the end of each chapter we provide a summary list of the main notions studied.

Finally, the book concludes and anticipates on future trends in the domain of RDF storage and the Semantic Web.

GUIDELINES FOR USING THIS BOOK

We identify three distinct readings of this book that are mainly motivated by a reader's expertise in either database management or Semantic Web technologies. Of course, readers not confident about their knowledge on any of these domains should read both background knowledge chapters—that is, Chapters 2 and 3.

In the case of a reader with database expertise, Chapter 2 can be skipped, but we warn that several different forms of database management systems are studied. For example, most readers with a database profile may already master all notions considered in the section dedicated to the relational model, but it may not be the case on the sections addressing *NoSQL* and novel extensions of the relational model.

If a reader's profile corresponds to a Semantic Web literate, then reading Chapter 3 may be optional because it spends most of its content presenting RDF, SPARQL, and ontology languages such as RDFS and OWL, as well as associated reasoning services.

The second part of the book is its cornerstone. All readers should be interested in reading its content and learn about the different approaches to address selected dimensions.

IT project managers and developers will acquire knowledge on the main characteristics of existing, commercial, or open-source systems, while researchers will learn about the latest and most influential systems with references to publications.

CONVENTIONS USED IN THIS BOOK

This book contains the following typographical conventions:
- **Bold** highlights the first occurrence of a software, system, or company name within a chapter.
- `Code font` is used for queries (e.g., expressed in SPARQL or SQL) and URIs, and can also be found within paragraphs to refer to query or program elements.

SUPPLEMENTAL MATERIALS

Additional materials for this book can be found at http://igm.mlv.fr/~ocure/rdfstores/

ACKNOWLEDGMENTS

We would like to thank our technical reviewer, Dean Allemang, special thanks go to our editor: Andrea Dierna, Kaitlin Herbert, and Anusha Sambamoorthy. We are also grateful to David Celestin Faye for participating in the design of roStore.

A very special thanks go to our families for their support: Virginie, Noé, Jeanne, Axelle, and Charlie.

CHAPTER ONE

Introduction

If you have this book in your hands, we guess you are interested in database management systems in general and more precisely those handling *Resource Description Framework* (RDF) as a data representation model. We believe it's the right time to study such systems because they are getting more and more attention in industry with communities of Web developers and *information technology* (IT) experts who are designing innovative applications, in universities and engineering schools with introductory and advanced courses, and in both academia and industry research to design and implement novel approaches to manage large RDF data sets. We can identify several reasons that are motivating this enthusiasm.

In this introductory chapter, we will concentrate on two really important aspects. An obvious one is the role played by RDF in the emergence of the *Web of Data* and the *Semantic Web*—both are extensions of the original *World Wide Web*. The second one corresponds to the impact of this data model in the *Big Data* phenomenon. Based on the presentation of these motivations, we will introduce the main characteristics of an RDF data management system, and present some of its most interesting features that support the comparison of existing systems.

1.1 BIG DATA

Big Data is much more than a buzzword. It can be considered as a concrete phenomenon that is attracting all kinds of companies facing strategic and decisional issues, as well as scientific fields interested in understanding complex observations that may lead to important discoveries. The *National Institute of Standards and Technologies* (NIST) has proposed a widely adopted definition referring to the data deluge: "a digital data volume, velocity and/or variety that enable novel approaches to frontier questions previously inaccessible or impractical using current or conventional methods; and/or exceed the capacity or capability of current or conventional methods and systems" (NIST Big Data, 2013). Most Big Data definitions integrate this aspect of the three V's: volume, velocity, and variety (which is sometimes extended with a fourth V for veracity).

Volume implies that the sizes of data being produced cannot be stored and/or processed using a single machine, but require a distribution over a cluster of machines. The challenges are, for example, to enable the loading and processing of exabytes (i.e., 10^3 petabytes or 10^6 terabytes) of data while we are currently used to data loads in the range of at most terabytes.

Velocity implies that data may be produced at a throughput that cannot be handled by current methods. Solutions, such as relaxing transaction properties, storing incoming data on several servers, or using novel storage approaches to prevent input/output latencies, are being proposed and can even be combined to address this issue. Nevertheless, they generally come with limitations and drawbacks, which are detailed in Chapter 2.

Variety concerns the format (e.g., **Microsoft**'s *Excel* [XLS], *eXtended Markup Language* [XML], *comma-separated value* [CSV], or RDF) and structure conditions of the data. Three main conditions exist: structured, semi-structured, and unstructured. Structured data implies a strict representation where data is organized in entities, and then similar entities are grouped together and are described with the same set of attributes, such as an identifier, price, brand, or color. This information is stored in an associated schema that provides a type to each attribute—for example, a price is a numerical value. The data organization of a *relational database management system* (RDBMS) is reminiscent of this approach. The notion of semi-structured data (i.e., self-described) also adopts an entity-centered organization but introduces some flexibility. For example, entities of a given group may not have the same set of attributes, attribute order is generally not important in the description of an entity, and an attribute may have different types in different entity groups. Common and popular examples are XML, *JavaScript Object Notation* (JSON), and RDF. Finally, unstructured data is characterized by providing very little information on the type of data it contains and the set of formatting rules it follows. Intuitively, text, image, sound, and video documents belong to this category.

Veracity concerns the accuracy and noise of the data being captured, processed, and stored. For example, considering data acquired, one can ask if it's relevant to a particular domain of interest, if it's accurate enough to support decision making, or if the noise associated to that data can be efficiently removed. Therefore, data quality methods may be required to identify and clean "dirty" data, a task that in the context of the other three V's may be considered one of the greatest challenges of the data deluge. Surprisingly, this dimension is the one that has attracted the least attention from Big Data actors.

The emergence of Big Data is tightly related to the increasing adoption of the Internet and the Web. In fact, the Internet proposes an infrastructure to capture and transport large volumes of data, while the Web, and more precisely its 2.0 version, has brought facilities to produce information from the general public. This happens through interactions with personal blogs (e.g., supported by **WordPress**), wikis (e.g., **Wikipedia**), online social networks (e.g., **Facebook**), and microblogging (e.g., **Twitter**), and also through logs of activities on the most frequently used search engines (e.g., **Google**, **Bing**, or **Yahoo!**) where an important amount of data is produced every day. Among the most stunning recent values, we can highlight that Facebook announced that, by the beginning of 2014, it is recording 600 terabytes of data each day in its 300 petabytes data warehouse and an average of around 6,000 tweets are stored at Twitter per second with a record of 143,199 tweets on August 3, 2013.

The *Internet of Things* (IoT) is another contributor to the Big Data ecosystem, which is just in its infancy but will certainly become a major data provider. This Internet branch is mainly concerned with *machine-to-machine* (M2M) communications that are evolving on a Web environment using Web standards such as *Uniform Resource Identifiers* (URIs), *HyperText Transfer Protocol* (HTTP), and *representational state transfer* (REST). It focuses on the devices and sensors that are present in our daily lives, and can belong to either the industrial sector or the consumer market. These active devices may correspond but are not limited to smartphones, *radio-frequency identification device* (RFID) tagged objects, wireless sensor networks, or ambient devices.

IoT enables the collection of temporospatial information—that is, regrouping temporal as well as spatial aspects. In 2009, considered an early year of IoT, Jeff Jonas in his blog (Jonas, 2009) was already announcing that 600 billion geospatially tagged transactions were generated per day in North America. This ability to produce enormous volumes of data at a high throughput is already a data management challenge that will expand in the coming years. To consider its evolution, a survey conducted by **Cisco** (Cisco, 2011) emphasized that from 1.84 connected devices per person in 2010, we will reach 6.58 in 2020, or approximately 50 billion devices. Almost all of these devices will produce massive amounts of data on a daily basis.

As a market phenomenon, Big Data is not supervised by any consortium or organism. Therefore, there is a total freedom about the format of generated, stored, queried, and manipulated data. Nevertheless, best practices of the major industrial and open-source actors bring forward some popular formats such as XLS, CSV, XML, JSON, and RDF. The main advantages of JSON are its simplicity, flexibility (it's schemaless), and native processing support for most Web applications due to a tight integration with the *JavaScript* programming language. But RDF is not without assets. For example, as a semi-structured data model, RDF data sets can be described with expressive schema languages, such as *RDF Schema* (RDFS) or *Web Ontology Language* (OWL), and can be linked to other documents present on the Web, forming the *Linked Data* movement.

With the emergence of Linked Data, a pattern for hyperlinking machine-readable data sets that extensively uses RDF, URIs, and HTTP, we can consider that more and more data will be directly produced in or transformed into RDF. In 2013, the *linked open data* (LOD), a set of RDF data produced from open data sources, is considered to contain over 50 billion triples on domains as diverse as medicine, culture, and science, just to name a few. Two other major sources of RDF data are building up with the *RDF in attributes* (RDFa) standard, where attributes are to be understood in an (X)HTML context, and the **Schema.org** initiative, which is supported by Google, Yahoo!, Bing, and **Yandex** (the largest search engine in Russia). The incentive of being well referenced in these search engines already motivates all kinds of Web contributors (i.e., companies, organizations, etc.) to annotate their web page content with descriptions that can be transformed into RDF data. In the next section, we will present some original functionalities that can be developed with Linked Data, such as querying and reasoning at the scale of the Web.

As a conclusion on Big Data, the direct impact of the original three V's is the calling for new types of database management systems. Specifically, those that will be able to handle rapidly incoming, heterogeneous, and very large data sets. Among others, a major advantage of these systems will be to support novel, more efficient data integration mechanisms. In terms of features expected from these systems, Franklin and colleagues (2005) were the first to propose a new paradigm. Their *DataSpace Support Platforms (DSSP)* are characterized by a pay-as-you-go approach for the integration and querying of data. Basically, this paradigm is addressing most of the issues of Big Data. Later, in Dong and Halevy (2007), more details on the possible indexing methods to use in data spaces were presented. Although not mentioning the term *RDF*, the authors presented a data model based on triples that matches the kind of systems this book focuses on and that are considered in Part 2 of this book.

1.2 WEB OF DATA AND THE SEMANTIC WEB

The Web, as a global information space, is evolving from linking documents only, to linking both documents and data. This is a major (r)evolution that is already supporting the design of innovative applications. This extension of the Web is referred to as the *Web of Data* and enables the access to and sharing of information in ways that are much more efficient and open than previous solutions. This efficiency is due to the exploitation of the infrastructure of the Web by allowing links between distributed data sources. Three major technologies form the cornerstone of this emerging Web: URIs, HTTP, and RDF. The first two have been central to the development of the Web since its inception and respectively address the issues of identifying Web resources (e.g., web pages) and supporting data communication for the Web. The latter provides a data representation model, and the management of such data is the main topic of this book.

The term *semantics* is getting more and more attention in the IT industry as well as in the open-source ecosystem. It basically amounts to providing some solutions for computers to automatically interpret the information present in documents. The interpretation mechanism is usually supported by annotating this information with vocabularies the elements of which are given a well-defined meaning with a logical formalism. The logical approach enables some dedicated reasoners to perform some inferences. Of course, the Web, and in particular the Web of Data, is an important document provider; in that context, we then talk about a Semantic Web consisting of a set of technologies that are supporting this whole process. In Berners-Lee et al. (2001), the Semantic Web is defined as "an extension of the current web in which information is given well-defined meaning, better enabling computers and people to work in cooperation" (p. 1). This emphasizes that there is no rupture between a previous non-semantic Web and a semantic one.

They will both rely on concepts such as HTTP, URIs, and the stack of representational standards such as *HyperText Markup Language* (HTML), *Cascade Style Sheets* (CSS), and all accompanying programming technologies like JavaScript, *Ruby*, and *HyperText PreProcessor* (PHP).

The well-defined meaning aspect is related to RDF annotations and vocabularies expressed in RDFS and the OWL standards. These languages are enabling the description of schemata associated to RDF. Together with such vocabularies, reasoning procedures enable the deduction of novel information or knowledge from data available in the Web of Data. In fact, one of the sweet-spots of RDF and other Semantic Web technologies is data integration, which is the ability to efficiently integrate new information in a repository. This leverages on the Linked Data movement, which is producing very large volumes of RDF triples, dereferenceable URIs (i.e., a resource retrieval method that is making use of Internet protocols such as HTTP), and a flexible data model. This will support the development and maintenance of novel mashup-based applications (i.e., mixing distinct and previously not related information resources) that are going far beyond what is used today.

A first question one may ask is, how popular the Semantic Web is getting? First, the fact that the principles or even the main technologies of the Semantic Web may not be known by the general public cannot be considered a setback of the overall approach. Semantic Web technologies are expected to be present on the server side, not on the client side (i.e., web browsers). So it should not be transparent to the general public and should only be known to application designers and developers. The emergence of semantics can be found in different domains. For instance, it's spreading throughout the search process performed at Google. Rapidly after the announcement in May 2012 of using its *Knowledge Graph* to improve search by providing smarter answers, Google was claiming to answer almost 20% of its total search directly using semantics. In fact, these searches try to understand the context of a given phrase by analyzing its language and terms. This analysis is based on the Knowledge Graph, a graph database originating from the **Freebase** project, Wikipedia, and the **CIA World Factbook**. It consists of a semantic network, the kind of technology RDF and RDFS enable to design, to describe over 600 million objects and 20 billion facts about them as well as their relationships. Note that Google is not the only Web company tackling this issue; for instance, Facebook proposes a similar approach with its *Open Graph Protocol* (OGP), and Microsoft's Bing engine is using its so-called Satori Knowledge Base.

Web technologies such as HTML, CSS, and JavaScript address a wider spectrum of people involved in Web content consultation and creation. The rapid success of the Web in its early days can, in part, be attributed to the ease of designing web pages and websites with computerized tools, so-called *what you see is what you get* (WYSIWYG) editors, that are automatically generating the lines of codes from interactions with the system. This may only partially happen for the Semantic Web, which requires some computer science knowledge for someone to apprehend the whole stack of standards. For example, one may have difficulties apprehending ontology languages (e.g., RDFS or OWL) and their reasoning services without any understanding on concepts such as entailment regimes and open/closed world assumption. Even efficient and elegant methods to annotate web pages with metadata processable by agents were not identified until recently. Now, with the emergence of the RDFa *World Wide Web Consortium* (W3C) standard, one is able to add information to a web page that will be used for both rendering and structured description. Several *content manager systems* (CMSs), such as **Drupal** or WordPress, have already integrated this aspect in their recent implementations, and therefore allow any-one to contribute to the Semantic Web project without being aware of it.

The use of semantic technologies can also be spotted at *The New York Times*, which, since 2009, publishes large *Simple Knowledge Organization System* (SKOS, a W3C Se-mantic Web recommendation) vocabularies about articles and topics proposed in the 150 years of the newspaper's history. In addition, **BBC** provides RDF descriptions of its TV and radio programs.

1.3 RDF DATA MANAGEMENT

So far, we have highlighted that the generation of large volumes of RDF data is increasing but we have not considered storage and processing issues. The volume and velocity of produced RDF data have a major positive impact on the Semantic Web. But it can also be a limit to its deployment if we do not consider issues such as scalability, availability, query answering, data exchange, and reasoning in an efficient way. In fact, since the first W3C's RDF recommendation in 1999, more than 50 data management systems have been proposed and developed for RDF data. Among them, some have been implemented by the three major database vendors: **Oracle**, **IBM**, and Microsoft (yet another proof of maturity of RDF technology that addresses important expectations of the IT market). Other systems are being produced by smaller companies that are more or less specialized on RDF standards: **Ontotext** with the **OWLIM** (now GraphDB) system suite, **OpenLink** with the **Virtuoso** system, **Systap LLC** and its **Bigdata** solution, **Franz Inc.** with its **Allegrograph** database, and **Clark & Parsia**'s **Stardog** system. Finally, a large number of systems frequently released under open-source licenses have been implemented in universities and research institutes, such as **RDF-3X** (Neumann and Weikum, 2008), **Hexastore** (Weiss et al., 2008), and **BitMat** (Atre et al., 2009).

These systems are designed using quite different technologies. For example, concern-ing backend storage and indexing, some are adopting a so-called native approach—that is, they are not relying on another management system—while others go for a non-native approach and benefit from existing systems, such as RDBMSs or NoSQL stores. Simi-larly, different approaches to address query processing, reasoning, data distribution, and federation have been identified and implemented. In the context of a given application, this makes the selection of an adapted RDF data management system a nontrivial task, probably harder than for a RDBMS. Over the last few years, we have met and worked with IT project managers and developers who were facing hard decisions on which RDF stores to use. We consider that a thorough investigation of the main dimensions differentiating existing systems can be useful when deciding which systems to integrate in an application. All these aspects are investigated in Part 2 of this book.

1.4 DIMENSIONS FOR COMPARING RDF STORES

We have defined a set of dimensions on which existing RDF stores should be analyzed and compared. The identification to these dimensions is mainly motivated by the discrepancies in the approaches adopted in certain systems. For example, our first dimension concerns the dictionary aspect. In most RDF data management systems, the RDF triples, mainly composed of URIs, are not stored as is. This is mainly motivated by two properties of URIs: the number of their occurrences over a triples set can be fairly high, and they generally correspond to rather long strings of characters. Therefore, for data compression reasons, almost all systems encode, using so-called dictionaries, these URIs into integers (enabling them to gain storage space). Nevertheless, the manner in which these encodings are processed and stored can be quite different from one system to another. Moreover, some systems propose a clever approach to this encoding that supports some form of almost free inferences and enables the efficient processing of simple regular expressions.

A second dimension considers the storage of RDF data. This has been the subject of an important number of research articles, which unsurprisingly have been published for both Semantic Web and database conferences. Many approaches have been presented, some storing the triples in raw files, RDBMSs, and recently *NoSQL* stores. But even within a given storage approach, several logical approaches have been proposed—for example, there exists at least half a dozen logical solutions over the relational model.

Just like in any database management systems, indexing the data is an important solution to speed up its access. Given the schema flexibility of RDF data and the combination of possible indexes over RDF triples, many approaches have been implemented and each comes with its set of advantages and drawbacks.

The next dimension, query processing, is highly related to the previous data indexation. It contains several aspects that discriminate systems—for example, query optimization with both the definition of logical and physical query plans, as well as query execution.

The distribution dimension addresses the data deluge aspect and considers that the volumes of RDF data we are dealing with must be distributed over a set of machines. Several approaches have been envisaged, some pertaining to standard management systems (e.g., range or hash-based), while others are more settled down into graph theory with graph partitioning.

The federation dimension is an important aspect of the Web of Data and the use of Linked Data. The goal of database federation is to enable the querying of a database over several databases in a transparent way. The use of dereferenceable URIs together with the SPARQL query language and SPARQL endpoints supports an unbounded form of data federation that enables the integration of data and knowledge efficiently and in an unprecedented manner.

So far, the dimensions we have presented are anchored in database management considerations. This is the main reason for the presence of Chapter 2, which presents some important notions on both relational and NoSQL stores.

The final dimension we are considering focuses on reasoning services that enable the enrichment of result sets when querying an RDF repository. Such inference considerations are almost never addressed in other existing data management systems, except with the integration of a *datalog* engine in an RDBMS. The understanding of the peculiarities of this dimension depends on a clear comprehension of the available ontology languages and their associated forms of reasoning in the Semantic Web, which is presented in Chapter 3.

CHAPTER TWO

Database Management Systems

The objective of this chapter is to provide some background knowledge on database management systems, a software the purpose of which is to define, create, manage, query, and update a database. We present certain aspects of systems that have been the most widely used in production for the last couple of decades. We also consider some trends that have emerged during the last few years. We limit this investigation to systems that are currently being used or have been in the past as the backend of existing *Resource Description Framework* (RDF) database management systems. Due to space limitations, we cannot provide a thorough presentation of these systems, therefore we concentrate on some peculiar characteristics that motivated their adoption in RDF data management and are main differentiators among these systems.

The first category of systems we consider is the *relational database management system* (RDBMS). It is a very popular family of systems that has dominated the database market for the last 30 years. We provide a short introduction on this topic for readers coming with a (Semantic) Web background, but a complete presentation is out of the scope of this book, (Elsmari, 2010) and (Kifer, 2005) are good introductions. Nevertheless, we define some notions and terms that are going to be used throughout this book. Then, we introduce concepts that are needed for understanding the particularities of the different RDF systems that are studied in Part 2 of this book. These concepts are generally presented in books investigating the internal description of RDBMSs, and are usually not considered in classic RDBMS books that concentrate more on how to model for and use these systems.

The second kind of systems we address corresponds to *NoSQL* systems. These systems only appeared a couple of years ago but already benefit from a high adoption rate in many IT infrastructures. They are used in many different application domains and are far from being limited to the issues of Web companies. This presentation concerns the four main families of NoSQL systems and also introduces some tools that are frequently associated with these systems, such as the popular parallel *MapReduce* processing framework.

Finally, we provide trails on the evolution of RDBMS and NoSQL systems. For instance, we present an introduction to some novel approaches in developing RDBMSs. Here, we are mainly concerned with implementing systems that leverage on the evolution of the hardware environment—for example, the availability of larger main memory spaces, the emergence of *solid-state drives* (SSDs), and the emergence of cloud-based systems. We also emphasize on the appearance of novel functionalities in NoSQL database systems. All these aspects may play a role in the evolution of RDF database management systems in the near future.

2.1 TECHNOLOGIES PREVAILING IN THE RELATIONAL DOMAIN

2.1.1 Relational model

The relational model was introduced by Edgar F. Codd in the early 1970s (Codd, 1970) and is the foundation of RDBMSs. In this model, the first-class citizen is a specific structure named a *relation* that contains tuples (a.k.a. *records*). All the tuples in a relation have the same set of *fields* (a.k.a. *attributes*) where each field has a certain type, such as an integer, a date, or a string. This matches the definition of structured data presented in Chapter 1. The operations performed over this model are handled by an algebra that principally serves as a query language to retrieve data. A selection operation retrieves information from a single relation or a set of relations. In this last case, relations are generally joined over some common-type attributes. An important aspect of this algebra is that it produces an output that takes the form of a structure that is itself a relation. Thus, this approach enables the composition of relational queries one into another—that is, using the result of a query as the input of another one.

The concepts pertaining in the relational model are transposed into an RDBMS using the following term translation: *relations*, *attributes*, and *tuples* correspond respectively to *tables*, *columns*, and *rows* (but these terms can be used interchangeably to denote the same notions). In an RDBMS, the query language is named *Structured Query Language* (SQL), and it implements most of the operations available in the relational algebra but also provides additional ones. Many consider that SQL is a major reason for the success and dominance of this type of data management system. This is mainly due to its short learning curve and its expressivity which has been defined to support good computational complexity properties. In other words, a lot of practical questions can be expressed with few concepts and answered relatively rapidly even over large data sets. Moreover, the wide adoption in most existing RDBMS systems of a common, standardized subset of SQL is another major advantage. Therefore, it enables one user to easily switch from one RDBMS to another with relative ease, such as from **MySQL** to **Oracle** or the other way around. SQL also extends the relation algebra by update operations, which are the ability to delete, insert, or modify information.

For example, we consider an oversimplified blog application containing the following information. Blog entries are being written by users, themselves being characterized by an identifier, first and last names, and a gender. For each blog entry, we store the content of the entry (i.e., the text it contains), its storage date (i.e., the date at which it's being stored in the database), the user who has produced the entry, and the category of the entry. A category corresponds to a subject area, such as sports, technology, or science. Finally, a subscription feature enables end-users to follow the blog entries of other users. Many solutions are available to represent the corresponding conceptual data model (e.g., an *entity relationship* (ER) *diagram*), but we have opted for a *Unified Modeling*

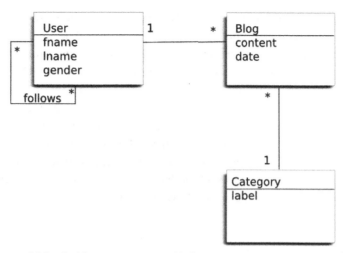

Figure 2.1 Data model for the blog use case using UML notation.

Language (UML) notation using a class diagram, see Figure 2.1. Note that in this diagram, we consider that identifiers are explicit (e.g., user identifier), and we therefore do not display them in the figure.

When the target database is an RDBMS, the conceptual model is translated into a relation schema. This is presented with some sample data in Figure 2.2. The schema contains four tables, namely `User`, `Category`, `Blog`, and `Follows`. The first three are direct translations from the classes proposed in Figure 2.1. The latter corresponds to the `follows` role the cardinalities of which are many-to-many (the two * symbols in

User

id	fname	lname	gender
1	Joe	Doe	Male
2	Mary	Smith	Female

Follows

followerId	followedId
1	2
1	3
2	1
2	4

Category

id	label
1	Sport
2	Science
3	Technology

Blog

id	content	date	userId	categoryId
1	Today..	10/13/2013	1	3
2	Science is	10/15/2013	1	2
3	My phone	10/16/2013	2	3

Figure 2.2 Sample data for the blog use case.

Figure 2.1), meaning that a user can follow as many users as he or she wants and he or she can also be followed by an unrestricted number of users. The attributes forming this relation correspond to user identifiers from both the follower and the followed users.

We can also see that some columns have been added to some relations. This corresponds to many-to-one relationships between entities (represented as 1 * associations between boxes in Figure 2.1). This is aimed to support joins between relations—for example, the `CategoryId` of the `Blog` relation enables joins with the `id` attribute of the `Category` relation. This approach implies column redundancy, which allows the definition of queries that may be useful when designing domain application. For example, the following query retrieves all the blogs belonging to the `Science` category and that have been written by persons followed by Mary:

```
SELECT b.content FROM category AS c, blog AS b, follows AS f
WHERE c.label LIKE 'Science' AND c.id=b.categoryId AND followerId=2
AND followedId=userId;
```

The capitalized terms correspond to reserved words of SQL. This query contains three clauses—SELECT, FROM, and WHERE—which respectively retrieve some columns to be displayed in the result set, specify the tables needed for the query to execute (AS is used for the creation of aliases for table names, which induces easier reading of the query), and can define some filters and/or joins. This query requires three tables and the WHERE clause contains two filters (i.e., on the `label` and `followerId` columns using the LIKE and equality operators) and two joins (e.g., on the columns `id` of `Category` and `categoryId` of `Blog`). Executed over the data sample of Figure 2.2, the query's result set contains the blog entry starting with `Science is`, which has been written by Joe (`userId = 1`), who is followed by Mary (`userId = 2`).

Note that an SQL query does not specify how to retrieve the answer set. We qualify languages that are adopting this approach as declarative because they just declare what to retrieve and from which source and under which conditions. This can be opposed to a procedural approach that describes the procedures to execute to obtain a result. An important consequence of being a declarative query language is that it leaves a complete freedom to a processor toward obtaining the answer set. This freedom generally implies that some optimizations are being processed, mainly to ensure fast executions. We will provide more details on the query processor of an RDBMS in Section 2.1.3.

Other forms of SQL queries correspond to update operations such as UPDATE, INSERT, and DELETE, which respectively modify, insert, or remove one or more tuples from a table. The following are examples for each of these operations on the blog example:

- `INSERT INTO User VALUES(3, 'Susan','Doe', 'Female');` introduces a novel row in the `User` table.

- `DELETE FROM Category WHERE id = 1;` removes the row corresponding to Sport from the `Category` table.
- `UPDATE Blog SET userId = 2 WHERE id = 1;` modifies the first row of the `Blog` table by stating that this blog entry has been written by the user whose `id` value is 2—that is, Mary Smith.

In the next section, we discuss the mechanisms developed to efficiently query large data sets.

2.1.2 Indexes

Agents (i.e., end-users or programs) interacting with a database management system expect that the execution of queries is optimal and will be performed as fast as possible. In cases of large data sets, a naive approach, such as reading all tuples of a given relation to find a particular one, to query execution is far from guaranteeing optimal performance. Because data persistence is taken care of by secondary storage, usually *hard-disk drives* (HDDs) even if SSDs are more and more common, the cost of transferring disk blocks (i.e., the basic disk storage unit for an RDBMS) to the main memory generally exceeds the other query processing operations.

For example, let's assume that the users relation of the blog example contains 100,000 tuples, each record being about 160 bytes long, and that disk blocks are 16 kilobytes per block. This means that 100 records fit into a disk block and that the relation occupies 1,000 blocks. Moreover, only 10 users have Smith as their last name. Consider the following simple query: `SELECT fname, gender FROM users WHERE lname LIKE 'Smith'`. To retrieve all users having Smith as their last name, our naive approach induces the transfer of all 1,000 blocks to the main memory. It's obvious that most of these disk transfers are unnecessary because, at most, 10 of them may contain all the Smith users. A clever approach will consist in identifying these disk blocks and proceeding to at most 10 disk blocks transferred to obtain the correct answer set.

This clever method of identifying the tuples of a given attribute value limits to its minimum the number of *input/output* (I/O) operations, and is enabled by the notion of *indexes*. Intuitively, an index is a data structure the goal of which is to facilitate the discovery of relevant disk blocks needed for the query to execute efficiently. Note that this is the same notion of searching for a given term in a large book. No one would read all the book pages to find all term occurrences. If it's available, one would go to the index section and efficiently find in an alphabetically sorted entry a line for that term. That line would contain all page numbers where the term appears. Most RDBMSs propose, through SQL operators, the creation of different types of indexes that are used for speeding up queries, for example, to efficiently access some values of a given attribute or to improve joins involving a set of attributes.

The definition of indexes comes at a certain price corresponding to their maintenance cost. That is, whenever an update is performed on an indexed attribute (a.k.a. search key), both the relation and the index have to be properly modified. Within the book metaphor, a change of the content involving an indexed term would imply an index maintenance, precisely to add or remove the page number of the content modification. Therefore, the selection of attributes to index has an important impact on the overall performance of the database. This selection requires an estimation of the importance of the queries to be executed over the database. Intuitively, one only needs the definition of indexes over attributes that are used and filtered in the most frequent queries executed over the database.

There are several indexing organization types. For example, a so-called *clustered index* ensures that the order of tuples in the file storing the data matches the order of the entries in the index. Therefore, only one clustered index is possible on a given file. This is opposed to an *unclustered index* where the physical order of the tuples is not the same as the indexed ones. Thus, several unclustered indexes are possible for a given relation. An index can also be qualified as *dense*, if there is a least one data entry per search key, otherwise it's called *sparse*.

Finally, several implementations are possible, the most frequent ones being balanced trees, B-trees or one of its variations (e.g, B+trees), and *hashes*. But the research has been prolific on this topic and some other indices are particularly adapted to certain domains, such as an *R-index* and other *generalized search trees* (GiSTs). To select one instead of another, the *database administrator* (DBA) generally needs to be acknowledged on the kind of queries that will frequently be executed. For example, if one popular query requires the access to a range of attribute values, then a balanced tree index is preferable to a hash-based one. This is due to the fact that hash indexes only support equality comparison. In Part 2 of this book, we will see that many RDF stores are using B+tree to index triples, therefore we only present this approach.

A B+tree is a structure that organizes its blocks in a tree like manner. The structure is composed by three components: a root node, internal nodes, and leaves. In a nutshell, the structure of each of these components is common, and composed of n search keys and $n + 1$ pointers. The pointers of the root or of any internal node point to other internal nodes or leaves. The pointers of leaves lead to the tuples. The main reason for the popularity of this structure in a database management system lies in the fact that it's *balanced*. This property means that all paths from the root to any leaf have the same length and ensures a worst-case complexity of $O(\log(n))$ for the search, insert, and delete operations, and $O(n)$ for space occupied by the structure.

Finally, note that the disk block approach is adopted in both HDDs and SSDs. That is, the manner in which data is retrieved from an HDD resembles the one of SSDs but with an average of two orders of magnitude more I/O per second for the latter. Nevertheless, even if your financial situation allows for SSDs, it would be a big mistake not to use indexes. After all, the objective is the transfer of data from a secondary storage to the main memory, and *random access memory* (RAM) is still three orders of magnitude faster than SSD. So in our all SSD scenario, your performance bottleneck will still be I/O transfer and indexes are an important helper in that case.

2.1.3 Query processing

To fully appreciate the architecture of RDF database systems, it's important to present the common components found in most RDBMSs' query processing (Figure 2.3). The two main components of query processing are *query compilation* and *execution*. Two steps are distinguished by the query compiler: *parsing* and *optimizing*.

Parsing involves scanning a query to make sure that it's well formed—that is, it complies to a set of syntactical rules and makes sure that all entities, such as tables, views, attributes, and functions, referred to are known by the system.

In the case where a query passes the parsing stage, the query is transformed into an internal format that generally takes the form of an algebra operator tree. This internal representation, which uses most of the operators of the relational algebra as well as some additional ones (e.g., for handling aggregation operations), aims at facilitating the optimization step. Several tree representations are possible for a given query and a component is responsible for selecting the most cost-effective logical query plan. This is performed using a set of rules that are defined over the relational algebra and its operations.

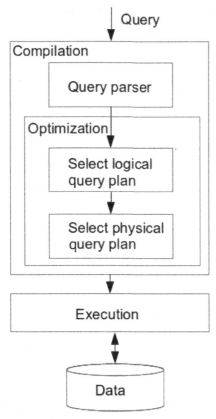

Figure 2.3 Overview of query processing.

The query plan is qualified as "logical" since it only defines the order on which the different operations will be performed and does not specify anything about which methods will be used for accessing stored data. To address this issue, another optimization form is required by the system and amounts to the translation of logical query plans into operations performed on the files containing the data, what is referred to as the *physical query plan*. Again, several physical query plans can be envisaged from a single logical query plan, and the selection of the most efficient one is based on an estimation of their execution duration. This implies a cost-estimation approach that takes the form of a set of heuristics that are using different parameters, such as the relation sizes, index availability, or join types. For example, histograms corresponding to statistics on the distribution of standard values of a relation are extensively used. They use information on indexes available for the involved relations. The order of joins is also the responsibility of this component, and it results in identifying the join algorithms that are being selected. The goal of this selection is not limited to the definition of operations required for the query to execute but also specifies the order on which they are performed.

Once a physical query plan is selected, it's sent to the query execution component, which communicates with the stored data to produce an answer set. This component executes the algorithms specified in the physical plan. There exists an important number of different algorithms that can be distinguished by whether one of the relations to be joined fits or not into the main memory, or whether the join requires a sort of one of the involved relations. This motivates whether a one-, two-, or multiple-pass algorithm can be used. For some of these algorithms, sorting or hashing the content of relations may be required for speeding up query executions.

2.1.4 ACID transactions and OLTP

In this section, we are not directly interested in the internal aspect of RDBMSs, but rather consider their usages. We can consider that they can be partitioned into two big categories: the category that is mainly handling transactions, called *online transactional processing* (OLTP), and the one concerned with the analysis of important workloads, called *online analytical processing* (OLAP).

An objective of OLTP systems is to properly maintain the different states of a real-world model in the context of possibly concurrent transactions. In this setting, the notion of a transaction corresponds to a non empty set of operations performed in SQL over the database. The set of operations is usually less important than the number encountered in an OLAP system, but the number of transactions per second can be very important, meaning that the state of the database is constantly evolving. To maintain the database in a coherent state, a set of properties are expected from such systems. This is characterized by the *atomicity*, *consistency*, *isolation*, and *duration* (ACID) properties.

Atomicity is an all-or-nothing approach on the set of operations constituting the transaction. This means that if one of the transaction operations cannot be properly executed, then every operation before that one has to be canceled and the transaction is not performed at all. Atomicity is tightly related to the consistency property, which states that the execution of a transaction must lead the database to a consistent state. We will see in the next section that this consistency is a very important aspect of the NoSQL ecosystem. Intuitively, a database state is consistent if it does not violate integrity constraints that can be defined in SQL or in some programming language. The isolation property is related to interferences that can occur between transactions that are executed in the same time window. It states that until a transaction is properly terminated (committed in the database jargon), all concurrent access on the same data is hidden—that is, other users will see the older data values, not the one being modified by the transaction. The duration property induces that all committed transactions are persisted on a secondary storage, most frequently an HDD. In general, OLTP applications are best described by relatively frequent updates, short and simple transactions accessing usually a small portion of the database. A ubiquitous example using OLTP databases is e-commerce applications.

The goal of OLAP, together with data mining, is to analyze the data contained in a database such that decisions and predictions can be taken by end-users or computer agents. These systems are implemented in so-called *data warehouses* and are frequently used in fields such as *business intelligence* (BI). In general, transactions are rare in OLAP (e.g., write operations are not frequent), but when some are performed they usually involve a very large number of operations. The execution of a million rows on a weekly or monthly basis is not rare. Therefore, the state of a database is more stable because it changes less frequently than in the OLTP context. This reduces the effort to maintain data consistency.

Because OLAP systems are read-intensive, they can be highly denormalized. This means that the conceptual schema of the database is modified in such a way that some queries require less joins (which is a bottleneck of query processing). This comes at the price of data redundancy, but it's usually not a problem for servers supporting data warehouses. Therefore, OLAP solutions usually do not need the whole ACID machinery because their write and update transactions are performed adopting a scheduled batch-processing approach—that is, every indicated time period a large chunk of data is inserted in the data warehouse. Retail stores make intensive use of OLAP data warehouses, for example, to identify product consumptions.

Both OLTP and OLAP are being queried with SQL, although more procedural approaches with a programming language can be used. The standard set of SQL operators is extended for OLAP systems because the queries can be more complex than in OLTP and can access a significant fraction of the database. These queries frequently handle multidimensional operations where a dimension corresponds to an attribute in a table. For instance, in a retail database, product sales would have the store location, product and time identifiers as dimensions. This could be represented as a cube where the quantity sold of a product at a location at a certain time would be stored in cells of that matrix. Typical operations performed on such cubes are *consolidation, drilling-down, rolling-up, slicing, and dicing*. Consolidation aggregates data that can be computed in one or several dimensions. The drill-down and rolling-up techniques allow a navigation along those dimensions, e.g., along the time dimension (weeks, months or quarters). Finally, slicing and dicing respectively retrieves and views slices from different points of view. The efficiency of performing these analytical operations is supported by efficient implementations of new SQL operations, e.g., GROUPY BY CUBE and GROUP BY ROLLUP, denormalized schemata and materialized views. These are the main reasons why OLTP systems are highly inefficient at performing similar analysis operations.

2.1.5 Row versus column stores

To summarize what we have already expressed in this chapter, an RDBMS persists its data in secondary memory (principally in an HDD, but SSDs are more and more frequent), and transferring data to the main memory is required whenever we want to do something useful with the data. So far we have indicated that the unit of transfer is a disk block (a.k.a. a page), and that a page contains a set of tuples. That approach corresponds to a row store—that is, a page stores some tuples. Another approach consists in storing columns of a relation separately so that they can be accessed independently—that is a page stores some columns.

The row store approach has been the most dominant in RDBMS history, but things are evolving toward the adoption of its column counterpart, mainly due to the need to analyze very large data sets as encountered in Big Data. Some systems are also proposing hybrid RDBMSs where the DBA can specify which of the two approaches makes more sense. For example, a table T1 may physically be stored as rows because some important queries frequently executed by an application must retrieve all its columns at a time. At the same time, another table T2 may adopt a column-oriented approach because many queries are retrieving a subset of its columns. The fact that T1 and T2 are respectively frequently or rarely updated would confirm this physical layout.

The context of adopting a row store is related to the use cases of OLTP—that is, domains requiring both fast reads and writes. In contrast, column stores are optimized in the context of OLAP—that is, they are characterized by mostly read queries with infrequent writes. These systems propose reasonably fast load times, which work efficiently for batch jobs but do not possess the capacity to handle high update rates. The kind of queries generally executed over a data warehouse involve big aggregations and summarizations over an identified number of columns. This matches cases where a column store is particularly efficient compared to a row store.

The storage layer is an important differentiator of row and column stores. Consider the tuples of the User relation in Figure 2.2. A row store would organize the tuples as displayed in that figure—that is values of the User table attributes are stored together in the same structure. Although different column store approaches exist among existing systems, a standard representation would be the following:

```
(userid) 1, 2, …
(fname) Joe, Mary, …
(lname) Doe, Smith, …
(gender) Male, Female, …
```

Note that the tuples are stored in several (one for each attribute) structures, denoted as *files* in this section, which correspond to a set of disk blocks. Moreover, the values in each of these files are ordered, which enables the reconstruction of the tuples if required. For example, the second values of each file support the retrieval of the information of the second tuple of the original table. To match values based on their position in the corresponding files, this approach imposes that columns that are undefined for a particular row must explicitly store a NULL value in the corresponding file. This storage organization clearly presents some advantages and drawbacks.

As advantages, queries that only retrieve a small subset of the attributes of a relation will transfer to the main memory a higher rate of useful information than a row store that transfers all attributes of some tuples. Another advantage is the possibility to compress the data of each column because all values have the same domain. For example, consider the compression possibilities on the gender column in Figure 2.2 where only two values are possible. Note that in certain use cases, query answering can be performed without decompressing the data. A typical example consists in counting the number of entries in data clusters—for example, counting the number of blog entries in each category. As a major disadvantage, tuple updates are slow because they may require the reorganization of several files.

Comparatively, row stores present the assets of more efficient update operations over a relation's tuple because a tuple is stored over a small number of disk blocks. An important drawback is related to the fact that most useful queries rarely retrieve all the information from a given tuple, but rather retrieve only a subset of it. That implies that a large portion of the tuple's data is unnecessarily transferred into the main memory. This has an impact on the I/O efficiency of row stores.

In Abadi (2007) the author states that column stores are good candidates for extremely wide tables and for databases handling sparse data. The paper demonstrates the potential of column stores for the Semantic Web through the storage of RDF. Based on these remarks, it's not a surprise that the current trend with database vendors emphasizes that column stores are getting more popular and can, in fact, compete with row stores in many use cases. Many recent systems have emerged in this direction, such as **Sybase IQ**, **Vertica**, **VectorWise**, **MonetDB**, **ParAccel**, and **Infobright**, together with older systems, such as **Teradata**.

Note that a new breed of RDBMS is trying to enjoy both worlds of row and column data storage. Systems such as **Greenplum** propose a so-called *polymorphic data storage* approach where a DBA can specify the storage, execution, and compression associated to each table.

2.1.6 Distributed and parallel DBMS

So far we have assumed that an RDBMS is running on a single server. In this context, issues related to the support of a concurrent access are handled using transactions and their ACID properties. Nevertheless, due to scalability, security, or location aspects, it may be necessary to distribute the data over a set of machines. In this section, we consider such situations and present some special kind of database systems that integrate distribution and related processes at their core.

A distributed database corresponds to an integrated set of databases that is physically distributed over different sites of a computer network. The software that manages such databases is denoted as a distributed management system, and its main characteristic is to make the different interactions with end-users and applications totally transparent from the distribution aspect—that is, the end-user does not have to know about the organization of the data over this network. This approach is obvious for certain organizations where the data is naturally (geographically) distributed over a network. In some cases, this is so profoundly anchored in the business model that it may not even be possible to deploy a centralized system. The advantage of this approach is to reinforce the autonomy of each site (e.g., by administering its own data), which reduces the communication overhead because the data is most of the time retrieved from a user's own local site. Finally, the availability of the data is increased, because in case a site falls down, the other functioning sites can potentially ensure data retrieval and query processing on replicated data.

Distributed systems typically involve replication of data across a number of physical (as opposed to virtual) machines. There exists several reasons that motivate the adoption of a replication approach. Some, as we have already seen, aim to design a more robust system, one that is more tolerant to parts of the system failing, or aim to build a system with higher availability properties by ensuring close location of machines needed for some processing. Another motivation is to support a form of parallelism that could be valuable when different processes are simultaneously operating on the same data by providing each of them with their own copy.

We can distinguish two types of data replications that depend on whether the copy of data is performed synchronously or asynchronously. A *synchronous replication* is performed via atomic write operations and therefore assures that no data is lost in the process. To guarantee completeness of the write operations, both the original and replica machines need for emission a form of acknowledgment (referred to as a *handshake*). This approach frequently implies that applications wait for completeness before accepting other operations. Thus, synchronous replication is frequently associated with latencies and poor performances. In *asynchronous replication,* the goal is to prevent latencies at the cost of possibly losing some data. This is performed with a different completeness strategy. Intuitively, a write is complete as soon as the original data is updated. Then the replica is updated, but one does not need to wait for any form of acknowledgment. The first systems designed with the concepts of a distributed database were **SSD-1** and **Distributed INGRES** in the 1970s. But the first mature systems can be considered as appearing in the mid-1980s with **INGRES/Star** and **Oracle version 7**.

A parallel database system manages data stored on a multiprocessor computer. It generally implements all the functionalities of a standard database management system. The main principle of such a system is to partition the data over the different multiprocessor nodes. Advantages of this approach consist in improving the performance and availability through parallelism and replication. By being able to address these operations efficiently, a parallel database management system is able to support very large volumes of data, a prerequisite in the current data deluge.

In DeWitt and Gray (1992), the authors stress ideal properties expected from a parallel database: linear speed-up and linear scale-up. The former means that "twice as much hardware can perform the task in half the elapsed time," (p. 3) while the latter implies that "twice as much hardware can perform twice as large a task in the same elapsed time" (p. 3) Ensuring such properties usually comes at the cost of providing an adapted hardware architecture. Stonebraker (1986) proposes a taxonomy that, although defined more than 25 years ago, has never been as relevant as now. It defines the following three architectures. The *shared-nothing* architecture (Figure 2.4a) consists of a set of connected, via an interconnection network (e.g., a gigabit ethernet), processors that can access their own memory and disk. Alternatives are the *shared-memory* architecture (Figure 2.4b) where a set of processors share, through an interconnection network, a common main memory and all disks. This facility of global memory and disks eases the design and implementation of the database software, but it comes at several scaling limitations. Two of these limitations are the interference of shared resources (e.g., lock tables and buffer manager) and the fact that the memory system can rapidly become a bottleneck. Finally, in a *shared-disk* architecture (Figure 2.4c), each processor has its own private memory but they can all access all disks via an interconnection network. Such an architecture induces a coordination of accesses to shared data that is implemented with a complex distributed lock manager. Oracle's *Real Application Clusters* (RAC) is one implementation of the shared-disk approach. Among the three possible architectures, the shared-nothing approach is, by far, the most adapted to parallel databases, and we will soon see that it's widely used in the NoSQL ecosystem and in cloud computing architectures.

The main advantages of the shared-nothing approach are that it minimizes interference between each machine—that is, no exchanges of information stored in main memories and disks are needed—and it can be scaled out to thousands of machines, by adding new commodity machines to the cluster, without impacting the global infrastructure's

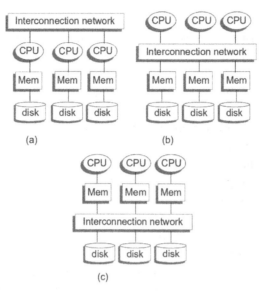

Figure 2.4 Taxonomy of parallel architectures: (a) shared nothing, (b) shared memory, and (c) shared disk.

performance. For example, it's known to be really difficult to scale shared–disk and shared–memory systems to more than respectively 10–20 and 100 nodes. Nevertheless, increasing the number of machines also increases the probabilities of failover of the architecture—that is, the more machines you get in your cluster, the more likely one will break down. Guaranteeing a quality of service for applications developed over such clusters comes at the cost of defining clever partitioning (e.g., an efficient data skew) and replication strategies.

Data partitioning is an operation performed at the relation level involving the distribution of its set of tuples over a set of disks. The main partitioning strategies are *round-robin*, *hash*, and *range* based. They respectively map the ith tuple of a relation to the (i *modulo n*) disk, each tuple to a disk identified by a hash function, and contiguous attribute ranges to distinct disks. Other partitioning approaches can be defined but are less frequently implemented. In the case of graph-oriented data, several strategies can be applied using graph operations (e.g., graph centrality), which are denoted as *graph partitioning*. In Part 2 of this book, we will present some uses of these techniques over RDF graphs.

Few open-source systems exist in this category. Most systems are commercial and are generally very expensive. This forces many Web actors to develop their own parallel storage and processing infrastructure, mostly on a shared-nothing architecture. The first systems, such as Teradata, date back to the end of the 1970s. Recently several systems emerged in this parallel database environment: Vertica, Greenplum, and **Xtreme Data**.

2.2 TECHNOLOGIES PREVAILING IN THE NOSQL ECOSYSTEM

2.2.1 Introduction

The term *NoSQL* was coined in 2009 to advertise a meeting in the Silicon Valley on novel data stores that are not based on the relational model. At the time, the acronym was standing for "NO SQL" and was reflecting a situation where programmers and software engineers were complaining about RDBMS and object-relational mapping (ORM) tools that prevent them to concentrate on their original mission, i.e., programming or designing systems. Among others, this fatigue could be justified by the omnipresence of SQL code in programming code lines, the impedance mismatch between data stored in the RDBMS and the programs, the hardness to distribute relations and their processing over a cluster of machines, and the inadequacy of the relational data model to some application domains (e.g. graph data). Therefore, the NO SQL movement was interpreted as a rejection of RDBMSs with their SQL and ACID machinery.

Since then, the term has evolved slightly toward a less controversial definition. It's now interpreted as "Not only SQL" (hence the small "o" in our spelling). This recognizes that RDBMSs have many qualities that justify their presence in the IT ecosystem, but that other forms of data management systems are needed to reply to expectations motivated by the Big Data phenomenon. This clearly indicates that there is room for more than one database management system type and that their coexistence will be required in many IT architectures. This corresponds to the notion of polyglot persistence on which we will come back to several times in Part 2 of this book.

Even if the NoSQL/NOSQL term appeared in 2009, the first database systems (we will use the term *store* interchangeably) considered to be part of this ecosystem were presented in papers published in research conferences in 2006 and 2007. These papers were respectively describing the **BigTable** database designed at **Google** (Chang et al., 2006) and the **Dynamo** system implemented at **Amazon** (DeCandia et al., 2007). It's not a surprise to see that these systems were pioneered by Web companies with Big Data issues.

It's important to understand what motivated the design of these first systems. In the previous section, we emphasized that parallel database systems are required for companies managing very large data sets. But available parallel database management systems are very expensive and are not open source. While many (Web) companies are able to run their business from off-the-shelf database systems, the likes of Google and Amazon are in need of special tuning, data, and processing distributions, and modification and extension capabilities of existing systems. Therefore, they need complete control over the frameworks running in their data infrastructure. This requisite motivates them to use open-source solutions for security and extensibility reasons—that is, they have the ability to study, modify, optimize, maintain, and distribute source codes, as well as to build contributing communities around them. Moreover, they are facing a data deluge that forces them to consider storing and processing very large volumes of data and arriving at high throughput, with novel approaches. The need to distribute the workload on distant data centers could not be handled efficiently by only relying on RDBMSs, although they are widely used by these companies (e.g., MySQL or **MariaDB**). Therefore, they engaged into contributions to this field up to a point where it now represents an essential part of their technology stack. This approach allows an increase in their productivity in terms of application development and scalability. We will see in this chapter that other large Web companies have contributed to this ecosystem, such as **Facebook** with **Cassandra** and **Twitter** with **FlockDB**.

NoSQL does not correspond to a single form of database system and does not follow any standard. Rather, it covers a wide range of technologies and data architectures for managing Web-scale data while having the following common features: persistent data, nonrelational data model, flexible schema approaches, individual (usually procedural) query solutions rather than using a standard declarative query language, avoiding join operations, distribution, massive horizontal scaling, replication support, consistency within a node of the cluster and eventually across the cluster, and simple transactions. We will now clarify each of these notions.

The concept of *persistent data* is the same as the one presented in the context of RDBMS. It mainly states that data aims to be stored in a nonvolatile memory, such as secondary memory, which used to be exclusively HDDs but are now sometimes replaced with SSDs. For some NoSQL systems, such as the **Aerospike** store (`http://www.aerospike.com/`), the use of SSDs is an important feature and motivates design decisions that are announced as the main reason for high performances.

None of the NoSQL systems follows the relational data model. Rather, they are influenced by key-value structures (e.g., hash tables) and are sometimes referred as *distributed hash tables* (DHTs). At least three out of four NoSQL system families adopt this approach, and they are mainly differentiated by the type of information they can store at the value position. The other quarter of NoSQL systems rely on the graph model and have a set of totally different properties and use cases.

An important aspect of the application domains motivating the emergence of NoSQL stores was the need for flexibility in terms of database schema. In fact, the designers of these systems pushed this characteristic to its logical limit by not providing facilities to define a schema. This schemaless property facilitates an important feature needed in many data management approaches: the integration of novel data into the database. For example, consider a relation where one can add as many attributes as needed. In an RDBMS, this would imply a high rate of NULL values for tuples where some attributes do not apply or are not known. In many NoSQL stores, one simply does not assign values for the attributes he or she does not want or know.

This flexibility imposes the design of novel query methods. In general, early NoSQL systems were supported by the application programmer community (as opposed to the database community) who were eager to access databases using their favorite programming language rather than a query language like SQL or an ORM solution, such as **TopLink** and **Hibernate**. In fact, until recently, most NoSQL stores were not proposing a dedicated query language, and the only method supported to retrieve and update data was through a set of *application programming interfaces* (APIs) and code written in some programming language. Because, in this context, queries are procedurally defined, as opposed to declaratively with a language like SQL, it's not possible anymore to automatically optimize them. This means that the optimization responsibility totally rests on the shoulders of the programmers! We consider this one aspect has to be taken care of very seriously when adopting such a database system.

For performance reasons, NoSQL database instances are frequently accessed by a single application. This enables users to fine-tune the model to handle, as previously identified, a set of queries required by the application. The goal is thus to model, as early as possible, the database to efficiently perform these peculiar queries. This usually comes at the cost of having poor performances for other queries. This approach is reminiscent to the denormalization step (see section 2.1.4), which is usually encountered at a tuning stage of an RDBMS. In this chapter, we already emphasized that denormalization aims at limiting the number of joins present in the most frequently executed queries. For example, consider that a frequent query in the blog application retrieves, for a given user, blog entries with the associated label category. For Joe Doe, our query would be: `SELECT b.content, b.date, c.label FROM category AS c, blog AS b WHERE b.userId = 1 AND c.id = b.categoryId`. In this case, storing the label category in the blog relation would enable us to write the more efficient following query: `SELECT content, date, label FROM blog WHERE userId = 1`. NoSQL systems go one step further by not supporting joins. Practically, join operations are programmed into the applications, giving again a complete freedom in terms of data structures and algorithms to the programmers. The impact of denormalization is not limited to reducing the number of joins; it also implies to increase data redundancy and support atomic transactions more efficiently—that is, transactions that occur at the atomic level of the entities supported by the NoSQL store (e.g., a document in a document store).

Except for graph databases, NoSQL systems integrate data distribution as a main feature through the adoption of the shared–nothing architecture. The scalability issue can be addressed in two different ways. The first way, known as *vertical scaling* or *scaling up*, upgrades a given machine by providing more *central processing unit* (CPU) power, more memory, or more disks. This solution has an intrinsic limit because one can reach the limit of upgrading a given machine. This approach is also considered to be very expensive and establishes a strong connection with a machine provider. The second approach, known as *horizontal scaling* or *scaling out*, implies buying more (commodity) machines when scalability issues are emerging. This solution has almost no limit in the number of machines one can add, and is less expensive due to low prices of commodity hardware.

In terms of data distribution, two main approaches are identified: *functional scaling* and *sharding*. With functional scaling, groups of data are created by functions and spread across database instances. In our running example, functions could be users, categories, and blogs. Each of them would be stored on different machines. The sharding approach, which can be used together with functional scaling, aims at splitting data within functions across multiple database instances. For example, suppose that if our user function is too large to fit into one machine, we can create shards out of its data set and distribute them on several machines. The attribute on which we create the shards is named the sharding key. In our running example, this could be the last name of the users. A second factor of this sharding-based distribution is the number of machines available. Let's consider that we have two machines. A naive approach could be to store all users with a last name starting with letters from A to M included on the first machine and with letters from N to Z on the second machine. This approach may not be very efficient if users' last names are not evenly distributed over the two machines. That is, there may be 80% of the names in the A to M range and only 20% in the N to Z range, causing some load-balancing issues—that is, the first machine stores and certainly processes a lot more data than the second machine.

In addition to these two distribution approaches, replication strategies can be used to store more than one copy of the data. Suppose we are replicating the A to M user's data set on three machines that are situated on different data centers. Then, if one machine (or data center) breaks down, we can still access the data set from the two remaining machines. Note that it's also possible to balance the read operations on these three machines and therefore provide better performances. In our running example, consider that the blogs of Joe Doe are stored on a server S1 (in Europe) and that Mary Smith, a follower of Joe Doe, is accessing Joe's blog entries using another server S2 (in the United States). At a certain time, Joe is entering a new blog entry, and before any replication can be performed between S1 and S2, there is a network failure—that is, communications between the nodes of S1 and S2 are not possible anymore. In a case where Joe's blogs are replicated on some nodes of S2, then Mary will be able to access any of Joe's blogs but the last one. Once the partition is solved and the data transfer between S1 and S2 is completed, Mary will be able to access Joe's last blog entry.

High replication also comes with some limitations, the main one being latencies related to the data replication. One kind of approach is to have a single machine accepting the write operations (denoted the master) and several slaves that are only accepting read operations from their clients. A simple running principle is the following: each time the slave receives a write, it will communicate with all the slaves to provide an update, therefore enabling them to stay up-to-date. The replication strategy can be synchronous or asynchronous, as presented in section 2.1.6, implying different latencies that may be more or less acceptable given the frequency of updates at the master. Of course, multiple replication solutions are possible, which more or less prevent some problems, such as architecture with multiple masters.

The final term of our description refers to the notion of consistency, which corresponds to the C in the ACID transaction properties. In the context of the CAP theorem (introduced in the next section), most NoSQL systems address consistency in a different manner than in RDBMS—that is, not using the machinery associated with the ACID properties.

According to their data model, distribution and replication strategies, we distinguish four NoSQL categories. Each one having its own peculiarities and facilitating the management of some particular kind of data: view of a database as a storage solution for persisting a value (*key-value stores*), allowing more flexibility about stored data (*document stores*), managing use cases like relationships (*graph databases*), or aggregating data (*column databases*). These systems have frequently been used to store various system logs, some components of social networks, or shopping carts in e-commerce web applications. But recently, new domains such as science and finance have started to be interested in these systems. NoSQL systems are becoming so popular that even database giants like Oracle, **IBM**, and **Microsoft** are enriching their offers to match some of the NoSQL features.

2.2.2 CAP and BASE

The *CAP* conjecture was proposed by Eric Brewer in 2000 (Brewer, 2000). This conjecture became a theorem after Gilbert and Lynch provided a demonstration in 2002 (Gilbert and Lynch, 2002). The CAP acronym corresponds to the three properties expected from a distributed system: *consistency*, *availability*, and *partition tolerance*. Intuitively, the theorem states that one cannot embrace the full potential of all three properties at the same time in a distributed system. To understand its impact on the design of distributed systems, we provide the definitions proposed in Gilbert and Lynch's 2002 paper. *Consistency* is defined as the fact that a service operates fully or not at all. This matches the notion of *atomicity* rather than *consistency* of ACID, but CAP sounds better than AAP. *Availability* is described as "every request received by a nonfailing node in the system must reply a response result" (p. 3). Note that this definition does not state anything about the amount of time needed to return the response. For many, the real constraint on availability is the notion of *latency*—that is, how is it going to take the nonfailing node to return the response? Finally, partition tolerance is specified as the fact that "no set of failures less than total network failure is allowed to cause the system to respond incorrectly" (p. 4). Here, a total network failure means that none of the nodes of the network can respond to a request. This theorem clearly had and still has a big influence on current database management systems, most notably in NoSQL stores.

The consequence of this theorem is that one has to identify which properties are the most relevant in a given system implementation. That is, if we cannot get all three properties at the same time, which one can be abandoned to still obtain a valuable system? In fact, there is not a single reply to this question, and the following configurations correspond to practical system requirements:

- We retain the consistency and availability properties (so our system is qualified as CA), but we renounce tolerance to network partitions. These systems typically correspond to standard RDBMS, such as MySQL and **Postgresql** to name open-source systems.
- We retain consistency and tolerance to network partitions (CP), but we accept that the system may not be available. Obviously, the idea here is that, in cases of network partitions, the system gives up availability and prefers consistency. Systems in this category are BigTable, **MongoDB**, **HBase**, and **Redis**.
- We retain the availability and tolerance to network partitions (AP), but we are ready to neglect consistency. Again, this defines another trade-off between availability and consistency where one prefers to be available rather than consistent. Systems adopting this approach are Dynamo from Amazon, Cassandra, **CouchDB**, and **Riak**.

In practice, the way consistency is handled is more subtle. In Vogels (2009), the author presents several forms of consistency that can be implemented in distributed services or data stores. Here, we focus on the two main ones. *Strong consistency* is the notion that we have considered in RDBMS with the ACID properties. This approach increases latencies in favor of data consistency. *Eventual consistency*, probably the most adopted in NoSQL stores, states that if no further updates are performed on the same data object, eventually all accesses are going to retrieve the last updated value. Said differently, all machines will be consistent after a given amount of time, denoted as the *inconsistency window*. In our running example, consider that Joe Doe has just added a new science blog entry that is stored in Europe on the S1 server. Before the replication to S2 (in the United States) is performed, Mary Smith is refreshing her science page. Because we are in the inconsistency window—that is, the time taken by the replication process to guarantee that Joe Doe's science entries are the same in all replica—Mary's science page will not display the last entry from Joe. At another time, outside of the inconsistency window, the most recent blog on Mary's science page will contain the last entry from Joe. These various consistency definitions are generally defined over three parameters:

- N, the number of nodes storing a replica of the data.
- W, the number of replicas needing to submit an update acknowledgment before the update is considered complete.
- R, the number of replicas that must be contacted for a read operation.

The different consistency strategies can be expressed in terms of relations among N, W, and R.

The term *basically available, soft state, eventually consistent* (BASE) has been presented by Pritchett (2008) and obviously aims to be opposed to ACID. Except for availability, the concepts composing BASE have not been precisely defined. Pritchett clearly presents BASE as a method to develop distributed systems using some dedicated design patterns. This interesting approach enables us to define services that can reject synchronization in favor of fast response times and therefore accepts some form of inconsistencies. These services usually possess their own methods to correct these inconsistencies—for example, by merging contradicting customer orders in an e-commerce situation. The main thing to retain is that a whole spectrum of architecture can be defined between the ACID and BASE extrema by implementing these design patterns into the application code.

2.2.3 NoSQL systems

In this section, we present the principal characteristics of the four main NoSQL families. The first three—key-value store, document store, and column family—can be considered as one family that is sometimes referred to as DHT or aggregate-oriented databases (Sadalage and Fowler, 2012), because they can all be viewed as key-value stores differing on what can be recorded and accessed at the value position. We will compare these systems on the following dimensions: *data structure, consistency, scalability, transaction support, indexing methods*, and *query facilities*. Because there does not exist any standard for any of these families, we will, for each family, consider the approach generally assumed for each dimension. Moreover, for each family, we will exhibit typical use cases and concisely present the most popular existing system.

Key-value stores

The *key-value store* family is the simplest category of NoSQL databases in terms of model and query facilities. This family corresponds to a hash table that is mainly used to access data stored using a primary key. This key is, in general, the only available index created for this kind of database. It can be represented in an RDBMS using a single table with two columns: one for the key and another one for the value. Like any hash table available in most programming languages, it's very efficient to retrieve a value given a certain key but is not adapted if one needs to obtain the key from a given value or to access values of a range of keys. Therefore, the main operations performed over this model are `get`, `put`, and `delete`, which respectively correspond to retrieve a value from a key; add a key-value pair in the case where the key does not exist, otherwise replace the value for that key; and to delete a key-value pair.

Many key-value stores exist, popular ones are: **Memcached**, Redis, **BerkeleyDB** (Oracle), **DynamoDB** (Amazon), **Voldemort** (Project), and Riak. Existing systems support different types for a value. Most of these systems can be of any type, ranging from simple types like a string of characters or a numerical value, to more complex objects like JSON and XML, and can possibly use lists or sets. In general, there is no native method to access a specific field in a complex value—that is, one cannot directly retrieve a section of a JSON document or access the ith element of a list. Given the three available operations, consistency can only be addressed on a single key. Some systems, like Riak, adopt the eventual consistency approach. In that case, conflict resolution is handled by either a newest-writes-win strategy or by retrieving all possible values and letting the end-user resolve the conflict.

Sharding the data is the principal solution to address scalability. A classic approach is to distribute given key-value pairs to determine on which machine the key-value pair is stored. Although this can improve performance by adding more machines, this method also comes with several problems. For example, if a node goes down, then its data is not accessible anymore and no data can be further stored on it. Another problem is related to data skew, which is the fact that the data as well as the workload are not evenly distributed over the nodes. In certain systems, a configuration based on the N, W, and R properties of the cluster can be defined to ensure performances for read and write operations. Usually transactions on write operations are not guaranteed in key-value stores. Nevertheless, some systems implement special approaches to overcome this limitation. For instance, Riak uses a write quorum approach. It amounts to setting certain values to N, W, and R such that not all replicas have to acknowledge an update, but rather half of it is sufficient. This can be stated as W > N/2. Typical use cases for key-value stores are domains with a low-granularity model such as a Web session, shopping-cart information, and user profiles. For models in need of more fine-grained modeling, the next two systems—document store and column family store—may be preferable.

We can now try to model the blog running example with a key-value store. It's first important to note that these kinds of database systems are considered special-purpose and are not designed to replace an RDBMS. Nevertheless, to bring to light the assets and drawbacks of key-value stores, we present a complete model of the blog example with an abstraction of a key-value store that possesses some of the characteristics of the Redis system. Our representation takes the form of a unique, very large DHT where all keys are being stored. To differentiate among key entries that are going to store users, categories, as well as blogs, we prefix the keys with respectively uid, cat, and blog. The right table in Figure 2.5 displays the different entries associated to a given key. The value entries follow the pattern label/value, where the label corresponds to an attribute in an RDBMS table. The left table in Figure 2.5 contains seven keys and respectively identifies two users, a username, two categories, and two blog entries.

The username:msmith needs some clarification. Recall that a key-value store only allows us to access information from a key. Therefore, if the system only provides a user-related key based on its identifier (e.g., uid:1), there will be no way to access information given its username. This is the main motivation behind the creation of a username-based key for each of the users. For instance, consider that Mary logs in the system by providing her msmith username and her password. The system needs to check if the username and password match an entry in the store. This is performed by searching for a key with username:msmith, which has a match, and checks if the retrieved value contains a password corresponding to the user-submitted password. Of course, with this mechanism, both the absence of an account for a user and the detection of login with an incorrect password are easily detected. Once the login step for Mary is performed, we also retrieved her user identifier. This enables us to search the key-value store for all

Keys   Values

uid:2	username/ msmith	fname/ Mary	lname/ Smith	gender/ female	following/ [uid:1, uid:4]	blogs/ [blog:102, ..]
uid:1	username/ jdoe	fname/ Joe	lname/ Doe	gender/ male	following/ [uid:2, uid:3]	blogs/ [blog:100, blog:101,...]
...						
username:msmith	uid/ uid:2	password/ *******				
...						
cat:1	label/ Sport					
cat:2	label/ Science					
...						
blog:100	date/ 10/13/2013	content/ Today...	uid/ uid:1	cat/ cat:3		
blog:101	date/ 10/15/2013	content/ Science is...	uid/ uid:1	cat/ cat:2		

Figure 2.5 Key-value store of the blog example.

her information—that is, accessing the value of the `uid:1` key. Thus, we are able to personalized her homepage with her first and last names, list of followers, etc. Finally, to display all the blog entries that Mary follows, we retrieve the list of `uids` that she follows and which are stored under the following attribute. The application then accesses all these users, retrieve the list of their blogs, and search all of their blogs in the store. All these operations have to be programmed because no join solutions are available. Note that our solution does not enable us to know by whom someone is followed. If this feature is important in the application, we can add an extract "column" in the value that will contain a list of followers.

This simple example has emphasized some modeling limits of key-value stores. For instance, these systems are not adapted to schema requiring one-to-many and many-to-many relationships, like those shown in Figure 2.1. One should limit the use of these stores to the efficient retrieval of atomic values from given keys. Such patterns are already quite frequent on the Web and by themselves justify the presence of Memcached-based key-value stores on a very large portion of the most frequented websites.

Document stores

Document databases focus on storage and access methods optimized for documents as opposed to rows or records in an RDBMS. The data model is a set of collections of documents that contain key-value collections. In a *document store* the values can be nested documents or lists, as well as scalar values. The nesting aspect is one important differentiator with the advanced key-value stores we just presented. The attribute names are not predefined in a global schema, but rather are dynamically defined for each document at runtime. Moreover, unlike RDBMS tuples, a wide range of values are authorized. A document stores data in tree-like structures and requires the data to be stored in a format understood by the database. In theory, this storage format can be XML, JSON, *Binary JSON* (BSON), or just about anything, as long as the database can understand the document's internal structure.

Several systems are available in that category with MongoDB certainly being the most popular and used in productions. Nevertheless, solutions such as CouchDB (Apache), **MarkLogic** (an enterprise-ready system that possesses all the features of a RDF store), and **RavenDB** are also active. MongoDB is an open-source, schema-free, document-oriented database using a collection-oriented storage. Collections are analogous to tables in a relational database. Each collection contains documents that can be nested in complex hierarchies and still support efficient query and index implementations. A document is a set of fields, each one being a key-value pair. A key is a string, and the value associated can be a basic type, a document, or an array of values. In addition, it allows efficient storage of binary data including large objects (e.g., photos and videos).

MongoDB provides support for indexes and queries for fetching data. Indexing techniques rely on B+trees and support multikey and secondary indexes. Dynamic queries are also supported with automatic use of indices, like in most RDBMSs. Each query goes through an optimization phase before being executed. MongoDB also supports MapReduce techniques for complex aggregations across documents. It provides access in many languages such as C, $C + +$, $C\#$, *Ruby*, *Java*, etc.

Other systems such as CouchDB propose a totally different query formalism through writing views in JavaScript using a MapReduce approach. Some systems support secondary indexes. MongoDB scales reads by using replica sets and it scales writes by using sharding. Here we present a possible design for the blog example using the JSON approach of MongoDB. Although the use case could be designed in many different ways, we propose one where all the information related to an end-user is stored in a single document. Note that our solution contains a mix of subdocuments and lists. In what follows, we only present the document of the Joe Doe end-user.

```
{
"userId" : "1", "fname" : "Joe", "lname" : "Doe", "gender" : "male",
"follows" : [2,3],
"isFollowedBy" : [2],
"writes" : [ { "content" : "Today ..", "category" : "Tech"},
      { "content" : "Science is ..", "category" : "Science"} ]
}
```

We have decided to store the label characterizing a blog entry in the value of the "writes" key. This enables us not to require any join when we are storing a new blog entry for an end-user. On the other hand, this approach is far from ideal if we want to retrieve all blogs of a given category, say, all Science blogs. This is a reason why some document stores, such as MongoDB, allow us to define secondary indexes and thus to bypass this access problem. Another aspect of our proposed solution is the storage of user identifiers in the "follows" and "isFollowedBy" keys. This clearly states that some forms of joins will be needed whenever one wants to retrieve the first and last names of an end-user following another one. As said earlier, most NoSQL databases do not propose query languages that natively support joins. Therefore, such joins will be handled in the application programs and the efficiency, in terms of algorithms used, will be the responsibility of the programmer. Another approach would have been to store the last and first names in the "follows" and "isFollowedBy" keys, but that approach would not have been efficient for other joins.

To generate Mary's science page, we are providing an extract of her document:

```
{
"userId" : "2", "fname" : "Mary", "lname" : "Smith", "gender" : "fname"
"follows", : [1,4],
"isFollowedBy" : [1],
...
}
```

Once, this document is accessed, the system will scan the entries of the "follows" list, and for each of those users, access their documents and filter the Science entries of the "writes" list.

Document stores present a particular interest in use cases such as blog applications, content management systems, Web and real-time analytics, and event logging.

Column family

Column family stores or BigTable-like databases (Chang et al., 2006) are very similar on the surface to relational databases, but they are, in fact, quite different because they are oriented differently to maximize disk performance. Note that these systems are not to be confused with the column stores described in Section 2.1.5. Therefore, we make a distinction between column stores and column family stores. Recall that a column store is a kind of RDBMS with a special storage layer, one where each column is stored in a distinct file. In a column family store, the term *store* is associated to a particular data structure that is called a "column" and that is regrouped into so-called column families. This approach is motivated by the fact that generally a query does not return every column of a record.

These systems store their data such that it can be rapidly aggregated with less I/O activity. A BigTable-like database consists of multiple tables, each one containing a set of addressable rows. Each row consists of a set of values that are considered columns. Among the systems other than BigTable adopting this approach, we can identify HBase (Apache), Accumulo (Apache), early versions of Cassandra (Apache and **DataStax**), **Hypertable**, and **SimpleDB** (Amazon). In this section, we concentrate on Cassandra and HBase. It's a column family stores having a data model that is dynamic and column-oriented. Unlike a relational database, there is no need to model all of the columns required by an application upfront, as each row is not required to have the same set of columns and columns can be added with no application downtime.

A table in HBase is a distributed multidimensional map indexed by a key. The value is an object that is highly structured and the row key in a table is a string. Columns are grouped together into sets called *column families*. Column families contain multiple columns, each of which has a name, a value, and a timestamp, and is referenced by row keys. While Cassandra was, originally, proposing two kinds of column families, denoted *simple* and *super* (intuitively a column family within a column family), the latest version of Cassandra is limited to simple column families, thus matching HBase and BigTable approaches. The column families are fixed when a HBase database is created, but columns can be added to a family at any time. The index of the row keys of a given column family serves as a primary index. It's the responsibility of each participating node to maintain this index for the subset of data it manages. Additionally, because each node is aware of ranges of keys managed by the others nodes, requesting rows can be more efficient. Cassandra supports secondary indexes—that is, indexes on column values.

Cassandra allows fast lookups, and supports ordered range queries. Cassandra is recognized to be really fast for writes in a write-heavy environment. However, reads are slower than writes. This may be caused by not using B+trees and in-place updates on disk unlike all major relational databases and some NoSQL systems. In terms of data access, Cassandra used to only propose a very low-level API that is accessed through its *remote procedure call* (RPC) serialization mechanism, such as Thrift. Recently, *Cassandra Query Language* (CQL) has appeared as an alternative to the existing API. Since its release, DataStax has promoted CQL (currently in version 3 in 2014) as the preferred query solution.

Figure 2.6 proposes a possible model for the blog example. It emphasizes the creation of four different column families. The gray boxes correspond to row keys (some of which are generated automatically by the system, for example, `1234xyz` in the `Blog` column family, while others are provided by the end-user) and the white ones represent columns. For readability reasons, we do not detail all three components of each column. We again consider the creation of Mary's science page. We assume that Mary logged in correctly to the website with her username msmith. This enables us to retrieve all the users she is following via the `Follows` column family—that is, `jdoe` and `mdavis`.

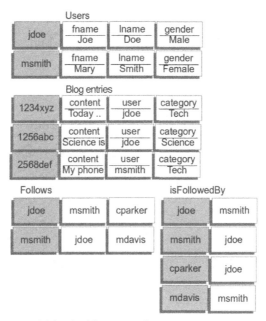

Figure 2.6 Column family model for the blog example.

Using the secondary indexing feature of HBase, we will be able to find all the blog entries with user `jdoe` (and `mdavis`) efficiently. For each of these blogs, we will only retain those with a `Science` category.

Column family stores have common ideal use cases with document stores: content management systems, blogging applications, and event logging. Their integration of a timestamp in columns suits them for handling counters and time-related information efficiently.

Graph database stores

A graph database stores a graph in the mathematical sense—that is, it deals with a set of nodes and relationships holding between these nodes. There are many available graph database store systems: **Infinite Graph**, **Titan**, **OrientDB**, **FlockDB** (Apache, originally developed at Twitter), and **Neo4J**, which is considered a leader in this category. Most systems addressing such representation use a traversing query approach by navigating along the nodes following the edges. Because edges are materialized in the graph, no computation, such as joins in RDBMS, are needed. This makes the traversing approach an efficient one. Nevertheless, to traverse a graph, one needs to find, among millions or billions of nodes, the one to start the search from, therefore indexes are required. In most systems, properties of a graph can be indexed to support fast lookups. The *Gremlin* query language is dedicated to traversing graphs and is used in many databases that implement the *Blueprints* property graph, which is a collection of interfaces, implementations, and

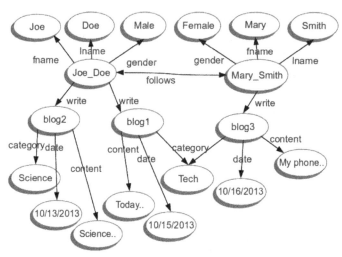

Figure 2.7 Graph for the blog example.

test suites for the property graph data model. Neo4J possesses its own query language called *Cypher*.

The transaction adopted by most graph databases conforms to the ACID approach. This is motivated by the fact that most of these systems do not distribute nodes among a cluster. Storing the whole graph over a single server enables us to address strong consistency. However, systems like Infinite Graph do propose distribution. In that situation, sharding and replication may be used as the main choice for scalability. Methods to split nodes on several machines are known but are very complex to maintain efficiently. Replication may be efficient with a master–slave approach if read operations dominate the write ones.

Figure 2.7 presents data for the blog example. All information corresponds to nodes with links between them represented as edges. To generate Mary's science page, we are using a navigation approach. That is, we will start from the `Mary_Smith` node and pursue all outgoing edges with the `follows` label. That leads the system to the `Joe_Doe` node from which the system follows the `write` outgoing edges. This points to two distinct nodes corresponding to blog entries. For each of them, the system will navigate through the `category` edge and will only retain those with a `Science` value—that is, in the figure, only `blog2` matches to our search.

Typical use cases of graph databases are social and e-commerce domains, as well as recommendation systems.

2.2.4 MapReduce

In the previous section, we emphasized on solutions that enable us to store data on cluster commodity machines. To apprehend the full potential of this approach, this also has to come with methods to process this data efficiently—that is, to perform the processing on the servers and to limit the transfer of data between machines to its minimum. MapReduce, a programming model that has been proposed by engineers at Google in 2004 (Dean and Ghemawat, 2004), is such a framework. It's based on two operations that have existed for decades in functional programming: the `map` and `reduce` functions.

In a MapReduce framework, the user programs the `map` and `reduce` functions in a given programming language, such as Java or C++. But abstractions to program these two functions are available using an SQL-like query language, such as *PIG LATIN*. When writing these programs, one does not need to take care about the data distribution and parallelism aspects. In fact, the main contribution of MapReduce-based systems is to orchestrate the distribution and execution of these `map` and `reduce` operations on a cluster of machines over very large data sets. It also fault-tolerant, meaning that if a machine of the cluster fails during the execution of a process, its job will be given to another machine automatically. Therefore, most of the hard tasks from an end-user point of view are automatized and taken care of by the system: data partitioning, execution scheduling, handling machine failure, and managing intermachine communication.

In this framework, the `map` function processes key-value pairs and outputs an intermediate set of key-value pairs. The `reduce` function processes the key-value pairs generated by the `map` function by operating over the values of the same associated keys. The framework partitions the input data over a cluster of machines and sends the map function to each machine. This supports a parallel execution of the `map` function. After all `map` function operations have been completed, a shuffle phase is performed to transfer to all `map` outputs to the `reduce` nodes—that is, all `map` outputs with the same key are sent to the same `reduce` node. Then the `reduce` jobs are executed and produce the final output.

Over the last several years, this framework has gained popularity and resulted in several implementations. *Hadoop* is currently the most popular of them and is a product of the Apache Software Foundation and is thus open-source. Given the features of MapReduce, some may consider it a database system. For instance, one may consider that the `map` and `reduce` functions respectively correspond to a `GROUP BY` clause and an aggregation function of SQL, such as a sum or average. Stonebraker and colleagues (2010) provide a complete comparison of Hadoop and existing parallel DBMSs. The paper emphasizes that they are not competitors but rather are complementary. In fact, MapReduce can be considered as an *extract transform load* (ETL) tool rather than as a complete DBMS. The framework is considered faster at loading data than parallel databases. Nevertheless, once loaded, the data is more efficiently operated on in a parallel database system.

At the time of writing this book, MapReduce is not a single framework anymore and comes with a full stack of technologies, libraries, and tools. We have already mentioned PIG LATIN as a solution to ease writing MapReduce tasks. But systems like Hadoop also depend on other components such as a distributed file system that is especially designed for very large data volumes, such as the *Hadoop Distributed File System* (HDFS), *Zookeeper* a centralized service providing coordination to distributed applications, i.e., maintaining naming, configuration information, and handling distributed synchronization. *Hive* as a data warehouse, and *Mahout* as a library to perform machine learning.

2.3 EVOLUTIONS OF RDBMS AND NOSQL SYSTEMS

Due to the Big Data phenomenon, data management systems are almost obliged to evolve to cope with new needs. In this section, we focus on evolutions that impact the two kinds of systems presented in this chapter and that will probably influence future solutions in the management of RDF data. Nevertheless, due to space limitations, we do not consider specific fields such as stream processing and scientific database systems.

During their long history, RDBMSs have faced several contenders, such as object databases in the 1990s and XML databases in the 2000s. Each time, they have adapted to the situation by introducing novel functionalities and retained their market dominance. These adaptations never involved deep architectural modifications and most of the main components of RDBMSs still rely on the design choices of the 1970s and 1980s.

NoSQL can be considered the latest threat for RDBMS dominance. To cope with the goals of NoSQL—that is, storing and processing large data sets on machine clusters—RDBMSs may have to rearchitecture at least some of their main components. In Stonebraker et al. (2007), the authors argue that the one-size-fits-all property of RDBMSs is over. In fact, the paper states that if they are not adapting rapidly, they could even lose their leading position in their OLTP niche market. The needed adaptations have to consider the evolution of hardware that has happened during the last few years—for example, the cost of main memory is decreasing so rapidly that servers with hundreds of gigabytes is not uncommon; SSDs are getting less expensive and are starting to replace disks in some situations; faster CPUs and networks are arising; computing with *graphics processing units* (GPUs) is easier through APIs and programming languages; and dominance of shared-nothing architecture is being confirmed. The main components responsible for the performance bottleneck of current RDBMS systems have been identified in Harizopoulos et al. (2008) and are related to ACID transactions (i.e., logging, locking, and latching), as well as buffer management operations. In the new hardware era, all these components could be implemented to reside in the main memory. Such systems recently started to appear and are sometimes denoted as *NewSQL*. They share the high-performance and scalability characteristics with NoSQL and at the same time retain full ACID properties and the SQL language. Available systems are **VoltDB, Clustrix, NuoDB, MemSQL, NimbusDB, Akkiban,** and **SQLFire**.

With the accession to new markets, NoSQL systems are also facing the needs of new clients. Some of their requisites concern the integration of new features: declarative query languages, solutions for defining schemata, the ability to select different consistency characteristics (e.g., strong or eventual), and integrating integrity constraints to enhance data quality and business intelligence processing. The most successful NoSQL stores are all going this way. For instance, an important work has been conducted by the team at DataStax (the main contributor on the Cassandra database) on designing a declarative, SQL-influenced query language, namely *CQL*. Note that this language does not just provide a *Data Manipulation Language* (DML) but also a *Data Definition Language* (DDL) that enables us to create/drop keyspaces (i.e., databases), tables, and indexes. Other popular systems such as CouchDB are also proposing an SQL-like solution, denoted *UnQL*. MongoDB and Neo4J, potential leaders in document and graph stores, have proposed query languages for quite a while now. Considering the consistency aspect, systems like Cassandra and MongoDB already propose configuration tools that enable us to select a particular approach for a given database. In fact, most of these desired features are already present in RDBMSs and one can ask what NoSQL stores will look like if they are all added.

As a final direction on the evolution of database management systems, it's always interesting to look for innovations provided by major Web companies. During the last couple of years, many consider that the most innovative systems have been designed at Google. Thus, it's amusing to witness that after leading the NoSQL movement, Google, through its **Spanner** system, is going back a more conventional relational model. The Spanner system (Corbett et al., 2013) has been presented at the 2012 OSDI conference. It's an attempt to implement an ACID- and SQL-compliant relational database over a global scale and geographically distributed cluster of machines. An important contribution of the paper is to present the TrueTime API: the system's solution to support externally consistent distributed transactions at a global scale. Therefore, all data are versioned using the timestamp of its commit. The design of this database mainly responds to requests from Google employees who needed a solution that enables easier schema evolution and a strong consistency in the presence of wide-area replication than available solutions, such as BigTable and Megastore.

2.4 SUMMARY

- The database management system market is very active due to the emergence of Big Data.
- For almost 30 years, this market has been dominated by systems based on the relational model. Due to their long history, they are considered the most mature and robust approaches. They are constituted of many features, such as complete query language (SQL) and optimization facilities, indexes for speed-up queries, processing of transactions, and concurrency support.

- NoSQL is an emerging family of data storage solutions that is gaining traction in many organizations and companies dealing with a data deluge. Existing systems are quite diverse and do not rely on standards, but leaders are active and very responsive to the expectations of their clients.
- Innovative system approaches are appearing and some of their objectives are to address high throughput with data availability and distribution. Some of these systems are based on the relational model and tend to go through a rearchitecturing process to gain some of these properties.
- These systems serve as the storage backend of several RDF systems we will study in Part 2 of this book.

CHAPTER THREE

RDF and the Semantic Web Stack

In Chapter 2, we presented the main characteristics of database management systems available on the market. Recall that such a system corresponds to a complete software used to define, create, manage, query, and update some set of data. Of course, an RDF database management system (we use the term *RDF store* interchangeably) handles RDF data. To motivate and understand the details of these systems, we begin this chapter with a presentation of an important part of the Semantic Web stack. This stack regroups some general notions that have emerged in the context of Artificial Intelligence (AI), such as Knowledge Representation (KR), and that support the description of reasoning services over schemata and facts expressed in this extension of the current Web. Note that this inference aspect is a main peculiarity of the systems we are covering in this book—that is, standard database management systems do not natively support inference features.

3.1 SEMANTIC WEB

From its inception at the beginning of the 1990s, the Web has evolved. From a static version, mainly supported by HTML and CSS, it evolved into a more dynamic and write-intensive Web, qualified as 2.0. Nevertheless, both of these versions can be qualified as syntactic because the languages they are built upon only convey information toward rendering in web browsers. The Web evolution is far from being finished, and some obviously make reference to the next extension as Web 3.0, to include the addition of semantics-supported features. In this book, we prefer the term *Semantic Web* because it refers to a computer science field that emerged in the early 2000s (Berners-Lee et al., 2001). In contrast, the Semantic Web provides meaning to the information contained in Web documents.

This description and its interpretation are supported by a stack of technologies that have been designed and recommended by the World Wide Web Consortium (W3C) since 1999. This stack is frequently referred to as the *Semantic Web cake*, and one of its generally adopted current versions is presented in Figure 3.1. The layer organization of this technology stack implies that the elements described at a given layer are compliant with the standards defined at the lower layers. In this book, we are only concerned with the five bottom layers.

The lowest layer of this stack provides a global identification solution for the resources found on the Web. In Figure 3.1 they are referred to as *uniform/internationalized*

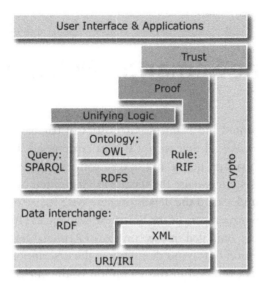

Figure 3.1 Semantic Web cake.

resource identifiers (URIs/IRIs). URIs and IRIs are now used interchangeably, so we will note in this book when a distinction is needed.

The second layer supports the definition of a syntax that is based on XML, a meta-language based on the notion of tags. Note that XML comes with some associated technologies that enable the definition of schemata for document instances, such as *document type definition* (DTD) or XML Schema, and a naming convention (i.e., namespaces) is supported to disambiguate the use of overlapping tags coming from different languages.

In the third layer, we really begin our journey in the Semantic Web with the RDF language. In Figure 3.1, it's qualified as data interchange because its objective is to enable the exchange of facts among agents. Note that RDF relies on both XML and the URI layer. This implies that several syntaxes are available for RDF: one based on XML, denoted RDF/XML, and other ones that we will present in this chapter.

The fourth layer provides a reply to the limitation that RDF represents facts only. With *RDF Schema* (RDFS), a first solution to define metadata on some elements of an RDF document instance is proposed. The features of this language do not support the specification of very expressive vocabularies but this aspect is taken care of in the next layer.

The fifth layer is composed of the *Web Ontology Language* (OWL). OWL enables us to define more expressive ontologies than RDFS does, but it comes at an increased computational complexity of reasoning.

Finally, spreading across layers four and five are SPARQL and the *Resource Interchange Format* (RIF). SPARQL is most widely used as a query language over RDF data. Therefore, it can be considered as the SQL for RDF stores. SPARQL is also a protocol that we will describe in Section 7 in the context of query federation. RIF supports an inference form that is based on the processing of rules (i.e., *prolog* and *datalog* like), and is usually not considered in RDF database systems. Therefore, we are not covering it in this book.

The remaining layers are not considered in RDF stores and are out of the scope of this book.

One term we need to clarify before delving into the standards of the Semantic Web is *ontology*. Ontology refers to the definition of a domain in terms of its concepts and their relationships. For instance, we can define an ontology for a bedroom where we would find concepts such as `bed`, `mattress`, and `pillow`. Some relationships among these concepts are `on` (to state that a pillow is on a mattress) or `composedOf` (to specify that a bed is composed of a mattress). Of course, ontologies can be defined for domains far more complex than a bedroom, such as medicine or biology. And some of the languages used to define these ontologies have to be more or less expressive. Expressivity characterizes the precision with which the concepts and relationships can be defined. For example, an RDBMS schema, expressed in an entity relationship (ER) diagram, can be considered as an ontology with a very low degree of expressiveness—that is, it's unable to represent constructors such as negation, disjunction, and quantifications. In our Semantic Web stack, RDFS is considered the least expressive language and, as will we see later on, OWL proposes several variants (called profiles) that present different degrees of expressiveness. An interesting aspect of the Semantic Web is that many quality ontologies are already available in these formats in fields as diverse as science, culture and economics to name a few.

We will highlight that it's possible to make inferences—that is, deduce information not explicitly stored in the source—over an ontology alone. But in general, it's more interesting to reason over data that is associated to a given ontology. This data is represented in RDF documents. In an AI terminology, the association of a schema and some data is referred as a Knowledge Base (KB). Additionally, in the context of *Description Logic* (DL), which is the logic underlying some of the OWL languages, one makes reference to an ontology as a terminological box (Tbox) and to a set of facts as an assertional box (Abox).

3.2 RDF

The first aim of the Resource Description Framework (RDF) was to provide a metadata data model to the Web. Nowadays, it emerges as a data model for the Web of Data and the Semantic Web providing a logical organization defined in terms of some data structures to support the representation, access, constraints, and relationships of objects of interest in a given application domain.

The underlying data model is quite simple, but, as we will see afterwards, nevertheless expressive. The basic unit of information is given as a triple (s,p,o) composed of a *subject* (s), a *predicate* (p), and an *object* (o). Each triple represents a fact on a thing being described

Table 3.1 RDF Triples Corresponding to User Table in Chapter 2

Subject	Predicate	Object
JD	firstName	Joe
JD	lastName	Doe
JD	gender	Male
MS	firstName	Mary
MS	lastName	Smith
MS	gender	Female

(i.e., the subject, which is also referred to as the resource), on a specific property (i.e., the predicate), and with a given value (i.e., the object). Table 3.1 provides a simplified overview of the RDF triples corresponding to the User table presented in Chapter 2.

A more compact way of representing a set of triples is using a directed, labeled graph representation. In such an RDF graph, a triple is represented by an edge between two nodes. The source node corresponds to the subject, the destination node to the object, and the edge to the predicate. As illustrated in Figure 3.2, any subject or object is represented by a single node and all its related information corresponds to a subgraph.

As previously mentioned, one of the main characteristic of the Web of Data movement is data distribution over multiple sources. This distribution induces a merging task whenever one wants to retrieve all information on a given set of resources. This merging process is facilitated by the representation of the unit of information in RDF. Indeed, in RDF, because any information is provided as a triple, merging data sources corresponds to merging sets of triples. The main problem that can arise is the identification of common resources among multiple sources. This problem is solved in RDF by the use of URIs or its generalization IRIs, which support encoding in Unicode rather than in ASCII.

URIs represent common global identifiers for resources across the Web. The syntax and format of URIs are very similar to the well-known *uniform resource locators* (URLs; e.g., `http://example.com/Blog#JD`). In fact, URLs are just special cases of URIs. Another form of URIs is a *uniform resource name* (URN), which identifies something that is not associated to a Web resource but on which people on the Web want to write about, such as a book or a tree.

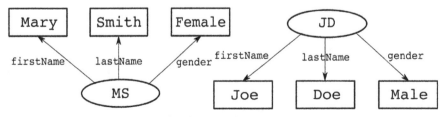

Figure 3.2 RDF graph representation of Table 3.1 triples.

Any two data sources on the Web can refer to the same resource by using the same URI. One of the benefits of the common form of URIs and URLs is that URIs may be *dereferenced*—that is, each part of the URI is a locator for the resource (e.g., server name, directories, filenames, etc.) where potential extra information can be found. For example, the URI `http://www.w3.org/standards/techs/rdf#w3c_all` specifies a protocol (i.e., http), a server name (i.e., www.w3.org), some directories on that server (i.e., standards/techs), a document (i.e., rdf), and a location in that document (i.e., w3c_all). The de-referencable quality of URIs is quite important in the context of the Semantic Web because it supports both the identification in a global Web infrastructure, and as an effect enables data integration at scale—that is, the ability to consider identifiers as links to other resources. Nevertheless, in RDF, the main objective of URIs is to provide a unique name for a resource or a property.

URIs will naturally support the related problem of distinguishing different senses of a word like "apple." The well-known computer brand and the delicious fruit will be differentiated by referring to different URIs, such as `<http://www.apple.com/public/RDF/#Apple>` or `<http://www.fruits.com/fall/#Apple>`. In these URI references, we can observe a fragment identifier that is preceded by the # symbol. Whatever appears before that symbol identifies a resource and the fragment identifier identifies a part of that resource. For ease of notation, in RDF, one may define a *prefix* to represent a namespace, such as `Fruits:Apple` where `Fruits` represents the namespace `<http://www.fruits.com/fall/#>`. Prefixes are not global identifiers and should be declared with their corresponding namespace (as similarly done with qualified names in XML).

While the prior aim of the Web was to provide access to information for humans via web pages, the aim of the Web of Data movement is to provide knowledge processing by nonhuman agents like software. For this purpose, one cannot rely only on strings and should be able to add structure and knowledge to the resource of interest. Thus, most of the information in RDF data sets will consist of URIs, for subjects, predicates, and objects. More precisely, non–URI values, namely *literals*, will only be supported for objects. A literal value may be accompanied with a *data type* (e.g., `xsd:integer`, `xsd:decimal`, `xsd:boolean`, `xsd:float`[1]) and will be referred to as a *typed literal*, or *plain literal* otherwise. Finally, while most of the resources are given an identifier (i.e., URI), RDF provides the possibility for resources to be anonymous. Such resources are represented as *blank nodes* (also called *bnodes*), which do not have a permanent identity. Blank nodes are defined with a specific namespace denoted by a _. The main purpose of such nodes is either to state the existence of some resources that we cannot name, or to group together some knowledge. For example, one would like to state that an anonymous follower added a comment to Joe Doe's blog about science.

---

[1]The `xsd` prefix corresponds here to the XML Schema namespace `http://www.w3.org/2001/XMLSchema#`.

Table 3.2 Prefixes `ex:` and `blog:` Respectively Correspond to `http://example.com/terms#` and `http://example.com/Blog#`

Subject	Predicate	Object
`blog:JD`	`ex:firstName`	`"Joe"`
`blog:JD`	`ex:lastName`	`"Doe"`
`blog:JD`	**`rdf:type`**	**`ex:Man`**
`blog:MS`	`ex:firstName`	`"Mary"`
`blog:MS`	`ex:lastName`	`"Smith"`
`blog:MS`	**`rdf:type`**	**`ex:Woman`**

The RDF standard provides a specific namespace often referred to with the `rdf` prefix name, such as `<http://www.w3.org/1999/02/22-rdf-syntax-ns#>`. Among the standard identifiers defined in this namespace, `rdf:type` is a predicate allowing elementary typing ability in RDF. That mechanism is quite useful to state the gender of Joe Doe and Mary Smith with respectively the `Man` and `Woman` concepts, as shown in Table 3.2.

The object of such triples will be understood as a type. As we will see, this mechanism will help us infer nonexplicit knowledge, such as Joe Doe and Mary Smith are persons, without the need to state it explicitly in the data but relying on the knowledge that `ex:Man` and `ex:Woman` are subtypes of `ex:Person`.

The identifier `rdf:Property` can be combined with `rdf:type` to indicate that a given resource may be used as a predicate rather than a subject or an object. In other words, it allows to introduce new predicates. In the blog running example context, it would be suitable to state that Joe Doe is following Mary Smith directly using a predicate named `blog:isFollowing`. The corresponding RDF declaration is given in Table 3.3.

Let's assume now that we want to express that Joe Doe is following Mary Smith since last January. Our main issue is that this extra information is specific to the previous statement. One would be tempted to add a `started` property to the `isFollowing` edge between the `blog:MS` and `blog:JD` nodes of our graph but this is not allowed in RDF graphs. One solution is to treat a statement as a resource. For this purpose, RDF provides

Table 3.3 Prefixes `ex:` and `blog:` Respectively Correspond to `http://example.com/terms#` and `http://example.com/Blog#`

Subject	Predicate	Object
`blog:JD`	`ex:firstName`	`"Joe"`
`blog:JD`	`ex:lastName`	`"Doe"`
`blog:JD`	`rdf:type`	`ex:Man`
`blog:JD`	**`blog:isFollowing`**	**`blog:MS`**
`blog:MS`	`ex:firstName`	`"Mary"`
`blog:MS`	`ex:lastName`	`"Smith"`
`blog:MS`	`rdf:type`	`ex:Woman`
`blog:isFollowing`	**`rdf:type`**	**`rdf:Property`**

Table 3.4 Prefixes `ex:` and `blog:` Respectively Correspond to `http://example.com/terms#` and `http://example.com/Blog#`

Subject	Predicate	Object
`blog:JD`	`ex:firstName`	`"Joe"`
`blog:JD`	`ex:lastName`	`"Doe"`
`blog:JD`	`rdf:type`	`ex:Man`
`blog:MS`	`ex:firstName`	`"Mary"`
`blog:MS`	`ex:lastName`	`"Smith"`
`blog:MS`	`rdf:type`	`ex:Woman`
`blog:isFollowing`	`rdf:type`	`rdf:Property`
`_:X`	**`rdf:type`**	**`rdf:Statement`**
`_:X`	**`rdf:subject`**	**`blog:JD`**
`_:X`	**`rdf:predicate`**	**`blog:isFollowing`**
`_:X`	**`rdf:object`**	**`blog:MS`**
`_:X`	**`blog:started`**	**`ex:January`**

a vocabulary—namely, `rdf:Statement`, `rdf:subject`, `rdf:predicate`, and `rdf:object`—that can be used to identify a given statement and refer to it in another statement. In other words, RDF allows making statements about RDF statements. This process is formally called *reification* and can be written as four statements (often referred to as the *reification quad*). An illustration is given in Table 3.4 and Figure 3.3.

One of the important properties of a reified triple is that assertion of a reified triple does not necessarily imply the assertion of the triple itself. Say that Joe Doe pretends that Will Smith is following Mary Smith; we can assert this knowledge without stating that Will Smith is indeed following Mary Smith.

For ease, we have only presented statements as three-column tables or RDF graphs. While the former is not easy to read, the latter is mostly provided for human readers. Nevertheless, graph visualization is known to be hard for human agents even for small graphs (i.e., tens of nodes). Let's now present the most conventional textual representation

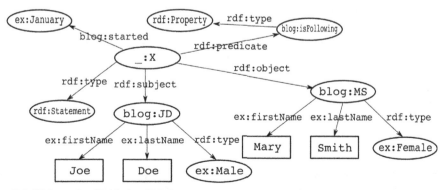

Figure 3.3 RDF graph of Table 3.4 RDF data set.

for publishing data in RDF on the Web. In the following, we will stick to the running blog context and consider the data presented in Chapter 2 for each format.

3.2.1 RDF/XML

The W3C recommendation for textual representation is using an XML serialization of RDF, a so-called *RDF/XML* (`http://www.w3.org/TR/rdf-syntax-grammar/`). Roughly, any resource can be defined as an `rdf:Description` XML element with an `rdf:about` attribute that states its URI. Multiple characteristics concerning a given subject are given as child elements of the corresponding XML element. To refer to a given URI, one should use the `rdf:resource` attribute. In the example shown in the following code, four statements about Joe Doe (`<http://example.com/Blog#JD>`) are given.

RDF/XML allows a more concise expression of the `rdf:type` predicate by replacing the `rdf:Description` element by an element directly named with the name-spaced element corresponding to the RDF URI of the `rdf:resource` attribute.

```
<?xml version="1.0"?>
<rdf:RDF xmlns:rdf="http://www.w3.org/1999/02/22 -rdf-syntax-ns#"
        xmlns:blog="http://example.com/Blog#"
        xmlns:ex="http://example.com/terms#">
  <rdf:Description rdf:about="htt p://example.com/Blog#JD">
      <rdf:type rdf:resource="http://example.com/Blog#User"/>
      <blog:hasGender rdf:resource="http://example.com/terms#Male"/>
      <ex:firstName>Joe</ex:firstName>
      <ex:lastName>Doe</ex:lastName>
  </rdf:Description>
</rdf:RDF>
```

Moreover, any predicate of which the value is a literal can be expressed as an XML attribute of the corresponding subject element. The previous example code can thus be rephrased as follows.

```
<?xml version="1.0"?>
<rdf:RDF xmlns:rdf="http://www.w3.org/1999/02/22-rdf-syntax-ns#"
        xmlns:blog="http://example.com/Blog#"
        xmlns:ex="http://example.com/terms#">
  <blog:User rdf:about="http://example.com/Blog#JD"
ex:firstName="Joe" ex:lastName="Doe">
      <blog:gender rdf:resource="http://example.com/terms#Male"/>
  </blog:User>
</rdf:RDF>
```

Finally, RDF/XML provides a vocabulary to manage groups of resources or literals. Groups are either defined with RDF *containers* or RDF *collections*. The main difference is

that RDF collections are groups containing only the specified members. Three kinds of
RDF containers are defined: an `rdf:Bag` corresponds to an unordered group allowing
duplicates, an `rdf:Seq` corresponds to an ordered `rdf:Bag`, and an `rdf:Alt` corresponds to alternative choices. Each member of a group is defined by an `rdf:li` element.
A full illustration based on the data presented in Chapter 2 is provided in the following code
block. In this example, note the presence the `rdf:ID` attribute, which enables us to define
a named node, therefore it's quite similar to `rdf:about`. Nevertheless, the latter is usually
preferred when one refers to a resource with a globally well-known identifier or location.

```xml
<?xml version="1.0"?>
<rdf:RDF xmlns:rdf="http://www.w3.org/1999/02/22-rdf-syntax-ns#"
xmlns:xsd="http://www.w3.org/2001/XMLSchema#"
xmlns:blog="http://example.com/Blog#"
xmlns:cat="http://example.com/Cat#"
xmlns:ex="http://example.com/terms#"
xml:base="http://blogs.com/">
  <blog:User rdf:about="JD" ex:firstName="Joe" ex:lastName="Doe">
    <blog:gender rdf:resource="ex:Male"/>
    <blog:isFollowing>
      <rdf:Bag>
        <rdf:li rdf:resource="MS"/>
        <rdf:li rdf:resource="#blogger3"/>
      </rdf:Bag>
    </blog:isFollowing>
  </blog:User>
  <blog:User rdf:about="MS" ex:firstName="Mary" ex:lastName="Smith">
    <blog:gender rdf:resource="ex:Female"/>
    <blog:isFollowing>
      <rdf:Bag>
        <rdf:li rdf:resource="JD"/>
        <rdf:li rdf:resource="#blogger4"/>
      </rdf:Bag>
    </blog:isFollowing>
  </blog:User>
  <blog:User rdf:ID="blogger3"/>
  <blog:User rdf:ID="blogger4"/>
  <cat:Category rdf:about="cat:Sport" cat:title="Sport"/>
  <cat:Category rdf:about="cat:Science" cat:title="Science"/>
  <cat:Category rdf:about="cat:Tech" cat:title="Technology"/>
  <blog:Blog rdf:about="blog1" blog:content="Today…">
    <ex:writtenOn rdf:datatype="xsd:date">10/13/2013</ex:writtenOn>
    <blog:owner rdf:resource="JD"/>
    <blog:category rdf:resource="cat:Tech"/>
  </blog:Blog>
  <blog:Blog rdf:about="blog2" blog:content="Science is">
    <ex:writtenOn rdf:datatype="xsd:date">10/15/2013</ex:writtenOn>
    <blog:owner rdf:resource="JD"/>
    <blog:category rdf:resource="cat:Science"/>
  </blog:Blog>
  <blog:Blog rdf:about="blog3" blog:content="My phone">
    <ex:writtenOn rdf:datatype="xsd:date">10/16/2013</ex:writtenOn>
    <blog:owner rdf:resource="MS"/>
    <blog:category rdf:resource="cat:Tech"/>
  </blog:Blog>
</rdf:RDF>
```

In the following sections, we present three additional serializations for RDF documents that do not suffer the verbosity of the XML syntax. They are frequently used for readability reasons but are also handled by most of the RDF tools we will see later in this chapter e.g., parser, serializer.

3.2.2 N-triples

N-triples is the simplest form of textual representation of RDF data but it's also the most difficult to use in a print version because it does not allow URI abbreviation. The triples are given in subject, predicate, and object order as three complete URIs separated by spaces and encompassed by angle brackets ($<$ and $>$). Each statement is given on a single line ended by a period (.). The following code illustrates the statements regarding the category `Science`.

```
<http://example.com/Cat#Science   http://www.w3.org/1999/02/22-rdf-
syntax-ns#type http://example.com/Cat#Category>.
<http://example.com/Cat#Science   http://example.com/Cat#title   "Science">.
```

3.2.3 N3

Notation 3, or *N3* for short, was proposed by Tim Berners-Lee as a compromise between the simplicity of N-triples with the expressiveness of RDF/XML. The notation is very similar to N-triples. The main syntactic differences are:

- The surrounding brackets have been removed.
- URIs can be abbreviated by prefix names.
- There is no restriction on the number of separating spaces.
- Shortcut syntax for statements sharing a predicate and/or an object have been introduced:
  - `"subject stuff ; morestuff ."` stands for `"subject stuff. subject morestuff ."`
  - `"subject predicate stuff, morestuff ."` stands for `"subject predicate stuff. subject predicate morestuff ."`
  - Blank nodes can be replaced by declared existential variables (see `http://www.w3.org/DesignIssues/Notation3` for more details).

N3 has other features unrelated to the serialization of RDF (e.g., RDF-based rules) that will not be presented in this book because they have been superseded by Turtle and SPARQL. A full illustration is given in the following code.

```
@prefix blog: <http://example.com/Blog#> .
@prefix cat: <http://example.com/Cat#> .
@prefix ex: <http://example.com/terms#> .
@prefix rdf: <http://www.w3.org/1999/02/22-rdf-syntax-ns#> .
@prefix rdfs: <http://www.w3.org/2000/01/rdf-schema#> .
@prefix xml: <http://www.w3.org/XML/1998/namespace> .
@prefix xsd: <http://www.w3.org/2001/XMLSchema#> .
<cat:Sport> a cat:Category ;
    cat:title "Sport" .
<cat:Science> a cat:Category ;
    cat:title "Science" .
<cat:Tech> a cat:Category ;
    cat:title "Technology" .
<http://blogs.com/blog1> a blog:Blog ;
    blog:category <cat:Tech> ;
    blog:content "Today…" ;
    blog:owner <http://blogs.com/JD> ;
    ex:writtenOn "10/13/2013"^^<xsd:date> .
<http://blogs.com/blog2> a blog:Blog ;
    blog:category <cat:Science> ;
    blog:content "Science is" ;
    blog:owner <http://blogs.com/JD> ;
    ex:writtenOn "10/15/2013"^^<xsd:date> .
<http://blogs.com/blog3> a blog:Blog ;
    blog:category <cat:Tech> ;
    blog:content "My phone" ;
    blog:owner <http://blogs.com/MS> ;
    ex:writtenOn "10/16/2013"^^<xsd:date> .
<http://blogs.com/#blogger3> a blog:User .
<http://blogs.com/#blogger4> a blog:User .
<http://blogs.com/MS> a blog:User ;
    blog:gender <ex:Female> ;
    blog:isFollowing [ a rdf:Bag ;
            rdf:_1 <http://blogs.com/JD> ;
            rdf:_2 <http://blogs.com/#blogger4> ] ;
    ex:firstName "Mary" ;
    ex:lastName "Smith" .
<http://blogs.com/JD> a blog:User ;
    blog:gender <ex:Male> ;
    blog:isFollowing [ a rdf:Bag ;
            rdf:_1 <http://blogs.com/MS> ;
            rdf:_2 <http://blogs.com/#blogger3> ] ;
    ex:firstName "Joe" ;
    ex:lastName "Doe" .
```

3.2.4 Turtle

Turtle (the Terse RDF Triple Language) is a simplified version of N3 that is becoming increasingly popular and is now a W3C recommendation. In Turtle, as a predicate, a is equivalent to the complete URI corresponding to rdf:type. RDF blank nodes can either be explicitly expressed as _:id, where id is the identifier of the blank node, or anonymously by putting all the triples that are subjects between square brackets ([and]).

Finally, Turtle provides a collection structure for lists as a sequence of elements separated by spaces and encompassed by parenthesis ((and)). The following code illustrates the statements regarding Mary Smith.

```
@prefix rdf: <http://www.w3.org/1999/02/22-rdf-syntax-ns#> .
@prefix cat: <http://example.com/Cat#> .
@prefix blog: <http://example.com/Blog#> .
@prefix ex: <http://example.com/terms#> .
...
blog:MS        a                  blog:User ;
               ex:firstName        "Mary" ;
               ex:lastName         "Smith" ;
               blog:hasGender      ex:Female ;
               blog:isFollowing    ( blog:JD  _:blogger4 ) .
_:blogger4     a                  blog:User .
...
```

3.2.5 Other serializations

Because a huge amount of data is already reachable on the Web, through HTML pages, some web page authors are interested in embedding information for agents (not necessarily human) to read and use. This is the aim of *microformats* (http://microformats.org/), which do not have effect on how the information is displayed through the browser but allow us to embed RDF data in a web page. This is done by the use of specific attributes of HTML/XHTML elements. A similar way to write RDF data in a web page is to use *RDF in attributes* (RDFa; `http://www.w3.org/TR/rdfa-core/`), which was proposed by W3C. This approach follows the style of microformats by minimizing repetition in a document—that is, the information is written once and both support extraction of metadata by agents and rendering in the web browser. RDFa defines existing and new HTML attributes where subjects, predicates, and objects should be stored and retrieved. RDFa has been adopted by search engines such as **Google**, **Bing**, **Yandex**, and **Yahoo!** (through the `http://schema.org/` initiative) to enable data extraction by agents. Microformats and schema.org provide vocabularies that cover a limited amount of domains (events, contact information, review, product). Moreover, RDFa is intrinsically not limited to any domain and can related to any well-formed compliant vocabulary.

3.3 SPARQL

We just presented RDF as the data model of the Semantic Web. In general, a data model comes equipped with a language to support queries over some data set. RDF follows that approach and *SPARQL*, which stands for SPARQL Protocol and RDF Query Language, corresponds to a group of specifications providing languages and protocols to query and manipulate RDF graphs. In the context of this chapter, we will concentrate on the query language aspect. To increase its adoption rate, the language borrowed part of its syntax from the popular and widely adopted Structured Query Language (SQL) of RDBMS. The standard `SELECT <result template> FROM <data set definition> WHERE <query pattern>` pattern of SQL is adapted in the context of SPARQL.

The peculiarity of SPARQL is to handle RDF graphs and to support a navigation-based approach to data retrieval. The idea is to start from a given node and move from node to node following certain edges until the goal node is reached. This approach is quite different from the SQL execution, which is based on joins between tables. To perform such operations, variables must be supported in the RDF triples patterns allowed in the query language, in particular in the `WHERE` clause. A *variable* is identified by a question mark (?) followed by the name of the variable. A variable will, on one hand, allow us to store any information resulting from the graph matching problem and, on the other hand, could be combined afterwards in other triples. As in Turtle, the use of prefixes declaration allows us to lighten the overall textual representation of the data. In fact, the triples pattern of the `WHERE` clause is based on Turtle. Following is a first simple query that retrieves the first names of users with a `Doe` last name. In this query, we have two variables, `?user` and `?name`, and only the latter is proposed in the result set since it is the only one presenting the SELECT clause (such a variable is qualified as distinguished).

```
PREFIX blog: <http://example.com/Blog#>
PREFIX ex:   <http://example.com/terms#>
SELECT ?name
WHERE {
  ?user      ex:lastName      "Doe" ;
             ex:firstName     ?name ;
}
```

While the `WHERE` part (i.e., the query pattern) of the query allows us to restrict the RDF subgraph of interest that should match the conditions, the `SELECT` part (i.e., the result template) allows us to moreover select the part of the result we want to exhibit. The clauses in the `WHERE` part are defined as the standard RDF triples pattern including variables. Variables not present in the `SELECT` part are used to connect up different triples patterns (similar to SQL's `JOIN`) and are qualified as non-distinguished. The following code presents a query requiring a join. Intuitively, it asks for the first names of persons with a `Doe` last name and who are following someone with a `Mary` first name. The join is supported by the co-occurrence of the `?user2` variable in both the third and fourth line of the query, respectively, at the object and subject positions.

```
PREFIX blog: <http://example.com/Blog#>
PREFIX ex:   <http://example.com/terms#>
SELECT ?name
WHERE {
  ?user      ex:lastName      "Doe" ;
             ex:firstName     ?name ;
             blog:isFollowing ?user2 .
  ?user2     ex:firstName     "Mary".
}
```

If the SELECT part contains the * symbol then, as in SQL, all the variables used in the WHERE clause are provided in the output. SPARQL also allows classic SQL LIMIT, DISTINCT, OFFSET, ORDER BY, GROUP BY, and HAVING arguments. Like it does in SQL, LIMIT allows us to restrict the number of results, DISTINCT forbids duplicate results, OFFSET skips a given number of results, ORDER BY sorts the results, GROUP BY groups sets of data to perform aggregate functions such as AVG(), MIN(), MAX(), or COUNT(), while HAVING specifies a condition restricting values to appear in the result. The following code provides a full example.

```
PREFIX blog: <http://example.com/Blog#>
PREFIX ex:   <http://example.com/terms#>
SELECT ?name
WHERE {
  ?user      ex:lastName      "Doe" ;
             ex:firstName     ?name ;
             blog:isFollowing ?user2 ;
             blog:owner       ?blog  .
  ?user2     ex:firstName     "Mary".
}
GROUP BY ?name
HAVING (COUNT(?blogs) > 2)
LIMIT 2
OFFSET 3
ORDER BY ?name
```

SPARQL also provides the following additional keywords: OPTIONAL, FILTER, and UNION. The OPTIONAL keyword allows us to retrieve data even in the absence of something matching for some triples patterns. The triples that are not obliged to find some binding are precisely expressed in the OPTIONAL clause, which is in the WHERE clause. Thus, it corresponds to an OUTER JOIN in relational algebra and SQL. The FILTER allows us to further verify if a variable meets a certain condition (e.g., string matching using *regex* expressions). The UNION keyword allows us to define intermediate results, provided by subqueries, that will be combined to produce a result containing any data satisfying at least one of those patterns. Each subquery must be enclosed in its own set of curly braces ({ and }). Following is an example of these notions. Intuitively, the query takes the union of a user name and a blog category name for: (1) users with a first name starting with the letters "Jo", who have written some categorized blogs and follow someone whose first name is "Mary" and (2) users who are being followed by a person with first name "Mary", have written some blogs but it is optional that these blogs are tagged with a category.

```
PREFIX blog: <http://example.com/Blog#>
PREFIX cat:  <http://example.com/Cat#>
PREFIX ex:   <http://example.com/terms#>
SELECT ?name ?cat
WHERE {
      ?user ex:firstName ?name ;
              blog:isFollowing ?user2 ;
              blog:owner ?blog.
      ?blog cat:category ?cat .
      ?user2 ex:firstName "Mary".
      FILTER (regex(?name,"Jo"))
      } UNION {
      ?user ex:firstName ?name ;
              blog:owner ?blog.
      ?user2  blog:isFollowing ?user ;
                ex:firstName "Mary" ;
      OPTIONAL {?blog cat:category ?cat}
      }
```

UNION should not be confused with subqueries. A *subquery* is a query inside a query where the outer query uses the results obtained by the inner query. SPARQL also borrowed the SQL *alias* (i.e., the AS keyword), as shown in the following code.

```
PREFIX blog: <http://example.com/Blog#>
PREFIX ex:   <http://example.com/terms#>
SELECT ?name   (COUNT(?blog) AS ?nbBlog)
WHERE {
      ?user     ex:firstName    ?name ;
                ex:lastName     "Dœ" ;
                blog:isFollowing ?user2 .
      ?blog blog:owner      ?user .
  {
    SELECT ?user2
    WHERE {
      ?user2   ex:firstName    "Mary".
    }
  }
}
```

Although in SQL, a data set corresponds to a relational table (or view), in SPARQL it correpsonds to a graph. The FROM keyword, as in SQL, is used to specify a data set to query. There may be more than one data set, and each of them should be declared with a FROM keyword. All data sets will be considered as a merged one from which the result will be pulled out. SPARQL also provides a nice mechanism to specify the data set of a given subquery with the use of the FROM NAMED keyword. As opposed to the previous merging behavior, this mechanism relies on a *named graph*, which corresponds to specific sets of triples of the data gathered under a common identifier. This important feature allows us to identify precisely the data we are dealing with.

While the FROM keyword allows us to retrieve data (from local or distant graphs) and apply a query to it, SPARQL's SERVICE keyword provides a way to remotely execute a query on a SPARQL endpoint. A *SPARQL endpoint* is a web service allowing the execution of SPARQL queries (e.g., *DBpedia* a central data set of Linked Open Data). Using SERVICE, the query will be sent to the SPARQL endpoint, which will execute the query and return the result. The following code illustrates the SERVICE and FROM keywords.

```
PREFIX blog: <http://example.com/Blog#>
PREFIX ex:   <http://example.com/terms#>
SELECT DISTINCT ?name ?nbBlog
WHERE {
  {
    SELECT ?name   (COUNT(?blog) AS ?nbBlog)
    SERVICE <http://someSPARQLendpoint.com>
    WHERE {
      ?user      ex:firstName     ?name ;
                 ex:lastName      "Doe" ;
                 blog:isFollowing ?user2 ;
                 blog:owner ?blog .
      {
        SELECT ?user2
        FROM <http://someURI.com/Blog>
        WHERE {
          ?user2   ex:firstName     "Mary".
        }
      }
    }
  }
}
```

By now, results to SPARQL queries were taking the form of a set of tuples, as in SQL, that is shaped from the SELECT template expression. In fact, SPARQL allows for other representations when used with ASK, CONSTRUCT, and DESCRIBE keywords. ASK allows us to obtain a Boolean answer to a SPARQL query depending on the possible match of a query pattern to the data set. The following code illustrates an ASK query.

```
PREFIX blog: <http://example.com/Blog#>
PREFIX ex:   <http://example.com/terms#>
ASK {
  ?user      ex:firstName     ?name ;
             blog:isFollowing ?user2 .
  ?user2     ex:firstName     "Mary" .
  FILTER (regex(?name, "Jo")) .
}
```

While ASK still provides a table result consisting of a single cell with a yes or no value, the CONSTRUCT and DESCRIBE keywords allow for a result as an RDF graph. CONSTRUCT has a similar syntax as SELECT except for the result template part, which will represent the RDF organization of the result using variables. CONSTRUCT will apply the query pattern to fill the values of variables of the result template and will return an RDF graph. If needed, aggregate functions can be called as part of a subquery in the CONSTRUCT's query pattern, an example of which is shown in the following code.

```
PREFIX blog: <http://example.com/Blog#>
CONSTRUCT {
  ?user <http://www.someserver.com/Blog#countOwnedBlogs> ?nbBlog .
} WHERE {
  {
    SELECT ?user (COUNT(?blogs) AS ?nbBlog)
    WHERE {
      ?user   blow:owner   ?blog .
    }
  }
}
```

A SPARQL DESCRIBE query asks for any RDF information related to some specific variables of the result template. The main point of this query form is to discover resources without knowing their schema. This approach is particularly useful when one tries to discover valuable information by following URIs from data sets to data sets. The following code illustrates a DESCRIBE query.

```
PREFIX blog: <http://example.com/Blog#>
DESCRIBE ?user {
WHERE {
  ?user   blog:firstName   "Mary" .
}
```

SPARQL 1.1 introduces a simple syntax for the support of negation. The MINUS operator enables us to remove some results from a first expression that has to be compatible with another expression. This corresponds to the difference operator of relational algebra, which is generally implemented with the MINUS or EXCEPT SQL operators. The following code shows an example of this first negation operator.

```
PREFIX blog: <http://example.com/Blog#>
SELECT ?user {
WHERE {
  ?user   blog:lastName   "Doe"
  MINUS { ?user blog:gender "Male".}
}
```

A second negation operator, namely EXISTS and NOT EXISTS, enables us to test the existence (or nonexistence) of a pattern in a given graph. Note with this approach, we introduce a triples pattern in a FILTER clause for the first time, as shown in the following code

```
PREFIX blog: <http://example.com/Blog#>
SELECT ?user {
WHERE {
  ?user    blog:lastName    "Doe"
  FILTER ( NOT EXISTS {?user blog:gender "Male".}) }
```

3.4 SPARQL 1.1 UPDATE

SPARQL 1.1 Update is intended to be used in conjunction with the SPARQL 1.1 query language as a language for updating RDF graphs in a graph store. A *graph store* is defined as a mutable container of RDF graphs managed by a RDF Store accepting and processing an update request. A graph store is by default composed of one anonymous graph (i.e., the default graph) and possibly zero or more named graphs (identified by URIs).

SPARQL 1.1 Update provides two categories of operations on a graph store: *graph update* and *graph management*. The former concerns update (i.e., insertion and deletion) operations on the content (i.e., triples) of an RDF graph, while the latter is related to adding or deleting a whole named RDF graph to the graph store.

3.4.1 Graph update

Insertion and deletion requests are very similar in their form. They are respectively expressed using INSERT and DELETE keywords accompanied with a template of the data concerned with possibly some request pattern that has to be respected by the resulting data. INSERT is thus also very similar to CONSTRUCT except that the resulting RDF graph will be merged to an existing RDF graph of the graph store. Because one may be interested in inserting new data without resting upon existing data, SPARQL 1.1 Update also allows inserting/deleting inline data with respectively INSERT/DELETE DATA keywords. By default, the operations are applied to the default RDF graph of the graph store. They can also be applied to an existing named RDF graph by providing the corresponding URI using the GRAPH keyword with INSERT and DELETE. The WHERE keyword can only be used in conjunction with

INSERT and DELETE to specify the pattern that the triples concerned by the modification should respect.

Finally, SPARQL 1.1 Update allows for batch insertion and deletion with respectively LOAD and CLEAR operations. LOAD operations retrieve a copy of all triples of a remote graph and insert it into a given named graph (using the INTO keyword) or the default RDF graph. CLEAR operations remove all triples of a given named graph (using the GRAPH keyword) or the default RDF graph, resulting in an empty RDF graph (which still belongs to the graph store). A request can be composed of multiple operations (each ended by ;) that should be performed as a single action. The following code provides an overall illustration.

```
PREFIX blog: <http://example.com/Blog#>
PREFIX ex:  <http://example.com/terms#>
CLEAR GRAPH <   http://example.com/Blog#NewUsers> ;
INSERT DATA {
  GRAPH <http://example.com/Blog#NewUsers> {
    blog:GB     ex:firstName     "Guillaume" ;
                ex:lastName      "Blin" ;
                blog:hasGender   ex:Male .
    blog:OC     ex:firstName     "Olivier" ;
                ex:lastName      "Cure" ;
                blog:hasGender   ex:Male .
  }
} ;
CLEAR GRAPH <   http://example.com/Blog#SomeUsers> ;
LOAD <http://example.com/Blog#SomeUsers> INTO <http://example.com/
Blog#Users> ;
INSERT { GRAPH <http://example.com/Blog#NewUsers> { ?s ?p ?o} }
WHERE {
  GRAPH <http://example.com/Blog#SomeUsers>{
    ?s      ?p               ?o ;
            blog:hasGender   ex:Male .
  }
} ;
DELETE WHERE {
  GRAPH <http://example.com/Blog#SomeUsers> {
    ?s      ?p               ?o ;
            blog:hasGender   ex:Male .
  }
} ;
```

3.4.2 Graph management

The creation and deletion of named RDF graphs of a graph store can be done using the CREATE/DROP GRAPH keywords respectively accompanied with the URI of the target named graph.

3.5 ONTOLOGY LANGUAGES

So far we have presented the RDF data model and how to query it using SPAR-QL. But we have not considered the value of elements present in the triples—that is, what subjects, properties, and objects represent. In fact, we will show in this section that describing some of these elements in vocabularies can support the design of several interesting features. Different languages are available to represent vocabularies used in RDF documents. In this book, we are interested in vocabularies corresponding to ontologies. The most widely used definition of an ontology is the one proposed by Thomas Gruber in 1993: "An ontology is a specification of a conceptualization." That is, it aims at conceptualizing a certain domain by rigorously specifying the entities it contains. Intuitively, it amounts to describing the concepts found in that domain together with all the relations existing between these concepts. In the blog running example, the concepts we have dealt with are `Man`, `Woman`, `User`, and `Blog`, and the property relating them is `isFollowing` and `owner`, which relate respectively two users and blog entry to a given user.

Within the Semantic Web, there is a large spectrum of ontology languages, RDFS and the OWL 2 family, which mainly differ in their expressiveness—that is, the logical operators and syntactical restrictions they are based upon to express the constraints of a domain. Figure 3.4 presents the containment of OWL 2 and RDFS languages in terms of their expressiveness.

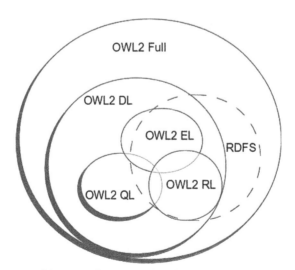

Figure 3.4 Expressiveness of OWL 2 and RDFS ontology languages.

3.5.1 RDFS

The least expressive language of the Semantic Web stack is *RDF Schema*, or *RDFS*. RDFS is a semantic extension of the RDF proposed by the W3C. We already discussed that `rdf:Property` and `rdf:type` provide elementary typing abilities. The aim of RDFS is to provide a mechanism allowing us to describe further the corresponding types. More precisely, it allows describing groups of related resources and their relationships. The former are called *concepts* or *classes* while the latter are called *properties*. All these descriptions are given in RDF format using a vocabulary defined in the namespace `<http://www.w3.org/2000/01/rdf-schema#>`, commonly associated with the prefix `rdfs`.

As already stated, a class corresponds to a group of resources, which is itself a resource (therefore identified by an URI) defined as an `rdfs:Class`. A resource belonging to a class is known as an *instance* of this class. An instance can be defined with the `rdf:type` property combined with the corresponding `rdfs:Class` element. The group of RDFS classes is itself a class named `rdfs:Class`. RDFS defines a set of predefined classes composed of `rdfs:Resource`, `rdf:Property`, and `rdf:Statement`. By definition, they are all instances of `rdfs:Class`. `rdfs:Resource` regroups all the resources, `rdf:Property` regroups all the relationships between resources, and `rdf:Statement` regroups the statements made on RDF triples. Both the subject and object of an RDF statement are instances of `rdfs:Resource`, while the predicate is an instance of `rdf:Property`.

The *literals* are represented by another instance of `rdfs:Class` named `rdfs:Literal`. Any literal is a resource and, therefore, `rdfs:Literal` is a subclass of `rdfs:Resource`. Formally, if a class A is a *subclass* of a class B, then any instance of A is also an instance of B; B is also called a *superclass* of A. The literals are moreover subdivided into two subclasses of `rdfs:Literal` named `rdfs:Datatype` and `rdfs:XMLLiteral`. `rdfs:Datatype` regroups all typed literals among which is `rdfs:XMLLiteral` (the only one defined in the recommendation). `rdfs:XMLLiteral` is thus an instance of `rdfs:Datatype`, which moreover allows for XML values.

RDFS defines several interesting instances of `rdf:Property`: `rdfs:range`, `rdfs:domain`, `rdf:type`, `rdfs:subClassOf`, `rdfs:subPropertyOf`, `rdfs:label`, and `rdfs:comment`. An *RDF property* is defined as a relation between a subject resource and an object resource. RDFS allows us to describe this relation in terms of the classes of resources to which they apply by specifying the class of the subject (i.e., the *domain*) and the class of the object (i.e., the *range*) of the corresponding predicate. The corresponding `rdfs:range` and `rdfs:domain` properties allow us to state that respectively the subject and the object of a given `rdf:Property` should be an instance of a given `rdfs:Class`. The property `rdf:type` is used to state that a given resource (i.e., an instance of `rdfs:Resource`) is an instance of a specific class (i.e., `rdfs:Class`). To summarize, by definition, the recursive definitions are provided in the following code.

```
PREFIX rdf: <http://www.w3.org/1999/02/22-rdf-syntax-ns#>
PREFIX rdfs: <http://www.w3.org/2000/01/rdf-schema#>
rdfs:range   rdfs:domain  rdf:Property ;
             rdfs:range   rdfs:Class .
rdfs:domain  rdfs:domain  rdf:Property ;
             rdfs:range   rdfs:Class .
rdf:type     rdfs:domain  rdfs:Resource ;
             rdfs:range   rdfs:Class .
```

The property `rdfs:subClassOf` is used to state that a given class (i.e., `rdfs:Class`) is a subclass of another class. As we will see later on, `rdfs:subClassOf` is moreover a transitive property. Similarly, using the property `rdfs:subPropertyOf`, one can state that any pair of resources (i.e., subject and object) related by a given property (`rdf:Property`) is also related by another property. The corresponding rules can be expressed in SPARQL as shown in the following code.[2]

```
PREFIX rdf: <http://www.w3.org/1999/02/22-rdf-syntax-ns#>
PREFIX rdfs: <http://www.w3.org/2000/01/rdf-schema#>
CONSTRUCT { ?x      rdf:type         ?d .
            ?c      rdf:type         rdfs:Class .
            ?d      rdf:type         rdfs:Class .
} WHERE {
            ?c      rdfs:subClassOf  ?d .
            ?x      rdf:type         ?c .
}
CONSTRUCT { ?x      ?p               ?y .
            ?p      rdf:type         rdf:Property .
            ?q      rdf:type         rdf:Property .
} WHERE {
            ?q      rdfs:subPropertyOf ?p .
            ?x      ?q               ?y .
}
```

Finally, `rdfs:label` and `rdfs:comment` properties are for human readability purposes to respectively provide a human-readable version (i.e., `rdfs:Literal`) of

---

[2]Expressing rules as SPARQL constructs was an original idea of Allemang and Hendler (2011) that we find very efficient and reuse in this chapter.

the name and the description of a resource (i.e., `rdfs:Resource`). The following code illustrates `rdfs:label`.

```
PREFIX rdf: <http://www.w3.org/1999/02/22-rdf-syntax-ns#>
PREFIX rdfs: <http://www.w3.org/2000/01/rdf-schema#>
PREFIX blog: <http://example.com/Blog#>
PREFIX ex:   <http://example.com/terms#>
ex:Male         rdfs:subClassOf    blog:Gender .
ex:Female       rdfs:subClassOf    blog:Gender .
blog:hasGender rdfs:domain         blog:User ;
                rdfs:range          blog:Gender ;
                rdfs:label          "Determine the gender of a User".
```

3.5.2 OWL

OWL is an ontology language that is far more expressive than RDFS. Through a set of W3C recommendations, two versions of OWL have been specified in respectively 2004 (OWL 1) and 2009 (OWL 2). The vocabularies of the OWL languages are a set of primitives, described in RDF, that are extending the expressive power of RDFS. These extensions enable us to define classes, properties, instances, and meta-descriptions with much more accuracy.

In OWL two types of properties are defined. The *object property* (`owl:ObjectProperty`) relates individuals (i.e., instances) of two OWL classes. The *data-type property* (`owl:DatatypeProperty`) relates individuals of an OWL class to a literal. One of the main provisions of OWL is defining a class by its description. The first mechanism provided for this purpose is based on *enumeration*. The enumeration constructor `owl:oneOf` specifies that all individuals of the described class should belong to the exact set of enumerated individuals (no more, no less). The following code illustrates the use of `owl:oneOf`.

```
PREFIX rdf: <http://www.w3.org/1999/02/22-rdf-syntax-ns#>
PREFIX owl: <http://www.w3.org/2002/07/owl#>
PREFIX blog: <http://example.com/Blog#>
_:X  rdf:type  blog:User ;
     owl:oneOf (blog:JD blog:MS blog:OC blog:GB) .
```

The second mechanism provided is a set of *property restrictions*. A property restriction defines a class by the set of all individuals that satisfy the corresponding restriction. A property restriction is defined by the `owl:Restriction` class and the `owl:onProperty` property indicates the restricted property. OWL distinguishes two kinds of property restrictions: *value constraints* and *cardinality constraints*.

A value constraint controls the range of the property when applied to a particular class description (to be compared to the general range restriction induced by `rdfs:range`). There are three value constraints in OWL. The value constraints `owl:allValuesFrom` and `owl:someValuesFrom` specify that respectively any and at least one individuals of the class described should be related by the corresponding property with an instance of the class description or a value in the specified data range. The value constraint `owl:hasValue` provides a restriction to a single given value. The following code illustrates these notions.

```
PREFIX rdf: <http://www.w3.org/1999/02/22-rdf-syntax-ns#>
PREFIX rdfs: <http://www.w3.org/2000/01/rdf-schema#>
PREFIX owl: <http://www.w3.org/2002/07/owl#>
PREFIX blog: <http://example.com/Blog#>
PREFIX ex:  <http://example.com/terms#>
PREFIX cat: <http://example.com/Cat#>
blog:scientificBlog  rdf:type          owl:Class ;
                     rdfs:subClassOf [
                       rdf:type         owl:Restriction ;
                       owl:onProperty  blog:category ;
                       owl:hasValue     cat:Tech .
                     ] .
blog:maleFollowers   rdf:type          owl:Class ;
                     rdfs:subClassOf [
                       rdf:type          owl:Restriction ;
                       owl:onProperty    blog:hasGender ;
                       owl:allValuesFrom ex:Male .
                     ] .
```

A cardinality constraint controls the number of values a property can take when applied to a particular class description. There are three cardinality constraints in OWL. The cardinality constraints `owl:maxCardinality`, `owl:minCardinality`, and `owl:cardinality` specify that all individuals of the described class can have respectively at most, at least, or exactly a given number of semantically distinct values (that can be individuals or data values). The following code provides an illustration.

```
PREFIX rdf: <http://www.w3.org/1999/02/22-rdf-syntax-ns#>
PREFIX rdfs: <http://www.w3.org/2000/01/rdf-schema#>
PREFIX owl: <http://www.w3.org/2002/07/owl#>
PREFIX blog: <http://example.com/Blog#>
PREFIX xsd: <http://www.w3.org/2001    /XMLSchema#>
blog:isOwning owl:inverseOf  blog:owner .
blog:activeBlogger  rdf:type          owl:Class ;
                    rdfs:subClassOf [
                      rdf:type          owl:Restriction ;
                      owl:onProperty    blog:isOwning ;
                      owl:minCardinality "3"^^<xsd:int> .
                    ] .
```

The third mechanism is provided by three sets of operators on classes allowing for a class description in terms of description logics. The `owl:intersectionOf`, `owl:unionOf`, and `owl:complementOf` specify that any individual of the described class is also an individual of respectively all, at least one, and none of the class descriptions in the list provided. The following code provides an illustration.

```
PREFIX rdf: <http://www.w3.org/1999/02/22-rdf-syntax-ns#>
PREFIX rdfs: <http://www.w3.org/2000/01/rdf-schema#>
PREFIX owl: <http://www.w3.org/2002/07/owl#>
PREFIX blog: <http://example.com/Blog#>
blog:unactiveBlogger   rdf:type        owl:Class ;
                       rdfs:subClassOf [
                         rdf:type           owl:Class ;
                         owl:intersectionOf (
                           blog:User
                           [
                               owl:complementOf  blog:activeBlogger .
                           ]
                         ) .
```

Finally, regarding individuals, in addition to the `owl:sameAs` equivalence constructor, OWL defines the `owl:differentFrom` property, which states that two URIs refer to different individuals, and the `owl:AllDifferent` class, which states that a given set of individuals are all different. The `owl:AllDifferent` class has to be combined with a special syntactical construct called `owl:distinctMembers` that should always be used with an `owl:AllDifferent` individual as its subject, as shown in the following code.

```
PREFIX rdf: <http://www.w3.org/1999/02/22-rdf-syntax-ns#>
PREFIX owl: <http://www.w3.org/2002/07/owl#>
PREFIX blog: <http://example.com/Blog#>
blog:JD  owl:differentFrom    blog:MS ,
                              blog:OC .
_:X      rdf:type             owl:AllDifferent ;
         owl:distinctMembers (blog:JD blog:MS blog:OC) .
```

3.5.3 OWL 2

OWL 2 is an extension and revision of OWL 1 providing a complete backwards compatibility with OWL 1. OWL 2 adds new functionalities, some being syntactic sugar, other offering new expressivity. The OWL 2 syntactic sugars simplify some common patterns in writing and are defined with the following class description constructors.

In OWL 2, the `owl:disjointWith` property allows us to specify that two classes do not share any instance. This disjointedness can be generalized to sets of properties using the class `owl:AllDisjointClasses`. The `owl:AllDisjointClasses` class has to be combined with a special syntactical construct called `owl:members`. The OWL 2 constructor `owl:disjointUnionOf` defines a class as the union of some classes that are pairwise disjoint. Finally, OWL 2 allows us to specify that a given property does not relate a given subject to a specific individual or literal. This is done by defining an RDF quad where respectively the subject, predicate, and object of the unsatisfied statement are related to the RDF quad using respectively the `owl:sourceIndividual`, `owl:assertionProperty`, and `owl:targetIndividual` properties, and where the type of property used in this negative assertion is defined by class `owl:NegativePropertyAssertion` or `owl:NegativeDataPropertyAssertion`. The following code provides an illustration.

```
PREFIX rdf: <http://www.w3.org/1999/02/22-rdf-syntax-ns#>
PREFIX owl: <http://www.w3.org/2002/07/owl#>
PREFIX blog: <http://example.com/Blog#>
blog:allFollowers owl:disjointUnionOf (
                                        blog:maleFollowers
                                        blog:femaleFollowers
                                        ) .
                        blog:OC .
_:X      rdf:type      owl:AllDisjointClasses ;
         owl:members   (blog:unactiveBlogger blog:activeBlogger) .
_:Y      rdf:type              owl:NegativePropertyAssertion ;
         owl:sourceIndividual  blog:JD ;
         owl:assertionProperty blog:isFollowing ;
         owl:targetIndividual  blog:OC .
_:Z      rdf:type              owl:NegativeDataPropertyAssertion ;
         owl:sourceIndividual  blog:Blog3 ;
         owl:assertionProperty blog:date ;
         owl:targetValue       "11/13/2013" .
```

OWL 2 provides new constructs for expressing additional restrictions on properties, new characteristics of properties, incompatibility of properties, and property chains and keys. The OWL 2 construct `owl:hasSelf` allows local reflexivity to be used in class descriptions, so-called *self-restriction*. The following code provides an illustration.

```
PREFIX rdf: <http://www.w3.org/1999/02/22-rdf-syntax-ns#>
PREFIX owl: <http://www.w3.org/2002/07/owl#>
PREFIX blog: <http://example.com/Blog#>
blog:blogAboutBlogs  rdf:type         owl:Class ;
                     owl:EquivalentClass [
                         rdf:type        owl:Restriction ;
                         owl:onProperty  blog:isAbout ;
                         owl:hasSelf     "true"^^<xsd:boolean> .
                     ] .
```

OWL 2 constructs `owl:minQualifiedCardinality`, `owl:maxQualified Cardinality`, and `owl:qualifiedCardinality` provide a means to restrain the class (on object properties) or data range (on data properties) of the instances to be counted, so-called *qualified cardinality restrictions*. They have the same behavior as the three OWL cardinality constraints previously defined. The data range can be expressed using the `owl:onDataRange` class and `owl:oneOf` property. OWL provides the `owl:oneOf` construct, which allows us to define a range of data values (commonly referred to as *enumerated data types*). The subject of `owl:oneOf` is a blank node of the `owl:DataRange` class and the object is a list of literals. The following code provides an illustration.

```
PREFIX rdf: <http://www.w3.org/1999/02/22-rdf-syntax-ns#>
PREFIX rdfs: <http://www.w3.org/2000/01/rdf-schema#>
PREFIX owl: <http://www.w3.org/2002/07/owl#>
PREFIX blog: <http://example.com/Blog#>
blog:isOwning          owl:inverseOf     owl:Class .
blog:activeGeekBlogger rdf:type          owl:Class ;
                       rdfs:subClassOf [
                        rdf:type owl:Restriction ;
                        owl:onProperty blog:isOwning ;
                        owl:minQualifiedCardinality "3"^^<xsd:int>;
                        owl:onDataRange [
                          rdf:type  owl:DataRange ;
                          owl:oneOf (
                                  blog:scientificBlog
                                  blog:TechnicalBlog
                                  ) .
                       ] .
                       ] .
```

OWL 2 provides three constructs allowing us to assess that an object property is respectively reflexive, irreflexive, or asymmetric: the `owl:ReflexiveProperty`, `owl:IrreflexiveProperty`, and `owl:AsymmetricProperty` classes. Respectively, it specifies that the property belonging to the corresponding class holds for all individuals, the property does not hold for any individual, and if the property holds between individuals x and y, then it cannot hold (which will not be induced by a non-symmetric property and therefore makes it stronger) between y and x.

The OWL 2 construct `owl:propertyDisjointWith` is a property with both range and domain on `rdf:Property` that specifies that two individuals cannot be connected by two different properties (both data and object properties). The `owl:AllDisjointProperties` class expands this concept to a list of properties and should be combined with `owl:members` as illustrated for `owl:AllDisjointClasses`.

The OWL 2 construct `owl:propertyChainAxiom` allows us to define properties as a composition of other properties using a *property chain*. A property chain is, as the name suggest, a succession of properties P_1, P_2, P_3, ..., P_n such that P_i relates the object of P_{i-1} with the subject of P_{i+1}. A classic example is to define the uncle of an individual as the brother of the father of the individual. The corresponding property chain could be (:hasFather, :hasBrother), which relates the subject of :hasFather to the object of :hasBrother with the :hasUncle property.

The owl:hasKey property allows us to specify that each named instance of a class is uniquely identified by a (data or object) property or a set of properties—that is, if two named instances of the class coincide on values for each of key properties, then these two individuals are the same. In OWL 2, owl:NamedIndividual is a class to state explicitly that a given entity is an individual. An owl:hasKey axiom is similar to an owl:InverseFunctionalProperty axiom, except that it's only applicable to named individuals and does not provide any inference mechanism.

Finally, OWL 2 supports a richer set of data types and restrictions of data types. OWL 2 data types (presented in http://www.w3.org/TR/owl2-syntax/#Datatype_Maps) include various kinds of numerical values both inherited from XML Schema data types (double, float, decimal, positive integer, etc.) and newly defined (e.g., owl:real) strings and useful data types such as binary data, date, time. Moreover, similar to the class description mechanism used to define a new class, OWL 2 provides a new construct to define data types with the rdfs:Datatype class and restriction definitions. On top of the so-called *facets*, borrowed from XML Schema data types (see http://www.w3.org/TR/2012/REC-xmlschema11-2-20120405/ for full details), OWL 2 also allows combinations of data ranges as intersections (owl:intersectionOf), unions (owl:unionOf), and complements (owl:complementOf) of data ranges, as shown in the following code.

```
PREFIX rdf: <http://www.w3.org/1999/02/22-rdf-syntax-ns#>
PREFIX rdfs: <http://www.w3.org/2000/01/rdf-schema#>
PREFIX owl: <http://www.w3.org/2002/07/owl#>
PREFIX blog: <http://example.com/Blog#>
:digit   owl:equivalentClass [
        rdf:type   rdfs:Datatype ;
        owl:onDatatype   xsd:int ;
        owl:withRestrictions (
            [ xsd:minInclusive "0"^^xsd:int ]
            [ xsd:maxInclusive "9"^^xsd:int ]
        ) .
        ] .
blog:biginnerBlogger   owl:equivalentClass [
                rdf:type   rdfs:Datatype ;
                owl:unionOf (
                  blog:rookieBlogger
                  blog:noviceBlogger
                  blog:newbieBlogger
                ) .
                ] .
```

We conclude this section here with a short presentation of two OWL languages, namely OWL 2 DL and OWL 2 Full. The DL acronym stands for Description Logics (Baader et al., 2003), a subset of first-order logic with interesting properties like decidability for an important number of its languages. That is a main difference with OWL 2 Full, which is not decidable and thus rarely used in practice to model vocabularies for the Semantic Web. Surprisingly, for someone not familiar with these technologies, the set of constructors of both languages are the same (i.e., they have identical sets of constructors). In fact, the decidability of OWL 2 DL comes from some constraints imposed in the definition of its ontologies. For instance, OWL 2 DL requires that the set of names of classes, properties, and instances are disjoint. This characteristic is not applied to OWL 2 Full and this is mainly motivated to provide a full compatibility with RDF. OWL 2 DL can be considered a very expressive language, and comes with high computational complexity of reasoning services. For this reason, this language is currently rarely considered in RDF database management systems.

3.5.4 OWL 2 profiles

OWL 2 defines three profiles—*EL*, *RL*, and *QL*—that are tackling description logics (the underlying logic of OWL) that have desirable computational properties. Profiles are maximal OWL 2 sublanguages that may better meet certain performance requirements or may be easier to implement. From a computational point of view, the main sources of intractability (i.e., nondeterminism) in OWL 2 are disjunctions (`owl:unionOf`), maximum cardinality restrictions, and combining `owl:someValuesFrom` and `owl:allValuesFrom` in a class description. Those features are not allowed in any OWL 2 profiles.

The OWL 2 EL profile is based on the EL++ description logic. It provides polynomial time reasoning for schema and data by focusing on terminological expressivity and is particularly useful for ontologies with a large conceptual part. OWL 2 EL defines restrictions on the type of class restrictions that can be used in axioms. It allows existential quantification to a class expression (`owl:someValuesFrom`) but not universal (`owl:allValuesFrom`) constructors. On one hand, it supports property domain restrictions, definition of classes and property hierarchies, intersections of classes, definition of disjoint classes and properties, `owl:hasSelf`, `owl:hasValue`, and keys. OWL 2 EL supports the following axioms: class inclusion, class equivalence, class disjointedness, object property inclusion with or without property chains, data property inclusion, property equivalence, transitive and reflexive object properties, domain and range restrictions, assertions, functional data properties, and keys. On the other hand, with inverse or symmetric properties, `owl:unionOf` and `owl:complementOf` are forbidden, and `rdfs:range` use and available data types are restricted. The main aspect of OWL 2 EL is that it can capture the expressive power used by many large-scale ontologies, such as SNOMED CT, a widely used ontology in the medical domain.

The OWL 2 RL profile is, as suggested by its name, an OWL-based rule language. Provided with restrictions on OWL 2, OWL 2 RL can be implemented using rule-based technologies such as rule-extended DBMS, Jess, and Prolog. The RDF-based semantics in OWL 2 RL is defined by first-order implications. OWL 2 RL is defined in terms of the set of supported constructs, and also restricts the places in which these constructs can be used. One of the main properties of OWL 2 RL is that it restricts class axioms asymmetrically: you can use constructs as a subclass that you cannot use as a superclass. Precisely, OWL 2 RL restricts the subclasses as being described as either class names, an enumeration of individuals (`owl:oneOf`), an intersection and union of class expressions (`owl:intersectionOf` and `owl:unionOf`), existential quantifications to a class (`owl:someValuesFrom`), a data range, or an individual (`owl:hasValue`). Superclasses can be described as either class names, an intersection of classes (`owl:intersectionOf`), negation (`owl:complementOf`), universal quantifications to a class expression, a data range (`owl:allValuesFrom`), existential quantifications to a literal or an individual (`owl:hasValue`), or at most a 0:1 cardinality restriction to a class expression (`owl:maxQualifiedCardinality` with 0 or 1). OWL 2 RL supports all axioms of OWL 2 apart from disjoint unions of classes (`owl:disjointUnionOf`) and reflexive object property axioms (`owl:owl:ReflexiveProperty`).

The OWL 2 QL profile is related to a standard relational query language. It allows query answering using SQL rewriting on top of a RDBMS. OWL 2 QL restricts both subclasses and superclasses to be defined as class names, existential quantifications to a class, or a data range, and moreover as intersection, complement of for superclasses. OWL 2 QL supports the following axioms: subclass axioms, class expression equivalence and disjointedness, inverse object properties, property inclusion (not involving property chains), property equivalence, property domain and range, disjoint, symmetric, (ir)reflexive, asymmetric properties, assertions other than individual equality assertions, and negative property assertions. Compared to OWL2 EL, OWL2 QL is particularly adapted to knowledge bases characterized by a large Abox and a relatively small TBox with an expressiveness corresponding to a UML class diagram or an entity relationship schema.

3.5.5 SKOS

There exists an important number of controlled vocabularies, taxonomies, folksonomies, subject heading systems, or thesauri that are being used within organizations, such as the Library of Congress Subject Headings (`http://id.loc.gov/authorities/subjects.html`). Although serving applications in an efficient manner, these knowledge organization systems (KOS) do not provide an exchange or linking facilities and are hard to distribute across the Web. To address these limitations, the W3C recommended *SKOS* (Simple Knowledge Organization System; `http://www.w3.org/TR/skos-reference/`) in 2009. Intuitively, SKOS corresponds to a data model that is expressed as RDF triples and views a KOS as a set of concepts identified by URIs, denoted as a concept scheme. These concepts are related by so-called semantic relations, such as `skos:narrower`, `skos, broader`, and `skos:related`, and are associated to labels using lexical labels, such as `skos:pref:label`, `skos`, and `altLabel`. Due to its simple and efficient approach to address an important problem, SKOS has been quite successful since the release of the W3C recommendation.

3.5.6 RDFS+

RDFS+ is a subset of the OWL Lite language, which was introduced in Allemang and Hendler (2011) and aims at providing a useful and quickly implementable subset of OWL. Not surprisingly, RDFS+ is expressed in RDF. RDFS+ provides a vocabulary to specify precise property characteristics (inverse, symmetric, and transitive properties) and equality between individuals, classes, and properties. As we will see, equality between instances may be derived from two other types of properties called *functional* and *inverse-functional*. All these resources are given in RDF format using a vocabulary defined in the namespace `<http://www.w3.org/2002/07/owl#>`, commonly associated with the prefix `owl`.

One property (i.e., `rdf:Property`) may be stated as the *inverse* of another property using the `owl:inverseOf` property. Roughly, the subject and the object of the former one can be stated respectively as the object and the subject of the latter. A property may be defined as *symmetric* using the `owl:SymmetricProperty` class. A symmetric property is a property that is its own inverse. Finally, a property may be defined as *transitive* using the `owl:TransitiveProperty` class. The corresponding rules can be expressed in SPARQL as shown in the following code.

```
PREFIX rdf: <http://www.w3.org/1999/02/22-rdf-syntax-ns#>
PREFIX owl: <http://www.w3.org/2002/07/owl#>
CONSTRUCT { ?y  ?q  ?x .}
WHERE {
          ?p  owl:inverseOf   ?q .
          ?x  ?p              ?y .
}
CONSTRUCT { ?p  rdf:type  owl:SymmetricProperty .}
WHERE {
          ?p  owl:inverseOf ?p .
}
CONSTRUCT { ?x  ?p  ?z .}
WHERE {
          ?x  ?p          ?y .
          ?y  ?p          ?z .
          ?p  rdf:type  owl:TransitiveProperty .
}
```

While RDF provides a global identity system (namely URIs) for resources, when merging RDF data from multiple sources, one should be able to state that several URIs actually refer to the same entity. RDFS+ provides three types of equality depending on the nature of the corresponding resources: instances of classes (a.k.a. individuals), classes, or properties.

Two individuals may be stated to be the same using the `owl:sameAs` property. Two classes having the same set of instances can be stated as equivalent using the `owl:equivalentClass` property. Two properties relating any individual to the same set of other individuals can be stated as equivalent using the `owl:equivalentProperty` property. Once we have remarked that the `owl:sameAs`, `owl:equivalentClass`, and `owl:equivalentProperty` properties are symmetric, we can express the corresponding rules as shown in the following code.

```
PREFIX rdf: <http://www.w3.org/1999/02/22-rdf-syntax-ns#>
PREFIX owl: <http://www.w3.org/2002/07/owl#>
CONSTRUCT { ?r  rdf:type  ?y .}
WHERE {
           ?x  owl:equivalentClass ?y .
           ?r  rdf:type              ?x .
}
CONSTRUCT { ?x  ?p  ?y .}
WHERE {
           ?p  owl:equivalentProperty  ?q .
           ?x  ?q                       ?y .
}
CONSTRUCT { ?s1 ?p1 ?x . ?x ?p2 ?o2 . ?s3 ?x ?o3 . }
WHERE {
           ?x  owl:sameAs  ?y .
           { ?s1  ?p1  ?y  .}
           UNION
           { ?y   ?p2  ?o2 .}
           UNION
           { ?s3  ?y   ?o3 .}
}
```

RDFS+ introduces two other types of properties, `owl:Functional Property` and `owl:InverseFunctionalProperty`, that allow inferring the sameness of different individuals. A property of type (i.e., `rdf:type`) `owl:FunctionalProperty` is a *functional* property—that is, for a given subject there is only one corresponding object (similar to surjective functions in mathematics). An `owl:InverseFunctionalProperty` is a property for which there is only one subject for a given object (similar to injective functions in mathematics). The corresponding rules can be expressed in SPARQL as shown in the following code.

```
PREFIX rdf: <http://www.w3.org/1999/02/22-rdf-syntax-ns#>
PREFIX owl: <http://www.w3.org/2002/07/owl#>
CONSTRUCT { ?o1  owl:sameAS  ?o2 . ?s1 owl:sameAs ?s2 .}
WHERE {
        {
        ?p   rdf:type owl:FunctionalProperty .
        ?x   ?p        ?o1 ,
                       ?o2 .
        } UNION {
        ?p   rdf:type owl:InverseFunctionalProperty .
        ?s1 ?p        ?y .
        ?s2 ?p        ?y .
        }
}
```

As in mathematics, a property that is both surjective and injective is a *bijective* function (also referred as a *one-to-one mapping*). Compared to an RDBMS, a knowledge base (e.g., expressed in RDF) does not use the *unique name assumption* (UNA) property. Intuitively, UNA states that an object can have a single identifier. Equivalence will be inferred using such kinds of properties. For example, considering a plane seat booking application, an RDBMS will make sure that a seat is booked by only one person at the time. In a knowledge base context, if two persons booked the same seat and they are not explicitly declared as distinct, then they will be considered as equal (`owl:sameAs`). We will come back to UNA in Chapter 8.

3.5.7 OWL Horst

OWL Horst (a.k.a. ρD⋆) was designed by Herman ter Horst (ter Horst, 2005). This work is an extension of Description Logic Programs (DLP), a proposal to support OWL inferences with rules. The semantics of this vocabulary extends RDFS with data types and a subset of OWL that includes the property-related vocabulary (i.e., functional, inverse functional, inverse, symmetric, and transitive), the comparisons (e.g., `sameAs` and `differentFrom`), and value restrictions (e.g., some values and all values). Entailment rules are provided and have been proved to be complete.

The main difference between OWL RL and OWL Horst is that OWL RL adopts an if and only if (`iff`) semantics (just like OWL), while OWL Horst adopts an `if` semantics reminiscent of RDFS.

These interesting properties have motivated several systems, such as **WebPie** and the GraphDB RDF store, to implement reasoning over OWL Horst ontologies. These systems and others are presented in detail in Part 2 of this book.

3.6 REASONING

A main feature of the Semantic Web is to support reasoning services over a given set of data and knowledge. This leverage from the technologies we have seen so far—that is, RDF as a simple data model—handles the representation of given facts and RDFS and OWL provide semantic interpretations to RDF facts. We will see that these interpretations enable the inference of additional RDF statements from the explicitly given ones. Moreover, the SPARQL query language enables us to retrieve explicit facts from the RDF data sets. Because SPARQL cannot by itself perform any inference tasks, it must interact with a reasoning component to extract implicit information. A detailed presentation of these interactions is the subject of Chapter 8.

Following is an example in the context of the blog use case to make the notion of an inference more concrete. Let's consider an ontology stating that running is a kind of sport (Running ⊑ Sport in a DL formalism where ⊑ corresponds to the subclass relationship) and that user Joe Doe is writing some blogs on his running activities that are annotated with this concept. Consider that the blog web page of Mary Smith is specified to retrieve all blog entries related to sports. Then equipped with some inference capabilities, her web page will contain the Joe Doe entries about running, because all pages typed with the Running ontology concept are also interpreted as being typed with the Sport concept. Note that this would not be the case without inferences. Intuitively, the inference mechanism can take two forms: either annotates each running blog entries with a new Sport type or it extends the query associated to Mary's web page to all specializations of sports. The general outcome of both these mechanisms is the same: all instances (i.e., blog entries) of the Running concept are also instances of the Sport concept. Of course, these mechanisms have to be performed with the help of some software component that is denoted as a *reasoner*.

This simple inference example is related to the task of answering a query and as such requires some facts (the Abox) and an ontology (the Tbox); recall that this is denoted as a knowledge base. This reasoning service is generally denoted as *retrieval* in a Semantic Web and DL context. It's certainly one of the most used services in a data store context. Intuitively, it aims at finding the individuals in a knowledge base that are instances of a given concept. While in a standard database only the explicit individuals are retrieved, in an inference-enabled store the implicit instances are also part of the answer set.

Three other important standard inference services requiring an Abox are *instance checking*, *realization*, and *knowledge base consistency*. The former checks whether a given individual is an instance of a given concept—for example, to check whether a Joe Doe blog entry on Running is an instance of a blog about Sport. Realization finds the most specific concept an individual is an instance of. For example, given an ontology with a SportTechnology concept defined as a subconcept of Sport and Technology

(SportTechnology ⊑ Sport ⊓ Technology in a DL formalism) and a blog entry annotated with the Sport and Technology concepts, then this blog has the SportTechnology concept as its most specific concept. Finally, knowledge base consistency verifies whether every concept in the knowledge base admits at least one individual. For example, if someone defines a RelaySport concept as being at the intersection of the IndividualSport and TeamSport concepts with both these concepts being disjoint (in DL formalism: RelaySport ⊑ IndividualSport ⊓ TeamSport and IndividualSport ⊑ ¬TeamSport), then the knowledge base is inconsistent because the RelaySport concept will never admit an instance in that ontology configuration.

There exists some standard reasoning services that are dealing with the Tbox only. In the context of the Semantic Web, they are mainly concerned with concepts that are described in terms of logical constructors (e.g., conjunction, qualifiers, etc.), properties, and other concepts. That is, properties are not first-class citizens of these services because their descriptions are expressed in terms of subsumption, domain, range, and a limited form of composition. The most important ones are *classification*, *concept satisfiability*, and *logical implication*.

Classification classifies a given concept in a concept hierarchy. For example, consider that we have the following hierarchy of concepts: Running ⊑ OutDoorActivity ⊑ PhysicalActivity ⊑ Activity. If we now add the concept Sport defined as a subclass of PhysicalActivity, then a reasoner should classify the Sport concept between the OutdoorActivity and PhysicalActivity concepts. Classification relies on the *subsumption* inference, which checks whether the set of individuals of a first concept is always a subset of the individuals of a second concept. *Concept satisfiability* verifies if a concept description does not necessarily designate the empty concept. Note that concept satisfiability can be seen as a special case of concept subsumption where the superconcept is the empty concept. Finally, the *logical implication* service checks whether a given relationship (e.g., subsumption or *equivalence* between two concepts) is a logical consequence of the Tbox description. For example, given our previous activity ontology extract, such a reasoning service can state that the subsumption relationship between the Running and Sport concepts (i.e., Running ⊑ Sport) holds while it does not hold between the Woman and Activity concepts. These reasoning services are quite useful in the process of designing an ontology, particularly in cooperative development. For example, an ontologist may need to check whether what he or she has defined is consistent with what other ontologists have described, to classify his or her set of concepts within a global hierarchy and to verify implied relationships between all defined concepts. They are useful in an integration context to assert interontology relationships and reason over the integrated class hierarchy.

Different types of reasoners coexist in the Semantic Web. They principally differ on the methods used to deduce implicit information from the explicit ones. Most methods are adapted to an underlying ontology language. Recall that the RDFS and different OWL languages mainly differ in their expressive power—that is, what they are able to express within their set of constructors and syntactic constraints. Obviously, this expressiveness directly influences the kind of deductions that can be performed within these languages. For example, the classification reasoning service really makes sense for ontology languages supporting the description of concepts (e.g., it's not useful for RDFS). Moreover, these different languages are motivated by a trade-off between their expressivity and reasoning complexity—that is, the more expressive the language, the harder the inference processing, therefore the longer the wait to obtain the results of the deductions. The main methods identified to perform reasoning tasks are *structural subsumption*, *semantic tableau, resolution, automata*, and translation to another logic.

Desirable properties for these reasoning methods are *soundness, completeness*, and *termination of the algorithm*. A concept or knowledge base is satisfiable, respectively consistent if there is a set of individuals, called a model, that satisfies all semantic constraints over that concept, respectively knowledge base. Soundness of an inference procedure is the property ensuring that inference rules prove only the formulas that are valid with respect to its semantics. The completeness property states that every truth (validity) is provable. Finally, the termination of an algorithm is related to the guarantee that it terminates for a given input. Of course, an ideal inference procedure is terminating, sound, and complete, but in certain situation constraints on completeness and less frequently on soundness can be relaxed. Finally, space and time complexities associated to performing inferences are preferably low—that is, the structures used by the procedure consume the smallest space on the computer's main memory and the processing duration is the shortest possible.

The structural subsumption algorithm compares the syntactic structure of a pair of concepts and is therefore being used for the subsumption and classification inference tasks. Although quite efficient, the method is only relevant for quite inexpressive DL— that is, it cannot handle disjunction, full negation (negation on complex concepts), and full existential restriction (existential restriction with an arbitrary concept).

As soon as expressive DL started to be studied, reasoning research concentrated on the semantic tableau method (a.k.a. tableau-based algorithm). This is a sound and complete method that tries to construct a representation of a model of a knowledge base by using a set of expansion rules that are addressing the different constructors of the underlying language. Thus, the algorithm is relevant for a range of description logics, including the two versions of OWL DL as well as OWL Lite. This method is the most widely used in the context of DL but has not been widely adopted in the context of retrieving data from an RDF store.

The resolution-based approach is influenced by prior work in logic programming and thus is widely used for rule-based ontology languages like OWL2 RL. Because this method is extensively used for inference-enabled query answering for RDF stores, its principle will be described in Chapter 8.

The last two methods, automata-based and translation to another logic, are rarely encountered in practical scenarios because they do not compare to the efficiency, due to optimization efforts, obtained in the tableau and resolution approaches. Intuitively, because most DLs correspond to a subset of first-order logic (FOL), it's possible, through a set of translation rules, to translate DL axioms to FOL ones and use a dedicated FOL prover. The Hoolet system (`http://owl.man.ac.uk/hoolet/`) is such an implementation of an OWL DL reasoner that uses the Vampire prover. Finally, the automata-based approach has mainly been used to determine the complexity of the lower bound of interesting problems but is not being used in practice.

3.7 BENCHMARKS

As it was done a while ago for RDBMS (`http://www.tpc.org/`), benchmarks for systems based on RDF have emerged. W3C keeps an up-to-date collection of RDF benchmarks available at `http://www.w3.org/wiki/RdfStoreBench-marking`. Next, we present the ones most frequently used in RDF stores research papers.

The *Berlin SPARQL Benchmark* (BSBM; `http://wifo5-03.informatik.uni-mannheim.de/bizer/berlinsparqlbenchmark`) includes a benchmark built around an e-commerce application. In this application, a set of products is offered by several vendors, and consumers can post reviews about products. The queries of the benchmark illustrate a typical search and navigation pattern of a consumer looking for a product. The data can be generated in several formats (e.g., N-triples, Turtle, XML, etc.) and scaled by the number of products (100 products make about 50,000 triples). The generator adds, by default, for each product an `rdf:type` statement with the most specific type of this product. Inclusion of the statements for more general classes can be done. The data generated can be split into multiple files. The data generator may, finally, include update transactions and may use named graphs.

The *Lehigh University Benchmark* (LUBM; `http://swat.cse.lehigh.edu/projects/lubm/`) includes a benchmark built around the university domain and includes a university domain ontology, customizable and repeatable synthetic data, a set of 14 test queries, and several performance metrics. The data generator allows us to indicate the number of universities to generate and the seed used for random data generation (for the repeatability purpose). The corresponding queries bear large inputs with both high and low selectivities, triangular patterns of relationships, explicit and implicit `sub-ClassOf` and `subPropertyOf`, and some OWL reasoning (transitive and inverse properties and some inferences based on domain and range).

The *University Ontology Benchmark* (UOBM; `http://www.springerlink.com/content/10wu543x26350462/University`) is designed as an extension of LUBM with a more complex ontology (i.e., supporting OWL Lite and OWL DL). While no generator of data sets of varying size is provided, the nature of the data is more complex. Resources of the data set are more linked (e.g., between persons from different universities), inducing a more challenging task for scalability tests. As in LUBM, 15 queries help testing scalability with search and reasoning across universities. Each query supports at least one different type of OWL inference.

The *SPARQL Performance Benchmark* (SP^{2}Bench; `http://dbis.informatik.uni-freiburg.de/index.php?project=SP2B`) includes a benchmark built around DBLP computer science bibliography scenario. The data is generated in *N*-triples format. The 12 provided queries include filtering requirements (inequality test) and an ASK query. The data generated includes blank nodes, containers, and long URIs. No use of inference is necessary.

The *Social Intelligence BenchMark* (SIB; `http://www.w3.org/wiki/Social_Network_Intelligence_BenchMark`) includes a benchmark built around popular social networks. The data generator is generating a huge volume of data (all data associated with one person, having on average 30 friends and a few hundred pictures and posts, is evaluated at 1 MB). The provided 20 SELECT queries include filtering requirements (range of value, regex, and equality test) and the optional use of transitive properties, negation, aggregation, and subqueries. Moreover, the benchmark includes 8 update queries including MODIFY, INSERT INTO, and DELETE FROM requests.

The *DBpedia SPARQL Benchmark* (DBPSB; `http://svn.aksw.org/papers/2011/VLDB_AKSWBenchmark/public.pdf`) includes a benchmark built on real data from the DBpedia database. The provided 25 SELECT queries include filtering requirements (equality test and regex) and correspond to queries indeed asked to DBpedia.

The *FedBench Benchmark* (`http://fedbench.fluidops.net/`) uses several data sets (around 10, among which there are DBpedia subsets, *New York Times*, LinkedMDB, and Drugbank) on cross and life science domains (news, movies, music, drugs, etc.). The major aim of FedBench is to test the efficiency and effectiveness of federated query processing.

Other benchmarks, such as *Linked Data Integration Benchmark* (LODIB) or *JustBench*, are designed to evaluate other properties of related systems, such as considering linked data (i.e., with real-world heterogeneities) or OWL capabilities of reasoners.

3.8 BUILDING SEMANTIC WEB APPLICATIONS

Jena (`http://jena.apache.org/`) is an open-source Semantic Web framework for Java and is widely used in the Java community. The Jena framework is composed of several components. We discuss here the main ones: Core RDF API, ARQ

(A SPARQL processor for Jena), Fuzeki, Jena rules engine, Jena Ontology API, and TDB (an RDF store within Jena).

The *Core RDF API* aims at creating and manipulating RDF graphs. Indeed, in Jena, all RDF information is provided as a collection of RDF triples in a data structure called a *model*. A model is a Java abstraction of an RDF graph. The API allows us to manipulate resources, literals, and blank nodes as graph nodes and provides a class (`Statement.class`) to represent a single triple. Accessors are defined in order to retrieve the subject, predicate, and object of any triple.

ARQ is a SPARQL query engine for Jena allowing us to query and update RDF models through SPARQL standards. ARQ can be used as a standalone application or as a library to integrate into a bigger application. ARQ considers both the SPARQL and SPARQL Update standards. ARQ can produce query results in several formats (XML, JSON, and column-separated output). ARQ can both read and query local and remote RDF data and SPARQL endpoints. ARQ supports custom filter functions, aggregation, `GROUP BY`, and assignment and federated queries.

Fuzeki is a SPARQL server built on ARQ that can present RDF data and answer SPARQL queries over HTTP. Its installation is easy and straightforward.

Jena provides a rules engine and other inference algorithms to derive additional RDF assertions. The inference system is pluggable with other reasoners. It allows supporting of RDFS and OWL, which allow inference of additional facts from instance data and class descriptions. There are several included reasoners: a transitive reasoner (i.e., dealing with `rdfs:subPropertyOf` and `rdfs:subClassOf`), an RDFS rule reasoner, some OWL reasoners (implementing partially OWL Lite), and a generic rule reasoner (for user-defined rules).

The *Jena Ontology API* aims at providing an ontology language–neutral programming interface for ontology applications. Specificities of each language are propagated through the notion of a profile that lists the permitted constructs, classes, and properties.

TDB is a component of Jena allowing a fast persistent triples store (directly to disk) supporting the full range of Jena APIs. This system is defined in detail in Chapter 5.

Similarly to Jena, Sesame is a framework for the development of Semantic Web applications and proposes an RDF store. Its mature set of APIs is used in several RDF stores, such as Virtuoso, GraphDB, and Bigdata.

To develop a Semantic Web application an ontology and knowledge base editor is necessary. *Protégé* seems to be the most relevant choice and is the most widely used editor. It's a free, open-source framework that can be envisioned as a plugin platform. Many plugins are available on the Protégé website (`http://protege.stanford.edu/`) concerning reasoners, visualization, and backends. Recently, a Web-based version of Protégé has been released and provides facilities to develop ontologies collaboratively.

An important number of other relevant tools, some of them open-source, belonging to categories such as visualization, programming environment (in programing languages as diverse as Java, C++, C#, Python, Ruby, Groovy, etc.), browser, converter, generator, Semantic wiki and annotation tool, and ontology engineering are listed in `http://www.w3.org/RDF/` and `http://semanticweb.org/wiki/Tools`.

3.9 SUMMARY

- RDF is the cornerstone of the Semantic Web and the Web of Data movements, two extensions of the current Web that aim to support novel functionalities.
- The data model of RDF is composed of triples composed of a subject, a predicate, and an object that mainly correspond to URIs, thus enabling data integration at the scale of the Web.
- The RDF ecosystem comes with schema languages (RDFS, OWL, etc.) that enable us to define vocabularies. They are generally named ontology languages.
- Together with facts, ontologies enable us to perform some inferences that will permit us to deduce implicit information from explicit information.
- The complexity of performing these inferences is related to the expressive power of the ontology languages—that is, the set of operators they support and the constraints they have to satisfy.
- The Semantic Web is also equipped with a full stack of technologies, such as a query language (SPARQL) for RDF data, benchmarks, APIs, and tools.

CHAPTER FOUR

RDF Dictionaries: String Encoding

As we already discussed, RDF data may be very verbose due to the use of string identifiers that are taking the form of URIs. Recall that URIs represent common global identifiers for resources across the Web. The syntax and format of URIs are very similar to the well-known *uniform resource locators* (URLs), for example, `<http://example.com/Blog#JD >`. In fact, URLs are just special cases of URIs (see Section 3.2 for more details on this topic). In a Semantic Web setting, URIs are intensively used in both RDF data (to represent facts) and in ontologies (i.e., using RDFS and OWL languages) to represent concepts and properties. Moreover, these URIs allow us to group related entities. Thus, it's not uncommon to handle terms of hundreds of characters in RDF data that may be used multiple times in the same document—for example, a subject may be associated to many RDF triples. Exchanging and storing such data naturally comes at the cost of a high memory footprint. This aspect is frequently handled by proposing efficient compression solutions.

The aim of this chapter is to present classic and enhanced encodings, as well as solutions handling big literals (**Lucene and Solr**) and Big Data sets (*MapReduce*-based encoding of Urbani et al. (2013)). Note that common operating systems propose a facility called *memory mapping*, which is independent of the index structure used in the RDF store but confers a significant performance advantage. Indeed, memory mapping is usually used to implement paged virtual memory subsystems. This facility provides optimized file accessing and keeps frequently accessed ones in memory.

4.1 ENCODING MOTIVATION

RDF database systems frequently try to store a database in a compact way. A common and basic approach consists in providing an integer value to each URI, blank node, or literal. The link between original values and encoded ones is usually stored in a data structure called a *dictionary*.

The underlying basic concept of a dictionary (which is not specific to the RDF model) is to provide a bijective function mapping long terms (e.g., URIs, blank nodes, or literals) to short identifiers (e.g., integers). More precisely, a dictionary should provide two basic operations: `string-to-id` and `id-to-string` (also referred to in the literature as `locate` and `extract` operations). In a typical use, a SPARQL engine will call `string-to-id` to rewrite the user query into a list to match the data encoding, while `id-to-string` will be called to translate the result into the original format. One can easily admit that this later operation will be more often called because

81

the number of terms to encode in a query will usually be smaller than the number of terms to be translated in the result. As a consequence, different approaches in the dictionary will be used for these two operations.

Considering the approach, one will end up with a "new" data set composed of the dictionary and the encoded data set. This new data set will provide a high-compression view of the data (Neumann and Weikum, 2010). Nevertheless, the size of the dictionary is not negligible at all, and may even be larger than the encoded data set itself, as pointed out by Martínez–Prieto et al. (2012), and thus may induce scalability issues by its own. Overall, an RDF dictionary must be optimized regarding two conflicting perspectives: minimizing its memory footprint and minimizing the answering time of `string-to-id` and `id-to-string` operations.

While, due to data heterogeneity, a constant compression ability cannot be achieved (Fernandez et al., 2010), some common features between data sets can be derived. Indeed, usually in a data set the proportion of predicates is often a small fraction of the dictionary. Moreover, one can achieve an overall compression improvement by uniquely encoding any term appearing both as the subject and the object. In the following, we present different approaches used in research and commercial solutions.

4.2 CLASSIC ENCODING

As pointed out in Martínez–Prieto et al. (2012), the approach used at **Oracle** (Chong et al., 2005), **3Store** (Harris and Gibbins, 2003), and **AWETO** (Pu et al., 2011), to name a few, is to rely on classic string dictionary techniques, as discussed next.

4.2.1 Classic string dictionary techniques

There are four classic string dictionary techniques: *hashing, front coding, grammar-based*, and *self-indexing*.

Hashing

The primary objective of a hash function is to generate deterministically a fixed-length representation (usually an integer) of an original data of arbitrary length. It is, therefore, a natural choice for key-value structures. On the one hand, it will provide an efficient `string-to-id` operation because it's the natural behavior of a hash function. On the other hand, hash functions are typically not invertible (i.e., reconstructing the original value from its hash value alone is impossible). Therefore, it will not provide a native way of answering `id-to-string` operations. Moreover, hashing does not provide any compression by itself. Let's first present a general compression solution based on the Huffman coding method.

Huffman coding is a popular encoding algorithm in lossless data compression. In the following, we consider a *code* defined as a function mapping a bit string to any symbol. Considering a text on a given alphabet (i.e., a set of symbols), the algorithm generates a *variable-length prefix* code, which is a code where different symbols of the alphabet may be represented with bit strings of different lengths. While variable-length codes tend to generate lower code word length than fixed-length codes, they need to be uniquely decodable to be practical. This is the aim of the prefix property, which states that given any two symbols (x,y) of the alphabet, the bit string mapped to x is not a prefix of the bit string mapped to y. In other words, even if the corresponding bit strings of two symbols share a common prefix, there will be a position in the bit strings where they will differentiate. Based on the probability of occurrence of each symbol in the text to be encoded, the Huffman algorithm moreover generates a code where the most common symbols are mapped to shorter bit strings than the ones mapped to less common symbols. The algorithm is usually presented as a binary tree (referred to as the Huffman tree) building process. The corresponding algorithm is described as a bottom-up process starting from a set of leaves. Each symbol of the alphabet is represented as a leaf node and is associated to its frequency. The Huffman tree is built in a repetitive process where a new node is inserted in the tree as the parent of the two parentless nodes with the smallest frequency, and associated to the sum of the frequency of its two node children. The process ends when only one parentless node is left.

Assuming the list of words common$, format$, and data$, Figure 4.1 proposes a Huffman encoding that is based on the Huffman tree in the figure.

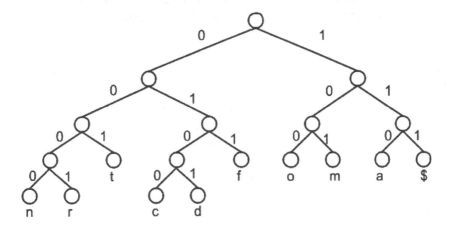

letter	frequency	code	letter	frequency	code
a	3	110	m	3	101
c	1	0100	n	1	0000
d	1	0101	r	1	0001
f	1	011	t	2	001
o	3	100	$	3	111

Figure 4.1 Symbol encoding and Huffman tree for the words common$, format$, and data$.

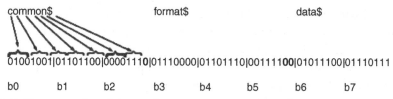

Figure 4.2 Huffman encoding of the words common$, format$, and data$.

Let's get back to our general solution. Considering a lexicographically sorted list of words that all end with a special $ symbol, all words are first Huffman encoded and their codes are concatenated in a byte-aligned way—that is, extra 0 bits (bold in Figure 4.2) are concatenated to the end of each code to obtain a binary word of an integral number of bytes. To retrieve the codes, byte-offsets and sizes of the words are stored in a hash table indexed by the coded words. Based on this character encoding, each word of our list can, in turn, be encoded with a certain number of bytes. A total of eight bytes is required in Figure 4.2.

A hash table H, based on an arbitrary hash function, is storing the respective byte-offsets. Table 4.1 represents the hash table where the index has m values. In the following, we consider that hash(010010010110110000000111) = m-3, hash(0101110001110111) = m-1, and hash(0111000001101110001111) = 2.

Provided with the encoded list of words, the Huffman code, and the hash table, one can answer the string-to-id operation as follows. First, the pattern is encoded using the Huffman code, then the hash table is accessed to retrieve the corresponding id (which is the byte-offset of the word in the dictionary). For example, string-to-id("format$") will return H[hash(0111000001101110001111)]—that is, b3. The id-to-string operation will only need to access the encoded list of words and decode, using the Huffman code, the string located at the corresponding byte-offset. For example, id-to-string(b3) will return HuffmanDecode(string[b3])—that is, format$. Indeed, using the prefix code described in Figure 4.1, the HuffmanDecode function will start decoding the bit string starting in byte b3—that is, 01110000.

By definition, the code word is uniquely decodable as illustrated in Figure 4.3. The decoding process will end when the $ symbol is decoded. Therefore, the extra 0 bits added for byte alignment purpose will not be considered.

Table 4.1 Hash Table H for the Running Example

Index	1	2	3	. . .	m-3	m-2	m-1	m
Value		b3			b0		b6	

Table 4.2 Compact Hash Table M

Index	1	2	3
Value	b3	b0	b6

The main issue of this general solution is that, depending on the hash function used, the corresponding hash table may contain a significant number of empty cells. The *HashB-dh* solution (Brisaboa et al., 2011) tends to resolve this issue as follows. Empty cells are removed from H to obtain a compact table, which we denote M. Note that in this table, the original cell order of H is preserved. Additionally, a bitmap B is added to mark with 1 bits all nonempty cells of H. Roughly, B will allow us to retrieve the original indices with a compressed cost (m bits, considering that H has m entries). Considering the previous example, H is replaced by the M and B structures.

Applied to the running example, this setting contains a bitmap B = 01000...1010 (that contains m bits) and the compact hash table M shown in Table 4.2.

The `string-to-id` operation is processed as before except that it will return the entry of M corresponding of the number of 1 bits present in B[1..X], plus one where X is the position returned by the hash function. As we will see later in this chapter, this operation can be done efficiently using the so-called `rank` operation on bit vectors. For example, `string-to-id("format$")` will return M[count(1,B[1..hash(01110000011011100011 11)])+1]. The `id-to-string` operation is not changed.

Note that if the hash function used ensures that the values in H are increasing, one can even get rid of M and replace it by a second bitmap B' marking with 1 bits the corresponding byte-offsets. For example, if one considers that the byte-offsets of interest are b0, b3, and b6 (but stored in that order in H), then M is replaced by the bitmap B' = 1001001000..0 of n bits, where n is the number of bytes of the encoded list of words. The *i*th entry of M corresponds to the position of the *i*th 1 bit of B'. The position of a given occurrence of a 1 bit in a bit vector can be retrieved efficiently using the so-called `select` operation on bit vectors. For example, `string-to-id("format$")` will return pos(1,count(1, B[1..hash(01110000011 01110001111)])+1).

Unfortunately, even this solution provides poor compression because it does not take advantage of long common prefixes that arise in URIs.

Figure 4.3 Code word encoding for the `format$` word.

Front coding

Front coding, unlike hashing, is a traditional technique for compressing a lexicographically sorted dictionary, which uses common prefixes between terms. It's also referred to in the literature as incremental encoding, front compression, or back compression. For efficiency purpose, based on the lexical order, it only encodes the difference between consecutive terms (also known as the delta encoding compression algorithm). Intuitively, common prefixes (or suffixes) and their lengths are stored together so that the common characters between two consecutive words in the lexicographically order are not duplicated.

In Table 4.3, we provide, given a set of words, two compressed outputs (composed of an information pair: the length of the common part and the differential part) based respectively on common prefixes and suffixes.

The list of words in Table 4.3 was derived from the abstract of this chapter and does not have any particular property. Nevertheless, there is already a small gain: six bytes and eight bytes for respectively common prefixes and suffixes cases. Note that because we considered that the lengths of the common prefixes are stored as characters as well (this is not optimal), any compressed output with a common prefix (or suffix) length smaller than 2 is, in fact, more expensive to store than the original word. In real applications, one could really gain in coding in a clever way with the pairs of information shown in the table.

Table 4.3 Prefix and Suffix Front Coding

Input Prefix Sorted	Common Prefix	Compressed Output
already	-	0,already
classical	-	0,classical
common	c	1,ommon
compression	com	3,pression
concept	co	2,ncept
context	con	3,text
data	-	0,data
data sets	data	4,sets
different	d	1,ifferent
distinguishing	di	2,stinguishing
efficient	-	0,efficient
encodings	e	1,ncodings
entities	en	2,tities
format	-	0,format
mapping	-	0,mapping
meanings	m	1,eanings
memory	me	2,mory
noticed	-	0,noticed
storing	-	0,storing
string	st	2,ing
(185 bytes)		(179 bytes)

(Continued)

Table 4.3 Prefix and Suffix Front Coding *(cont.)*

Input Suffix Sorted	Common Suffix	Compressed Output
data	-	0,data
noticed	-	0,noticed
enhanced	ced	3,enhan
distinguishing	-	0,distinguishing
mapping	ing	3,mapp
storing	ing	3,stor
string	ring	4,st
classical	-	0,classical
compression	-	0,compression
common	on	2,comm
entities	-	0,entities
encodings	s	1,encoding
meanings	ings	4,mean
data sets	s	1,data set
format	-	0,format
efficient	t	1,efficien
different	ent	3,differ
concept	t	1,concep
context	t	1,contex
already	-	0,already
memory	y	1,memor
(185 bytes)		(177 bytes)

A common optimization technique is to store the lengths with delta encoding as well (i.e., storing only the gaps between two consecutive lengths). In the so-called *plain front coding* approach, the prefix length is encoded on var-bytes and the suffixes are appended as plain chars (terminated with a null byte). Var-byte encoding uses an integral number of bytes to encode each length. Note that the "var" comes from the fact that lengths are encoded using a variable number of bytes. Considering the sequence of lengths to be encoded, each length entry is encoded as the difference with the previous length. For ease, the first one is encoded as a difference of 0. Consider, for example, that we have the following sequence of lengths: $12, 23, 283$. The sequence that will be stored is $12, 11, 260$, which respectively represents the gaps $12 - 0, 23 - 12$, and $283 - 23$. Each gap is encoded using possibly several bytes (e.g., 260 needs two bytes while 12 and 11 only need one byte). To handle a variable number of bytes, the first bit of each byte is dedicated to encode whether the corresponding byte is the last byte of the current length encoding or not. More formally, in each byte, the last seven bits are coding a part of the gap, while the first bit is a continuation bit. The continuation bit is set to 1 for the last byte of an encoded gap, and to 0 otherwise. Thus, for decoding a variable byte code, one reads a sequence of bytes with the continuation bit set to 0 ended by a byte with the continuation bit set to 1. The difference is obtained by extracting and concatenating the seven-bit parts. For

```
10001100|10001011|00000010|10000100
+12        +11         +260
(1100)     (1011)      (1 0000 0100)
```

Figure 4.4 Var-byte encoding for lengths 12, 23, 283.

example, consider that we have the following sequence of lengths: 12, 23, 283. Figure 4.4 provides its var-byte encoding.

The efficiency can even be expanded by performing the differential encoding on smaller sets of terms (referred to as *buckets*), which allow efficient targeted querying. The dictionary is partitioned into buckets of s strings. A binary search is done to locate the candidate bucket and a sequential bucket scan retrieves the required string.

The so-called *Hu–Tucker front coding* approach further compresses prefixes and suffixes using the Hu–Tucker compression algorithm (Hu, 1982). Roughly, the Hu–Tucker approach can be seen as an order-preserving variant of the Huffman coding. Indeed, it requires the ordering of the code words of the letters to be the same as their corresponding letters. The overall process is quite similar to the Huffman algorithm and starts with the frequency list of the letters. In the Huffman approach, each symbol of the alphabet is represented as a leaf node, and a new node is inserted in the tree as the parent of the two parentless nodes with the smallest frequency. In the Hu–Tucker approach, the leaves are ordered considering the lexical ordering of their corresponding symbols and a new node is inserted in the tree as the parent of the two parentless *compatible* nodes with the smallest frequency. Two nodes are compatible if there are no parentless leaves between them. The new inserted node acquires the rank of its smallest child in the lexical order. Consider the text `alabar-a-la-alabarda` and ASCIIbetical order (`-` < `a` < `b` < `d` < `l` < `r`). The frequency list is shown in Table 4.4.

At the very first step, each node is only compatible with its neighbors. The only pair of compatible nodes with the smallest frequency is the pair of nodes `(b;d)`, which give rise to a new node (referred to as `b,d`) in the third position in the ordering. For ease, in Figure 4.5, inserted nodes are highlighted in bold and their children are hidden. A star is used to notify that the corresponding node is not a leaf. In the second step, the only pair of compatible nodes with the smallest frequency is the pair of nodes `(l;r)`. Indeed, even if `(b,d;r)` would have induced a smaller frequency, it's not compatible due to `l`. In the third step, yet again, while the node pair `(-;b,d)` would have induced the smallest frequency, it's not compatible due to `a`. The only compatible pair of nodes with the smallest frequency is `(b,d;l,r)`. In the fourth step, `(-,a)` forms a compatible pair of

Table 4.4 Frequency List

Letter	-	a	b	d	l	r
Frequency	3	9	2	1	4	2

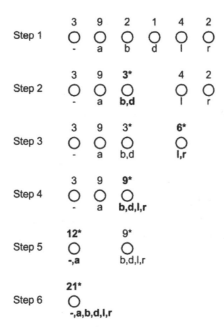

Figure 4.5 Hu-Tucker steps considering the text "alabar-a-la-alabarda"

nodes of the smallest frequency. Finally, one ends up with a unique parentless node after using the compatible pair (-,a;b,d,l,r).

In the end, the only information useful in this tree is the depth of each original leaf. Indeed, it provides the respective length of each code word that is used in the construction of the final coding. Let f(c) be a function returning the code word length of letter c computed as previously presented. In the running example, f(b) = f(d) = f(l) = f(r) = 3 and f(a) = f(-) = 2. The final step of the algorithm builds the unique alphabetic binary tree having these lengths. To do so, its starts by assigning the code 0^k to the smallest letter c, where k = f(c). In the running example, it assigns 00 to letter -. Then, for each letter in the lexical order, the code word is built from the last one built using the following procedure. First, remove any tail of consecutive 1 bits from the previous code. Then, replace the rightmost 0 with a 1. Finally, append enough 0 bits to the right of the constructed code to achieve the desired code length. Back to the running example, - is assigned 00. Then, the rightmost 0 has been replaced by a 1, and a is assigned 01. From 01, first the rightmost 1 bits are removed leading to 0, which is in turn replaced by 1, and two 0 bits are appended in order to achieve length 3; b is thus assigned 100. With a similar process, one ends up with the coding shown in Table 4.5.

Another interesting approach is the so-called *iterated front coding* (Bshouty and Falk, 1992). The method, as one may guess, consists of a series of nearly identical stages, where starting from a dictionary, a smaller dictionary is produced. In each stage, the dictionary

Table 4.5 Coding Chart

Letter	-	a	b	d	l	r
Code	00	01	100	101	110	111

is front coded, the suffixes are Huffman coded, and these codes are written to a temporary file along with the associated length information. Each stage produces a dictionary consisting of the list of suffixes resulting from the front coding. The method is applied repeatedly to the dictionary returned by the previous stage. When no further compression can be achieved on the dictionary, the process ends up by writing the suffixes at the last stage without Huffman coding. To obtain at each stage a list upon which the front coding technique can be applied, each word is reversed and then the list is sorted.

While the front coding technique is not specific to RDF, it's very adapted to URI encoding because it takes the benefit of long common prefixes.

Grammar based

Grammar-based compression is based on a context-free grammar for the strings to be compressed. One of the most famous solutions is *Re-Pair* (Larsson and Moffat, 2000), which is a greedy algorithm based on the strategy of most-frequent-first substitution. The most-frequent-first substitution is a text-compression technique first introduced by Wolff (1975) in which any two consecutive characters occurring the most often are replaced by a new one. By keeping in memory the corresponding rewriting rule, one will be able to retrieve the original text. The compression performance of the algorithm was improved by Larsoon and Moffat and led to the Re-Pair solution, although the main memory space is very large. Re-Pair will repeatedly find the most frequent pairs of consecutive symbols in the strings and replace them with a new symbol, until no more repeated pairs of consecutive symbols can be found. More precisely, Re-Pair over a string S will first identify the most frequent pair of consecutive symbols in S, say uv. It will then add a rule w→uv to the set of rules R, where w is a new symbol not appearing in S. Finally, it replaces every occurrence of uv in S by w. The process is iterated until every pair of consecutive symbols in S appears once. The Re-Pair method can be implemented in linear time and space with a compressed representation of the rules. Interested readers may refer to Larsson and Moffat (2000) for more details. Table 4.6 illustrates the corresponding process on the repetitive text alabar-a-la-alabarda, where, for ease, we replace spaces with dashes.

The resulting compression of alabar-a-la-alabarda is E-a-A-Eda and the set of grammar rules.

Self-indexing

Self-indexing is a representation using a structure that compresses the data and indexes it at the same time. The most popular self-indexing approaches are the FM-index

Table 4.6 Re-Pair Example on the String `alabar-a-la-alabarda`

Text Rule	Repeated Pairs of Symbols				Resulting Rule
`alabar-a-la-alabarda`	`(al,2)`	`(la,3)`	`(ab,2)`	`(ba,2)`	A→la
	`(ar,2)`	`(-a,2)`	`(a-,2)`		
`aAbar-a-A-aAbarda`	`(aA,1)`	`(Ab,2)`	`(ba,2)`	`(ar,2)`	B→Ab
	`(-a,2)`				
`aBar-a-A-aBarda`	`(aB,2)`	`(Ba,2)`	`(ar,2)`	`(-a,2)`	C→aB
`Car-a-A-Carda`	`(Ca,2)`	`(ar,2)`			D→Ca
`Dr-a-A-Drda`	`(Dr,2)`				E→Dr
`E-a-A-Eda`					

(Ferragina and Manzini, 2000) and the wavelet tree (Grossi et al., 2003), which uses space closer to the optimal compressed text while providing search functionalities. While they provide a high compression with less competitive performance for operations, this induces a more uniform effectiveness on literals than other solutions. This is mainly due to the fact that literals are characterized with less regularities than URIs and, thus, imply a more complicated compression.

An FM-index, which stands for full-text index in minute space, is a compressed full-text substring index based on the Burrows–Wheeler transform (Burrows and Wheeler, 1994) and created by Paolo Ferragina and Giovanni Manzini (Ferragina and Manzini, 2000). The main purpose of this structure is to allow us to efficiently count the number of occurrences of a pattern within the compressed text, as well as locate the position of each occurrence. These operations can be done both in sublinear time and space with respect to the size of the input data.

Considering a given input text, an FM-index is computed upon the Burrows–Wheeler Transform (BWT) of the input text. The BWT has been the unifying tool for string compression and indexing, producing many important breakthroughs (e.g., the popular bzip2). It was invented by Michael Burrows and David Wheeler in 1994. The transform is done by sorting all rotations of the input text in lexicographic order, then taking the last column read from top to bottom. For example, considering `missis-sippi$` input text, one obtains the encoding shown in Table 4.7.

The BWT of `mississippi$` is `ipssm$pissii` (the string created from the letters of the last column). Roughly, the BWT is a permutation of the characters of a string that is reversible and where characters with similar right-contexts tend to come together. This makes the BWT more compressible than the original text. The reversibility of the BWT is obtained via the so-called *last-to-front mapping* property, which states that the ith occurrence of a character `c` in the BWT of a text `T` (i.e., the last column of the sorted list of all rotations) corresponds to the ith occurrence of `c` in the first column of the sorted list of all rotations of `T` in lexical order. Let's mark each character with its rank in the original text as a subscript—that is, the third occurrence of `s` is denoted s_2.

Table 4.7 Permutations and Ordering of the `mississippi$`String

Rotations	Sorted Rotations	BWT
mississippi$	$mississippi	i
ississippi$m	i$mississipp	p
ssissippi$mi	ippi$mississ	s
sissippi$mis	issippi$miss	s
issippi$miss	ississippi$m	m
ssippi$missi	mississippi$	$
sippi$missis	pi$mississip	p
ippi$mississ	ppi$mississi	i
ppi$mississi	sippi$missis	s
pi$mississip	sissippi$mis	s
i$mississipp	ssippi$missi	i
$mississippi	ssissippi$mi	i

As shown in Table 4.8, s_2 is indeed the third occurrence of s in both the BWT and the first column of the sorted list of all rotations.

The BWT contains all the characters of the original text. Thus, retrieving the first column of the sorted list of all rotations of the text is trivial. One can just sort alphabetically the characters of the BWT. Then, the first and last columns together provide all pairs of consecutive characters in the text. Because the text can contain multiple occurrences of a character, one needs to determine the rank of each occurrence of a character. The reconstruction will be done from right to left—that is, from the last character to the first one. By definition, the first character of the BWT is the last character of the text (excluding $). According to the LF mapping property, in order to know which letter

Table 4.8 BWT for the `mississippi$` String

Rank of the Character in the First Column		Sorted Rotations		BWT	Rank of the Character in the BWT
		$m_0i_0s_0s_1i_1s_2s_3i_2p_1p_2i_3	i_3	1st	i
1st	i	$i_3$$m_0i_0s_0s_1i_1s_2s_3i_2p_0p_1	p_1	1st	p
2nd	i	$i_2p_0p_1i_3$m_0i_0s_0s_1i_1s_2s_3	s_3	1st	s
3rd	i	$i_1s_2s_3i_2p_0p_1i_3$m_0i_0s_0s_1	s_1	2nd	s
4th	i	$i_0s_0s_1i_1s_2s_3i_2p_0p_1i_3$m_0	m_0	1st	m
1st	m	$m_0i_0s_0s_1i_1s_2s_3i_2p_0p_1i_3$	$		
1st	p	p_1i_3m_0i_0s_0s_1i_1s_2s_3i_2p_0	p_0	2nd	p
2nd	p	$p_0p_1i_3$m_0i_0s_0s_1i_1s_2s_3i_2	i_2	2nd	i
1st	s	$s_3i_2p_0p_1i_3$m_0i_0s_0s_1i_1s_2	s_2	3rd	s
2nd	s	$s_1i_1s_2s_3i_2p_0p_1i_3$m_0i_0s_0	s_0	4th	s
3rd	s	$s_2s_3i_2p_0p_1i_3$m_0i_0s_0s_1i_1	i_1	3rd	i
4th	s	$s_0s_1i_1s_2s_3i_2p_0p_1i_3$m_0i_0	i_0	4th	i

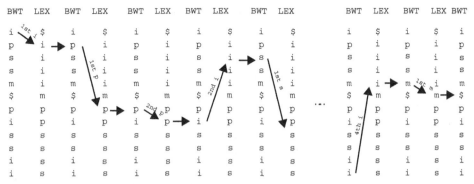

Figure 4.6 Reconstruction of the original text.

appears to its left (i.e., what is the character before the last), we only have to know the rank of the last character (i.e., how many occurrences of this character appear before in the BWT). Let's illustrate this on the previous example.

We know from the first character of the BWT that the original text ends with i$. Because the corresponding i is the first one in the BWT, it corresponds to the first rotation beginning with a i in the lexical order. We deduce that it's preceded by a p. By repeating this process until obtaining character $ in the BWT, one obtains the original text as shown in Figure 4.6.

The BWT is closely linked to the so-called *suffix array*. A suffix array is a compact representation of all suffixes of a text.

Definition 4.1 Given a text $T = c_1c_2c_3 \ldots c_n$, the suffix array SA of T is defined as a simple vector of integers storing the starting positions of all the suffixes of T in lexicographical order; SA[i] contains the starting position of the ith sorted suffix of T.

For ease of notation, let's denote T[i] the ith character of text T. Because the BWT of a text is also a text, we will denote BWT[i] the ith character of the BWT BWT of a text.

Lemma 4.2 BWT[i] = T[SA[i]−1], where BWT and SA are respectively the BWT and the suffix array of a text T.

For example, the suffix array of mississippi$ is SA = [12, 11, 8, 5, 2, 1, 10, 9, 7, 4, 6, 3], where SA[7] = 10 because pi$ appears as a suffix at position 10. Once we present side by side the BWT and the suffix array of a text T, one can indeed observe that the BWT can be derived from the suffix array and the original text easily (BWT[i] = T[SA[i]−1]). In Figure 4.7, BWT[7] is indeed p because T[SA[7]−1] = T[9] = p.

Ferragina and Manzini (2000) proposed to pair a BWT and a suffix array, creating the so-called *FM-index*, which enables a backward search. Roughly, backward searching is searching for occurrences of a pattern P in a self-indexed text T using only the FM-index structure. First, notice that in the suffix array all occurrences of a search pattern

Index	Sorted Rotations	Sorted Suffixes SA		BWT
1	$mississippi	$	12 i	
2	i$mississipp	i$	11 p	
3	ippi$mississ	ippi$ 8	s	
4	issippi$miss	issippi$ 5		s
5	ississippi$m	ississippi$	2	m
6	mississippi$	mississippi$	1	$
7	pi$mississip	pi$	10 p	
8	ppi$mississi	ppi$ 9	i	
9	sippi$missis	sippi$ 7	s	
10	sissippi$mis	sissippi$ 4		s
11	ssippi$missi	ssippi$	6	i
12	ssissippi$mi	ssissippi$	3	i

Figure 4.7 Correspondence between suffix array and BWT.

lie in a set of consecutive rows. Indeed, any pattern in the text is a prefix of a suffix, which is moreover lexicographically sorted. One only needs a clever way to use this property. In the backward search, the BWT is used via a series of paired rank operations. More precisely, the backward search consists in at most k pairs of rank operations, where k is the length of the searched pattern P. To find the rows beginning with the pattern P, we proceed repeatedly by finding the range of rows prefixed by successively longer proper suffixes of P. If P does not occur in T, the process will end up in an empty range. If P occurs in T, the process of the whole word P (i.e., the longest proper suffix of P) results in a range where all the occurrences of P appear. Therefore, the size of this range equals the number of times P occurs in T. Formally, for $|P| <= i <= 1$, the range of the proper suffix of size $|P| - (i-1)$ of P, denoted (s_i, e_i), can be computed from (s_{i+1}, e_{i+1}) as follows: $s_i = C[P[i]] + Occ(P[i], s_{i+1}) + 1$ and $e_i = C[P[i]] + Occ(P[i], e_{i+1})$, where C is a table containing, for each character c in the alphabet, the number of occurrences of lexically smaller characters in the text, and $Occ(c, j)$ returns the number of occurrences of character c in the prefix $BWT[1..j]$. Initially, $s_{|P|+1}$ is set to 1 and $e_{|P|+1}$ to the length of T. If P does not occur in T, the process will end up as an invalid range—that is, when $e < s$. If P does occur in T, the positions of P in T can be retrieved from the following entries of the suffix array: $\{SA[i] | s_1 <= i <= e_1\}$.

Let's illustrate this process in the search of pattern $P = si$ in the text $T = mississip$-$pi\$$. Table C will be defined as follows. Consider the lexical order $\$ < i < m < p < s$, $C = [0,1,5,6,8]$. $C['m'] = C[3] = 5$ means that there are five occurrences of letters belonging to $\{'\$', 'i'\}$; because $C['i'] = C[2] = 1$, one can deduce that there is one $'\$'$ and four occurrences of $'i'$. Note that, for efficiency purposes, one can store C using var-byte coding. Initially, we set $s_3 = 1$ and $e_3 = 12$. We then proceed by finding the range for the shortest proper suffix of P—that is, i. The range (s_2, e_2)

corresponds to $s_2 = C['i'] + Occ('i',1) + 1 = 1 + 0 + 1 = 2$ and $e_2 = C['i'] + Occ('i',12) = 1 + 4 = 5$. Note that, indeed, considering the sorted suffixes list, all the occurrences of 'i' appear between the second and the fifth positions. Now we look for the range for the final suffix of P—that is, si. The range (s_1, e_1) corresponds to $s_1 = C['s'] + Occ('s',2) + 1 = 8 + 0 + 1 = 9$ and $e_1 = C['s'] + Occ('s',5) = 8 + 2 = 10$. We can conclude that there are two occurrences of 'si' in T, one in position 7 (i.e., SA[9]) and one in position 4 (i.e., SA[10]).

Regarding query performance, the Occ operation can be performed using the so-called *wavelet tree* succinct data structure. This family of succinct data structure uses a compression rate close to the theoretical optimum, but simultaneously allows efficient decompression-free query operations on the compressed data. This property is obtained using a small amount of extra bits to store additional information. Bit vectors (a.k.a. *bit maps*) are useful to represent data while minimizing its memory footprint. In its classic shape, a bit vector (if stored consecutively in memory) allows us, in constant time, to access and modify a value of the vector. Munro (1996) designed an asymptotic optimal version where, in constant time, one can execute three additional interesting operations. One may count the number of 1 bits (or 0 bits) appearing in the first x elements of a bit vector. This operation is denoted rank(b,x) with $b \in \{0,1\}$. One may also find the position of the xth occurrence of a bit. This operation is denoted select(b,x) with $b \in \{0,1\}$. Finally, one may retrieve the bit at position x with the operation called access(x). Naturally, these operations on bit vectors would be of great interest for a wider alphabet.

The original solution was provided by Grossi et al. (2003) and roughly consists in using a balanced binary tree, the wavelet tree. The alphabet is split into two equal parts. One attributes a 0 to each character of the first part and a 1 to the other. The original sequence is written at the root of the tree using this encoding. The process is repeated in the left subtree for the subsequence of the original sequence only using characters of the first part of the alphabet, and in the right subtree for the second part. The process iterates until ending up on a singleton alphabet. Roughly, one has provided an encoding of each character of the alphabet. Using rank and select operations on the bit vectors stored in the nodes of the tree, one is able to compute the rank and select operations on the original sequence in O(log|alphabet|) by deep traversals of the tree. These operations can be easily adapted to only traverse until a given depth, referred to as rankprefix and selectprefix operations. Considering the mississippi$burning$ text, a corresponding wavelet tree is displayed in Figure 4.8.

Once the tree is constructed, the rank and select operations can be done with rank and select operations over the bit vectors stored in the nodes of the tree. For example, if we want to know the number of i's appearing until position 10 (i.e., rank('i',10)), we use the following procedure. We know that i is encoded as 100.

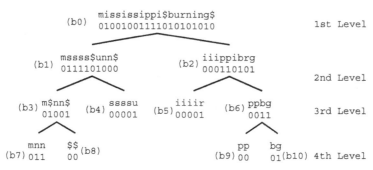

Figure 4.8 Wavelet tree for the `mississippi$burning$` string.

Therefore, we know that any potential occurrence of i in the first level corresponds to a 1 entry. Therefore, we count the number of 1's before position 10—that is, `rank(1,10)` on the corresponding bitmap b0. It should return 5. We further know now that any potential occurrence of i should appear as a 0 in the first five bits of b2. Thus, we count the number of 0's before position 5—that is, `rank(0,5)` on b2. It should return 3. Finally, we know now that any potential occurrence of i should appear as a 0 in the first three bits of b5. Thus, we count the number of 0's before position 3—that is, `rank(0,3)` on b5. It should return 3, which corresponds to the number of 's appearing until position 10. Now, if we want to know the position of the fourth occurrence of i (i.e., `select('i',4)`), we use the following procedure. We know that i is encoded as 100. Therefore, we know exactly where the fourth occurrence of i is—it corresponds to the fourth occurrence of 0 in b5. Therefore, we retrieve its position (i.e., `select(0,4)`) on the corresponding bitmap b5. It should return 4. We further know now that the fourth occurrence of i corresponds to a 0 in b2. In fact, it corresponds to the fourth one according to the previous operation. Thus, we retrieve its position (i.e., `select(0,4)`) on the corresponding bitmap b2. It should return 6. Finally, we know now that the fourth occurrence of i corresponds to a 1 in b0. In fact, it corresponds to the sixth one according to the previous operation. Thus, we retrieve its position (i.e., `select(1,6)`) on the corresponding bitmap b0, which corresponds to the position of the fourth occurrence of i. One can easily see that the number of operations is proportional to the depth of the tree, which induces the logarithmic complexity of the operations.

4.2.2 RDF dictionaries

In RDF dictionaries, three sets of components are considered: URIs, blank nodes, and literals. As we already pointed out, URIs potentially share long prefixes, while literals are strongly related to the knowledge represented in the data set. Moreover, those components have specific potential locations in a triple that allow RDF dictionaries to take into account this location in the encoding, such as by assigning similar identifiers to differently located elements.

Most RDF stores (e.g., **sw-Store** (Abadi et al., 2007a), **Hexastore** (Weiss et al., 2008), and **RDF-3X** (Neumann and Weikum, 2010b)) use two independent structures to efficiently answer to `string-to-id` and `id-to-string` operations. Often, B+trees are used for `string-to-id` operations, sometimes associated to a front coding compression, while structures supporting constant time–direct access (e.g., arrays) are used for `id-to-string` operations. This direct mapping is particularly adapted for identifier lookups and results in a better cache hit ratio. This is especially valuable when the query produces many results, because the cost of these lookups then becomes non-negligible compared to the rest of the query processing steps.

In TripleBit (Yuan et al., 2013), a prefix-compression method is adopted (quite similar to front coding) to obtain compressed dictionaries. The method starts by splitting each URI into a prefix and a suffix part (the last string appearing after the last / is considered the suffix). Each prefix is stored once with a corresponding integer representation called `prefix-id` in a mapping table. The position of a given prefix pair is obtained through a hash table indexed by the prefix. Each URI is stored once as a quad (`len, id, prefix-id, suffix`) in another mapping table. Given a URI, `prefix-id` is the identifier stored in the `prefix-id` table of the prefix, `suffix` is the suffix in its textual form, `id` is the overall identifier used for the whole URI, and `len` is the size in the mapping table of the quad. The overall identifier of a URI is obtained from an independent identifier space of the `prefix-ids`. The position of the quad corresponding to a given URI is obtained from another hash table indexed by strings obtained by the concatenation of `prefix-id` and `suffix` of the URIs. The main benefit of this solution is that any prefix is only stored once even if it's common to a huge number of URIs.

Let's now describe the `string-to-id` operation. During query translation, the URI, say `<http://www.w3.org/2004/02/skos/core#example >`, is decomposed into its prefix and suffix part. The `prefix-id`, say `12`, is obtained using the hash table over `http://www.w3.org/2004/02/skos/core`, which returns its position. The position of the corresponding quad is obtained using the second hash table over `12#example`. Then accessing the mapping table, the overall identifier is retrieved. Considering the `id-to-string` operation, looking for the `id` into the mapping table would be too costly. Therefore, two inverted tables are used. The first (respectively second) inverted table stores any `prefix-id` (respectively overall `id`) and its position in the corresponding mapping table. Roughly, these inverted tables play the same role as the hash table—that is, giving positions in mapping tables—but using an integer index rather than strings. Therefore, given an overall `id`, the corresponding inverted table, which is accessed in at most logarithmic time if it's stored sorted according to the `ids`, allows us to retrieve the position of the quad in the mapping table. In turn, the `prefix-id` retrieved from the quad is used together with the corresponding inverted table to retrieve the position of the prefix in the other mapping table. The URI is finally obtained by concatenating back the prefix and the suffix. Inverted tables make the `id-to-string` operation more efficient. However, the overall process can still be costly when the query result size is big.

As previously mentioned, RDF components have specific potential locations in a triple that can be used in RDF dictionaries to further compress the data set. An overall strategy has been defined as an RDF data-centric format, which reduces verbosity in favor of machine understandability and data management, the so-called RDF HDT format (see `http://www.w3.org/Submission/HDT/`). The HDT (header-dictionary-triples) format introduces a new representation for big RDF graphs that is based on three components: a recommended header, a dictionary, and the triples. In this chapter, we only consider the dictionary, but some further details may be found in Chapter 5, Section 5.2.

The HDT dictionary aims at organizing the vocabulary appearing in the RDF graph in such a way that it avoids as many repetitions as possible and allows for a rapid search with high levels of compression. The underlying basic observation of HDT is that the sets of subjects, predicates, and objects in RDF are not disjoint. Thus, HDT proposes to regroup common subjects/objects into a shared identifier, which avoids duplicating entries in the dictionary, and thus reduces the dictionary size. More precisely, given the set of subjects `S`, the set of predicates `P`, and the set of objects `O`, the set `SO` of common subjects/objects is coded with identifiers from `1` to `|SO|`, the set `(S-SO)` of uncommon subjects is coded with identifiers from `|SO| + 1` to `|S|`, the set `(O-SO)` of uncommon objects is coded with identifiers from `|SO| + 1` to `|O|`, and the set of predicates is coded with identifiers from `1` to `|P|`. The set of predicates is treated independently because of their low number and the infrequent overlapping with other sets.

4.3 SMART ENCODING

Mainly, two recent approaches investigated a nonarbitrary encoding: **Semantic Index** (Rodriguez-Muro and Calvanese, 2012) and **WaterFowl** (Curé et al., 2014). Both systems are based on the differentiation of the Tbox (i.e., the ontology) and Abox (i.e., the facts) in the dictionaries. While the terms of the Abox are still encoded in a classic way, the terms of the Tbox are encoded according to their corresponding hierarchies. Indeed, the concepts and properties defined in the Tbox are usually organized in hierarchies that specify inheritance properties. Regarding the concepts (respectively properties), one can specify that a concept (respectively property) is a subconcept (respectively subproperty) of another concept (respectively property). These subsumption relations are evaluated when inference on knowledge is needed.

For example, consider an RDF data set produced by **LUBM** (refer to Section 3.7 for more details), where there may be several statements about assistant and associate professors. With a classic encoding, a user who wants to retrieve all the professors, whatever their precise positions are, would either need to materialize the implicit knowledge of the data set (here, the fact that any assistant or associate professor is also a professor), which may be time and space consuming, or would need to explicitly request for any type of professor (also called *query rewriting*). One way of solving this issue gracefully is to derive an encoding of the entry of the Tbox that encompass the Tbox knowledge (subsumption, property domain, and range). While the objective is common—that is, providing a storage technique that allows for efficient querying of concepts and properties hierarchies—the techniques are different.

In the Semantic Index approach (Rodriguez-Muro and Calvanese, 2012), each entity (concept or property) in the corresponding hierarchy is assigned a numerical value according to a breadth-first visit of the hierarchy. Provided with this assignment, one is ensured that any subhierarchy is associated to a consecutive set of numerical values (i.e., an interval). In other words, each entity is associated to an interval covering the indexes of all its subentities. Considering `string-to-id` operations, an entity will be encoded using the smallest integer of its interval (i.e., the one induced by the breadth-first visit). The Semantic Index can be constructed in polynomial time in the size of the entity hierarchies. Using this Semantic Index, any query over entity hierarchies can now be expressed as a simple range query. Similar ideas have been considered in Agrawal et al. (1989) and DeHaan et al. (2003).

In WaterFowl (Curé et al., 2014) approach, the hierarchical relations are encoded as a prefix code. Roughly, any two TBox entities sharing a common prefix in their encoding have at least a common superconcept or superproperty. As for the Semantic Index, this process allows the WaterFowl system to infer some implicit knowledge without materialization and at low cost. One of the benefits of using prefix codes is inherent to the succinct data structures used in the system. Roughly, answering a request on the system induces the system to visit some data structures. These visits can be shortened whenever the smallest sufficient prefix of a code has been encountered (see Chapter 5, Section 5.2 for more details). The main drawback is that because the `id`s are guided by the hierarchies, a lot of the candidate integers cannot be attributed.

4.4 ALLOWING A FULL TEXT SEARCH IN LITERALS

Regarding literals, compared to URIs, the corresponding encoding strategy does not have the same purpose. Indeed, while compression is the main objective in URI encoding, the main feature sought in RDF stores related to literal is a full text search. The most popular solution for handling a full text search in literals is *Lucene*, integrated in RDF stores such as **Yars2**, **Jena TDB/SDB**, and **GraphDB (formerly OWLIM)**, and in Big Data RDF databases, but it's also popular for other systems, such as **IBM OmnifindY! Edition**, **Technorati**, **Wikipedia**, **Internet Archive**, and **LinkedIn**. Lucene is a very popular open-source information-retrieval library from **the Apache Software Foundation** (originally created in **Java** by Doug Cutting). It provides Java-based full-text indexing and searching capabilities for applications through an easy-to-use API. Lucene is based on powerful and efficient search algorithms using indexes.

A Lucene *index* is a collection of Lucene *documents*. A Lucene document contains Lucene *fields* of text. A Lucene field is textual content along with metadata describing the content. Typically, the original textual information is used to create a Lucene document, which is analyzed using a given Lucene *analyzer* and added to the index. The index is then used to perform a user textual query. The purpose of an analyzer is to convert the original textual data into essential units of searching referred as Lucene *terms*. Terms are stemming from so-called *tokens* obtained from the textual data after a series of operations: words extraction, common words, and punctuation removal.

Lucene provides many out-of-the-box analyzers, such as `SimpleAnalyzer`, `WhitespaceAnalyzer`, `StandardAnalyzer`, and more. They differ in the tokenizing and filtering process. For example, the `SimpleAnalyzer` divides text at nonletter characters and puts it in lowercase, while the `WhitespaceAnalyzer` splits tokens at whitespaces. The `StandardAnalyzer` uses a sophisticated grammar analysis that recognizes, among others things, email addresses, acronyms, alphanumerics, and more, and puts them in lowercase and removes stop words (e.g., `the`, `a`, `is`, etc. for the English language). While this process removes words before indexing, and thus decreases index size, it can also decrease query processing precision. One can get more control by implementing its own `Analyzer`. Figure 4.9 illustrates these differences on sample text.

Once the analyzer process has been done, the corresponding tokens can be indexed. In Lucene, the data of the index is stored in a so-called *inverted index*, on disk or in memory as a set of index files. An inverted index uses terms as keys and a list of corresponding documents containing them as values, which lets users perform fast keyword lookups. An inverted index stores terms and related metadata (position, number of occurrences, etc.) in a tunable manner via a field constructor.

The field constructor takes in as arguments the field name, a value, and a set of flags determining how this last field will be saved in the index. The first flag, so-called `STORE` (with typical values `YES` or `NO`), marks whether the raw value of the field is stored in the index or not. Storing raw values speeds up retrieving them at search time at the price of

```
SimpleAnalyzer
[joe] [doe] [is] [the] [owner] [of] [the] [australian] [b] [b] [blog] [joe]
[doe]                                    [example]                      [com]
WhitespaceAnalyzer
[Joe] [Doe] [is] [the] [owner] [of] [the] [Australian] [B&B] [blog] [-]
[joe.doe@example.com]
StandardAnalyzer
[joe] [doe] [owner] [australian] [B&B] [blog] [joe.doe@example.com]
```

Figure 4.9 Analyzing text "Joe Doe is the owner of the Australian B&B blog joe.doe@example.com."

space consumption. Any field must be indexed to be searchable but all fields do not have to be indexed. One can mark whether a field will be indexed or not with the `INDEX` flag (with typical values `NO`, `ANALYZED`, `NOT_ANALYZED`, `ANALYZED_NO_NORMS`, and `NOT_ANALYZED_NO_NORMS`). Only the value `NO` turns off indexing of a field. The values `ANALYZED` and `NOT_ANALYZED` cause respectively a field to be tokenized or treated as a single token. A `NOT_ANALYZED` field will not be decomposed into searchable terms. Lucene determines how relevant a given document is to a query by computing a score. Lucene allows influencing scoring and thus search results by *boosting*. Details regarding boosting are out the scope of this book but interested readers may refer to Gospodnetic et al. (2009). Lucene will ignore any boost and field length during score evaluation of any field flagged as `ANALYZED_NO_NORMS` or `NOT_ANALYZED_NO_NORMS`. Roughly, a matching token will always be worth the same, no matter the length of the field. The main benefit of these last two flags is decreasing memory usage during a search at the price of less-effective search results. The final flag, so-called `TERMVECTOR`, marks whether to store *term vectors*. A term vector is a list of terms along with metadata. Term vectors can store the number of occurrences of the term in the document and its positions. Each position corresponds to the number of previous terms in the document plus one, while the offset gives the relative textual position in the document in terms of characters. Typical values are `NO` (nothing), `YES` (only number of occurrences), `WITH_OFFSETS` (offsets), `WITH_POSITIONS` (positions), and `WITH_POSITIONS_OFFSETS` (both offsets and positions).

Considering a common usage, the body, title, and abstract of a document will be analyzed and indexed with term vectors including both positions and offsets; they will be stored except for the body (for memory reasons). Document characteristics such as the filename, URLs, and dates will be stored and indexed but not analyzed nor boosted. Finally, information such as document type will not be indexed but will be stored.

Once the index is built, one can run search queries against the index. An analysis will also be performed on the query. For efficiency purpose, the same type of analyzer that was used for creating the index should be used for the query. The search will result on a documents ranking where hits were found and ordered by the scoring function.

Readers interested in Lucene should also have a look at Lucene's sister package called *Solr* (see `http://lucene.apache.org/solr/tutorial.html`), which embeds Lucene in a client-server architecture. Solr is an open-source search server with XML/HTTP APIs, caching and replication functionalities, and a Web administration interface. Solr provides useful features such as a powerful full-text search, hit highlighting, and database integration. Solr is used in RDF stores such as **Allegrograph** and Jena TDB/SDB, but also in several commercial websites such as **Netflix**, **CNET**, and the **Smithsonian**.

4.5 COMPRESSING LARGE AMOUNTS OF DATA

Traditional centralized approaches have growing difficulties (both in terms of time and space efficiency) for handling very large input. Considering large amounts of data, a high-performance compression technique is required. In Urbani et al. (2013), the authors propose a distributed data compression based on a set of distributed MapReduce algorithms. The proposed prototype (based on a **Hadoop** framework) is able to build a dictionary over hundreds of millions of entries.

MapReduce is a programming model that was proposed by engineers at Google in 2004 (Dean and Ghemawat, 2004). Let's recall here some key properties of the system (detailed in Chapter 2, Section 2.2.4). It's based on two operations, namely the `map` and `reduce` functions to be programmed in a given programming language (e.g., Java or **C++**). When writing these programs, one does not need to worry about most of the hard tasks from an end-user point of view, because they are automatized and taken care of by the system (e.g., data partitioning, execution scheduling, handling machine failure, and managing intermachine communication). In this framework, all the information is encoded as `<key,value>` pairs. First, the `map` function processes the input (i.e., some `<key,value>` pairs) and outputs an intermediate set of possibly different `<key,value>` pairs. Then, the intermediate pairs are grouped together according to their key and each group is processed by the `reduce` function. The framework partitions the input data over a cluster of machines and sends the `map` function to each machine. This supports a parallel execution of the `map` functions. After all `map` functions have been completed, a shuffle phase is performed to transfer all `map` outputs to the `reduce` nodes—that is, all `map` outputs with the same key are sent to the same `reduce` node. Then the `reduce` jobs are executed and produce the final output.

The proposed MapReduce compression approach (i.e., a `string-to-id` operation) of Urbani et al. (2013) consists of a sequence of three MapReduce jobs. In a first job, the most popular terms are identified so that they can be compressed further than terms occurring only a few times. Because the input is supposed to be large, for efficiency purposes, the popular terms are extracted from a random sample of the input. Note that, because the approach supports incremental updates, the input of the first job consists of both the data to compress and possibly an existing dictionary. Roughly, the `map` function produces two types of `<key,value>` pairs. When an existing dictionary entry is processed, it's simply reemitted, while new entries (`s,p,o`) (which are RDF triples) are emitted as three `<key,value>` pairs: `<s,null >`, `<p,null >`, and `<o,null >`. To apply a sampling of the input, for new entries a random number is computed and compared to the sampling threshold. The `reduce` function will treat all entries regarding a common term and decide if it's a popular term (i.e., counting the number of occurrences of this last and comparing it to a given threshold) and assign it an identifier if it does has not already have an identifier assigned to it in a previous update (i.e., if in the group there is an entry with a non-null value). To avoid conflicts due to the incremental updates, a specific range of values is intended for popular terms.

In a second job, the statements will be deconstructed and identifiers will be assigned to each term. The corresponding `map` function will produces three types of `<key,value>` pairs. When an existing dictionary entry is processed, it's simply reemitted as a `<value,key>` pair—that is, the term is used as a key and its identifier as a value. If a statement is treated (i.e., `null` key) and an identifier `id_s` is associated to each new statement (using a counter), then three `<key,value>`pairs are emitted, one for each of the subject, the predicate, and the object—respectively, `<k,id_s + 0 >`, `<k',id_s + 1>` and `<k",id_s + 2 >`—where the corresponding key is either the term itself or an identifier computed in the first job depending on the popularity of the term. On the whole, the `map` function produces pairs with integer (for popular terms) or textual (for unpopular terms and dictionary entries) keys. The `reduce` function will treat all entries regarding either a common identifier or a common term. In the former case, it will simply reemit the pair. In the latter case, it will check whether there is already a dictionary entry for the term and retrieve its identifier, or create a new identifier for the term otherwise. A new pair will be emitted with the same value (i.e., a composition of the statement identifier and the nature of the term—the subject, predicate, or object) and the identifier as key.

In a last job, the numerical terms will be read to reconstruct the statements in their compressed form. In this job, the dictionary is not used anymore and all pairs are of the same type: the key is a numerical value associated to each term and the value contains both a statement identifier and the nature of the term. The `map` function decomposes the value and reemits a pair with the statement identifier as key and a composition of the numerical value of the term and the nature of this as value. The `reduce` function will treat all entries regarding a given statement and will thus be able to reconstruct the statement in its compressed form.

Note that, from a practical point of view, the authors use variable-length encoding for the different identifier, which consists in using the two to three most significant bits to store the number of bytes required to write the value.

The proposed MapReduce decompression approach (i.e., the `id-to-string` operation) of Urbani et al. (2013) consists of a sequence of four MapReduce jobs. The first and last jobs are similar to the one described for the compression approach and respectively identifies the popular terms (in terms of identifiers this time) and reconstructs the statements in the original format (from identifiers to textual form this time). The second job performs the join between the popular resources and the dictionary table. It aims at efficiently extracting the popular terms' translations from the dictionary table that may contain hundreds of millions of entries. The `map` function emits a pair for each popular term with its numerical value as key and its textual form as value. This task does not need a `reduce` function.

The third job deconstructs the statements and decompresses the terms performing a join on the input. The corresponding map function will produces three types of <key,value> pairs. When an existing dictionary entry is processed, it's simply reemitted as a <value,key> pair—that is, the numerical value is used as a key and its textual form as a value. If a statement is treated (i.e., null key) and an identifier id_s is associated to each new statement (using a counter), then three <key,value>pairs are emitted, one for each of the subject, the predicate, and the object—respectively, <k,id_s + 0 >, <k',id_s + 1 >, and <k",id_s + 2 >, where the corresponding key is either the numerical value of the term or the textual form computed in the first job depending on the popularity of the term. On the whole, the map function produces pairs with textual (for popular terms) or numerical (for unpopular terms and dictionary entries) keys. The reduce function will treat all entries regarding either a common term or a common identifier. In the former case, it will simply reemit the pair. In the latter case, it will retrieve the term of the corresponding identifier from the dictionary entry. A new pair will be emitted with the same value (i.e., a composition of the statement identifier and the nature of the term—the subject, predicate, or object) and the textual form as key. Note that the dictionary emits pairs with numerical values as key and in textual form as value.

4.6 SUMMARY

- RDF data may be very verbose due to the use of string identifiers in the shape of URIs. Therefore, storing triples as is may be very inefficient in terms of space occupied by the data.
- The underlying basic concept of a dictionary is to provide a bijective function mapping long terms (URIs, blank nodes, literals) to short identifiers (integers) through two basic operations: string-to-id and id-to-string.
- The size of the dictionary is not negligible at all and may even be larger than the encoded data set itself, and thus may induce scalability issues by its own.
- Classic string dictionary techniques—namely, hashing, front coding, grammar-based, and self-indexing—can be used, but specificity of RDF dictionaries may be taken into account to further obtain better compression.
- Very few solutions make a differentiation between the Tbox and the Abox of the knowledge base at the dictionary level. We consider that this aspect seems promising.
- When considering big literals and data sets, there exists well-defined frameworks that can handle these tasks efficiently.

CHAPTER FIVE

Storage and Indexing of RDF Data

5.1 INTRODUCTION

This chapter presents different physical organizations for storing and indexing RDF data. Apart from having an impact on the size required to store data sets, these design choices have an important influence on the performance of the main operations performed on an RDF store, such as query processing and reasoning, which are investigated in later chapters. Due to the relatively short history (at least compared to RDBMS where the first systems were released in the beginning of the 80s) of the RDF data model (i.e., the first W3C recommendation in 1999) and the emergence of the first RDF stores (i.e., **Sesame** in 2002), the research for an efficient storage backend is still considered an open problem. This is confirmed by witnessing the increasing number of system descriptions provided in proceedings of established databases (e.g., VLDB [http://www.vldb.org/], EDBT [http://www.edbt.org/], and SIG-MOD [http://www.sigmod.org/]) and Semantic Web (e.g., ISWC [http://www.informatik.uni-trier.de/~ley/db/conf/semweb/index.html] and ESWC [http://eswc-conferences.org/]) conferences during the last few years. Moreover, following the footsteps of Oracle, the recent involvement of computer science–industry giants like IBM and Microsoft highlights the importance of this field and a certain market health.

Among the plethora of existing systems, we can distinguish between solutions that are implementing their own storage backend, denoted as *native*, and those that are using an existing database management system, denoted as *non-native*. Figure 5.1 proposes a classification along these two axis for the storage and access of RDF data.

5.1.1 Native approaches

The native approach provides a way to store RDF data closer to its data model, eschewing the mapping to entities of a DBMS, such as relations. It uses the triples nature of RDF data as an asset and enables to tackle the specificities of its graph approach, such as the ability to handle data sparsity and the dynamic aspect of its schema. These systems can be broadly classified as *disk–based*, i.e., persisted, and *main memory–based*, i.e., volatile, systems.

The persistent disk–based storage is a way to store RDF data permanently on a file system. These implementations may use well-known index structures, such as B+trees,

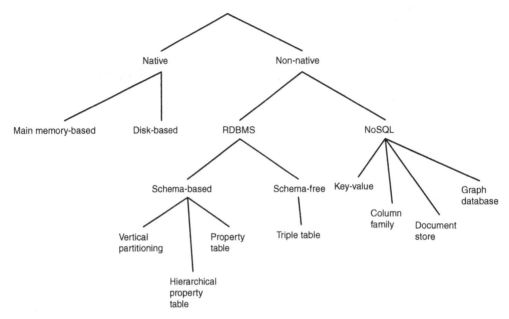

Figure 5.1 RDF storage classification.

which are extensively used in RDBMS. One may consider that reading from and writing to disks induces an important performance bottleneck. This consideration has motivated in-memory solutions that aim to store as much of the data, such as RDF triples, dictionaries, or ontologies, as possible in the main memory.

The in-memory storage of RDF data allocates a certain amount of the available main memory to store the whole RDF graph structure. Like the persistent disk–based storage, this approach relies on research results in the database domain (e.g., indexes or efficient processing) and multiple index–based techniques. When working on RDF data stored in the main memory, some of the most time-consuming operations are loading and parsing the RDF files, but also the creation of suitable indexes. Therefore, an RDF store must have a memory-efficient data representation that leaves enough space for the operations associated to query processing and data management.

5.1.2 Non-native approaches

The non-native approach makes use of a database management system to store RDF data permanently. Such an approach benefits from years of research and development on these DBMSs, and this is especially relevant for systems based on an RDBMS. For example, most RDBMSs are known to have industrial-strength transaction support and security considerations that most native approaches are lacking.

In the RDBMS category, we can distinguish between schema-based and schema-free approaches. With schema-free, we mean that a single table, denoted *triples table*, is responsible for the storage of all triples. In schema-based, unlike the previous representation that is quite straightforward, the schema's characteristics are used to split the set of triples into different tables. Such a split can be organized based on the intrinsic structure of triples, i.e., subject, predicate and object, or based on the RDFS or OWL schema properties or classes. For instance, we can distinguish two major schemas: the property table and the vertical-partitioning approach. Recently, some systems came to light with some NoSQL stores taking care of the storage backend. The main motivation behind these approaches, at least those based on a key-value, document, or column-family store, is to address the distribution of very large data sets over a cluster of commodity hardware. Considering the graph database category, they present the qualities of not providing an important mismatch with the RDF data model and they generally support ACID transactions but an efficient data distribution is hard to obtain in a totally automatic manner.

5.1.3 Native and non-native comparison

Systems following the native approach generally have to start their development from scratch, therefore heavy design and implementation efforts are needed if one wants to release a production-ready system. It is not a surprise to encounter the most efficient, in terms of query and inference performances, solutions in this native category. Compared to the native storage solution, non-native approaches are less demanding in terms of design and implementation efforts. That is, one can rely on existing index implementation, ACID support and SQL query processing and optimization. Nevertheless, to obtain satisfying overall performances, the handling of the mismatch between the two data models (e.g., graph to relational) as well as SPARQL to SQL, possibly for complex queries, have to be taken into consideration.

5.1.4 Chapter overview

In the remainder of this chapter, we focus on systems that propose query processing functionalities. Most of the time, the query language corresponds to the SPARQL 1.0 specification, but other languages such as SeRQL are present on some systems. In the near future, we can expect full support of the recent (March 2013) W3C SPARQL 1.1 recommendation, such as queries supporting updates, negation, and aggregations. In the following sections, our goal is to provide an overview of existing solutions through the different native and non-native approaches. Note that more details on systems for which data distribution and query federation exist are provided in Chapter 7.

Figure 5.2 provides a timeline of the emergence of the most influential RDF stores. The figure contains about 50 systems that are organized into the native or non-native dichotomy. In the non-native block, all systems are based on an RDBMS, except those regrouped in the NoSQL block. In the native block, a special block clusters some highly compressed systems. Finally, a block of production-ready systems covers both the native and non-native stores. Two kind of arrows are present in the figure: plain arrows

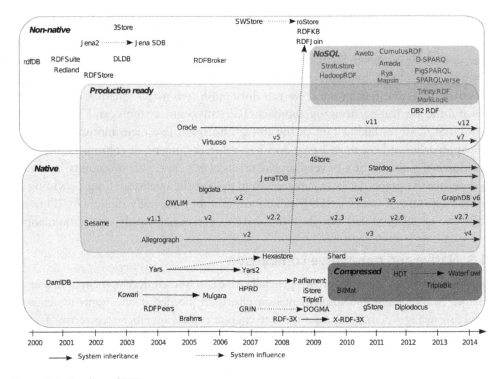

Figure 5.2 Timeline of RDF systems.

represent the evolution of a system, such as between RDF-3X and X-RDF-3X, and dotted arrows emphasize some influence from one system to another, such as **Hexastore** borrows from the data model of the **swStore** system and the indexing approach of **YARS**. The figure provides an interesting vision of the technological trends in RDF stores: RDBMS-based systems were the first to emerge in the early 2000s, but later on native ones became more and more important. Currently, NoSQL-based and highly compressed systems are emerging. In Chapters 7 and 8, we add some new boxes to this figure to respectively highlight distributed and inference-enabled systems.

5.2 NATIVE STORAGE APPROACH

5.2.1 RDF engines based on multiple indexes

Most of these approaches avoid mapping to an RDBMS and focus instead on indexing techniques specific to the RDF data model. They propose methods for rearranging data in memory and/or on disk such that query processing can be performed more efficiently compared to straight-forward approaches like triples tables. They are motivated by the fact that using a traditional RDBMS for RDF data storage results in propagating RDBMS deficiencies such as inflexible schemas, whereas avoiding these limitations is, arguably, one of the major reasons for adopting the RDF data model (Kolas et al., 2009). The corresponding proposals aim to be closer to the query model of the Semantic Web.

These systems, as well as most non-native ones, use multiple indexes. This is motivated by the nature of RDF data and the need address all forms of triple patterns efficiently at query processing time. Intuitively, depending on which triple positions are filled with a IRI or literal, it is going to be much more efficient to access the triples using a precise index. For instance, the binding for the variable ?x in the triple pattern '?x p s', i.e., a variable at the subject position and constant property and object, is going to be much more performant with a 'pos' or 'ops' than 'spo' or 'sop' ones. Of course, one can only use the indexes that are supported by the system. Thus some system adopt an aggressive multiple indexes solution, i.e., almost all access path are considered, while others consider that some graph patterns are rarely encountered in practical situations and only support the most common ones. This comes at the cost of heavy maintenance when data is updated in the former (an important portion of the indexes have to be maintained) and the incapacity to address efficientlly some triple patterns for the latter.

The remainder of this section presents existing systems that we have separated into two categories: those emerging from academia and production-ready systems. Note that the former can sometimes be considered more performant than the latter, but they may lack some features that are needed in a production setting, such as security issues, administration tools, or the absence of APIs or inference features.

5.2.1.1 Project emerging from academia

We first present solutions based on an aggressive indexing strategy. That is, the number of supported indexes is close to a theoretical upper bound. This will ensure good data retrieval performance, but it comes at the cost of designing clever strategies for index selection at query answering time. It also raises some issues for index maintenance when data is updated. The structures used for the indexes frequently correspond to B+trees, but bitmaps or hash-based indexes are also present.

RDF-3X (Neumann and Weikum, 2008) is certainly the system with the most aggressive indexing strategy. From a research point of view, it is currently considered the state of the art in RDF storage systems, and it is used in most research papers as a gold standard in evaluation sections. Although quite sophisticated, the system cannot be considered ready for production; an API interface is not provided for its use in production. It has even been integrated in some distributed systems as a standalone storage layout on nodes of a *MapReduce*-based cluster (more details are provided in Chapter 7 on this topic). RDF-3X has been designed, implemented, extended, and maintained at the Max Planck Institute in Germany. The system stores its triples in the classic triples table approach—that is, a single triples table with three columns. In RDF-3X, this huge table does not rely on an RDBMS, but rather depends on its own storage system that has been specifically designed for the purpose of RDF storage.

One identified problem with the triples table storage approach is the proliferation of self-joins in SPARQL queries. That is, because all triples are contained in a single table, joins are performed using "copies" of this table. This can be very costly or even saturate the main memory of a powerful server because these tables can potentially contain millions of triples and SPARQL queries can possibly imply tens of joins. The system prevents the proliferation of many self-joins by the use of exhaustive indexes for all per-mutations of subject-property-object triples—that is, SPO, SOP, OSP, OPS, PSO, and POS. All the triples of a data set are stored lexicographically in a compressed clustered B+tree, which is six duplicates, one per index. To limit the memory footprint, the solu-tion adopts a standard dictionary encoding approach and therefore obtains an interest-ing compression rate. But the indexing strategy of RDF-3X also contains nine other indexes: six store two out of three entries of a triple (SP, SO, PS, PO, OS, and OP) and are named *aggregated indexes*, and three one-valued indexes are created (S, P, and O). All of these nine indexes provide some selectivity statistics, such as a count of the number of triples satisfying the pattern is stored. Therefore, they can be used to identify the fastest index among the six clustered indexes. The overall claim of this multiple-index approach is that, due to a clever compression strategy, the total size of the indexes is less than the size required by a standard triples table solution. The system supports both individual update operations and updates to entire batches. More details on RDF-3X and its exten-sion **X-RDF-3X** are provided in Chapter 6.

The **YARS** (Harth and Decker, 2005) system combines methods from information retrieval and databases to allow for better query answering performance over RDF data. It stores RDF data persistently by using six B+tree indexes. It not only stores the subject, the predicate, and the object, but also the context information about the data origin. Each element of the corresponding quad (i.e., 4-uplet) is encoded in a dictionary storing mappings from literals and URIs to object IDs (object IDs are stored as number identi-fiers for compactness). To speed up keyword queries, the lexicon keeps an inverted index on string literals to allow fast full-text searches. In each B+tree, the key is a concatena-tion of the subject, predicate, object, and context. The six indexes constructed cover all the possible access patterns of quads in the form s, p, o, c, where c is the context of the triple (s, p, o). This representation allows fast retrieval of all triples access patterns.

The YARS system is also oriented toward simple statement–based queries and has limitations for efficient processing of more complex queries. The proposal sacrifices space and insertion speed for query performance because, to retrieve any access patterns with a single index lookup, each quad is encoded in the dictionary six times, in a dif-ferent sorting order. Note that inference is not supported. The same team of developers later developed **YARS2**, which, in 2007, was one of the first clustered RDF store engines. YARS2 distributed aspects are detailed in Chapter 7, but its indexing approach is identical (i.e., six indexes) to its predecessor YARS, but a different data structure is used to store the indexes.

The **Hexastore** system (Weiss et al., 2008) takes a similar approach to YARS, but only considers triples, not quads. The framework is based on the idea of main memory indexing of RDF data in a multiple-index framework. The RDF data is indexed in six possible ways, one for each possible ordering of the three RDF elements by individual columns. The representation is based on any order of significance of RDF resources and properties and can be seen as a combination of vertical-partitioning (Abadi et al., 2007 see Section 5.3.1.3) -and multiple-index approaches (Harth and Decker, 2005). Two vectors are associated with each RDF element, one for each of the other two RDF elements (e.g., [subject,predicate] and [subject,object]). Moreover, lists of the third RDF element are appended to the elements in these vectors. Therefore, a sextuple-index schema is created. As Weiss and colleagues emphasized, the values for O in PSO and SPO are the same (Weiss et al., 2008). Figure 5.3 proposes a representation of such an organization. Thus, in reality, even though six structures are created, only five copies of the data are really computed, because the object columns are duplicated.

To limit the amount of storage needed for the URIs, Hexastore uses the typical dictionary encoding of the URIs and the literals—that is, every URI or literal is assigned a unique numerical identifier. Hexastore provides efficient single triples-pattern lookups, and also allows fast merge-joins for any pair of two triples patterns. However, the space requirement of Hexastore is five times the space required for storing statements in a triples table. Hexastore favors query performance over insertion time. Update and

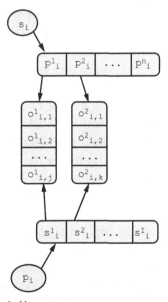

Figure 5.3 SPO and PSO indexing in Hexastore.

insertion operations affect all six indexes, and therefore can be slow. Note that Hexastore does not provide inference support. Recently, Weiss and Bernstein (2009) proposed an on-disk index structure/storage layout so that Hexastore performance advantages can be preserved. In addition to their experimental evaluations, they show empirically that, in the context of RDF storage, their vector storage schema provides significantly lower data retrieval times compared to B+trees.

The **Kowari** system (Wood, 2005) is an open-source, transaction-safe, purpose-built database for the storage, retrieval, and analysis of metadata. The system uses an approach similar to YARS. Indeed, the RDF statements are also stored as quads in which the first three items form a standard RDF triple and the fourth describes in which model the statement appears. The approach also uses six different orderings of quad elements acting as a compound index, and independently contains all the statements of the RDF store. In this ordering, the four quad elements can be arranged such that any collection of one to four elements can be used to find any matching statement or group of statements. However, Kowari uses a hybrid of AVL (a self-balanced binary search tree named after its inventors, Adelson, Velskii and Landis) and B-trees (instead of B+trees) for multiple-index purposes. The Kowari solution also envisions simple statement–based queries like YARS. Several versions of the Kowari system were released during active collaboration with Tucana Technologies Inc., which was bought in September 2005 by Northrop Grumman. The Kowari community then decided to fork the system and renamed it **Mulgara**. The system is open-source and licensed with **Apache 2**. It supports both the Jena and Sesame APIs to help in developing applications.

The **RDFCube** system (Matono et al., 2007) is a three-dimensional hash index designed for **RDFPeers** (Cai and Frank, 2004) which is presented in Chapter 7. RDFCube, is a distributed RDF repository that enables us to efficiently search RDF triples, i.e., it removes unrelated triples from candidates answers. In this Chapter, we only consider the storage aspect, not the distribution one. Each triple is stored by specifying its subject, predicate, or object as a key. The RDFCube storage schema consists of a set of cubes of the same size called *cells*. Each of these cells contains a bit called an *existence flag* indicating the presence or absence of triples mapped into the cell. During the processing of a query, by checking the existence flags of cells into which candidate answer triples are mapped, it is possible to know the existence of the triples before actually accessing remote nodes where the candidate answer triples are stored. This information helps to reduce the amount of data that is transferred among nodes when processing a join query because it is possible to narrow down the candidate triples by using the AND operator between existence flags bits and transfer only the actual present candidate triples. However, using a distributed hash table (DHT) for the indexation suffers from some problems, such as freshness of data and security. Dynamic insertion or deletion of RDF triples is not supported at present time.

BRAHMS (Janik and Kochut, 2005) is a main memory–based RDF storage system, specifically designed to support fast semantic association discovery (finding paths between two nodes in an RDF graph) in large RDF databases for which it uses graph algorithms like depth-first search and breadth-first search. BRAHMS has not been designed for modifications of RDF triples, but only for data retrieval–oriented queries. It employs six indexes, two per dimension (e.g., subject dimension ordered on [predicate, object] and [object, predicate]) to speed up these queries. The triples of instance resources are indexed as follows: [subject → object, predicate], [object → subject, predicate], and [predicate → subject, object]. These indexes are needed for a fast retrieval of node neighborhoods, as well as for merging them during the semantic association discovery process.

The **TripleT** (three-way triples tree) technique (Fletcher and Beck, 2009) adopts a partial indexing scheme—that is, not all triples combinations are considered—with the aim of limiting the memory footprint of the overall data structure. The proposal pays attention to data locality to avoid situations where a piece of data appears in multiple locations (e.g., a URI appearing at the subject and object positions of some triples), therefore spanning multiple data structures, and consequently negatively impacting storage and query processing costs. Concretely, a single B+tree secondary-memory data structure is created and contains every resource, either a literal or a URI, regardless of the position (i.e., subject, predicate, or object) they are occurring at in the triples set.

The position at which a resource occurs in triples is taken care of by three distinct buckets (each resource of the index is mapped to them). The buckets correspond to the (o,p), (s,o), and (s,p) pairs where the resource in question appears. To enable fast query processing, each bucket is sorted according to the following assumptions: subjects are more selective than objects, which are themselves more selective than predicates. This motivates the order of the previous bucket structures. Of course, this set of three indexes limits the options for efficient query optimization due to the absence of several orderings, compared with the aggressive indexing approaches of RDF-3X and Hexastore. Obviously, experimentations conducted on this system emphasize that the system is very efficient on the size required by the indexes, but also highlight interesting query performances for the most common query patterns—that is, those following the entity order assumption. Also note that the source code of the system is made available on a GitHub repository but does not seem to be actively maintained.

The **iStore** system (Tran et al., 2009) is an approach for data partitioning and join processing that uses an index structure automatically built from the data. This index, while being basically a compact representation of the data graph, can act as a schema, enabling the effective browsing and querying of schemaless Web data. The index structure is basically a graph that can be computed for general RDF graphs to capture different structure patterns exhibited by the data. The vertices of this graph represent groups of data elements that are similar in structure, where *structure* refers to the set of incoming and outgoing connections. Thus, the schema properties are used to perform vertical partitioning—that is, vertices are mapped to physical tables. This is done to obtain a contiguous storage of data elements that are structurally similar.

The processing of a given query begins by matching it against the structure index to identify groups of data satisfying the overall query structure (in other words, to filter candidates through structure-level processing). Then, these data groups are retrieved and joined. This needs to be performed only for some parts of the query. In fact, structure-level processing helps to prune the query and then process the pruned query using standard data-level operations. The whole query structure is taken into account for the retrieval of a candidate data group instead of retrieving data for every single triples pattern using a vertical table. Finally, structure-level processing may be very helpful because, in the case where no candidates can be found in the structure index, data-level processing can be completely skipped. Compared to vertical partitioning, where triples with the same properties are grouped together, the partitioning proposed by iStore results in the contiguous storage of triples that have the same structure.

Parliament (Kolas et al., 2009) is the open source extension of a system called damlDB which has been designed and used at BBN. It is a storage and indexing schema based on linked lists and memory-mapped files with a storage structure composed of three parts: the resource table, the statement table, and the resource dictionary. The resource dictionary follows the standard approach as presented in Chapter 4, i.e. a one-to-one mapping, bidirectional mapping between a resource and an identifier. The locate operation, i.e., from a resource to its associated identifier, is taken care of using the B-tree implementation of the BerkeleyDB system. The extract operation (form id to resource) uses a constant time reverse lookup approach. A memory-mapped file using a sequential, variable-length, null terminated string representations supports the implementation. The current approach stores each string representation twice. The resource table is a single file of fixed-length records (sequentially numbered with the numbers serving as the ID of the corresponding resources), each of which represents a single resource or literal. This allows direct access to a record given its ID via simple array indexing. Each record has eight components: three statement ID fields representing the first statements that contain this resource as a subject, predicate, and object, respectively; three count fields containing the number of statements using this resource as a subject, predicate, and object, respectively; an offset used to retrieve the string representation of the resource; and bit-field flags encoding various attributes of the resource. The first three values point to a position in the statement table.

The statement table, similar to the resource table, is a single file of fixed-length records (with an ID per statement), each of which represents a single statement. This table is composed of seven fields: three resources ID (those identifying entries in the dictionary) for respectively the subject, predicate and object positions, three pointers to the next position of this value at respectively the subject, predicate and object position, bit-field flag which help in supporting update operations. The mechanism for accessing files is optimized and keeps frequently accessed pages in memory. This schema is designed to balance insertion performance, query performance, and space usage. Parliament is designed as an embedded triples store and does not include a SPARQL or other query language processor.

Diplodocus (Wylot et al., 2011) is a native RDF data processing system that supports simple transactional queries and complex analytics. The main motivation of the system is data collocation to reduce I/O operations. This is performed by clustering data together in different data structures to provide several perspectives on the same data set and to retrieve all the data about a given perspective with a minimum of I/O operations. The storage model can be considered a hybrid because it is composed of three main concepts: RDF molecule clusters, template lists, and a hash table indexing URIs and literals. Intuitively, the hash table supports the functionalities of a dictionary as presented in Chapter 4. It uses the notion of a lexicographic tree to provide unique identifiers to URIs and literals and points to the two other data structures. A molecule cluster can be considered as a mix of RDF subgraphs and property tables (see Section 5.3). A template list stores literals in compact lists, in the manner of column-store RDBMS.

This organization envisions the triples in two dimensions: a horizontal one where each molecule cluster stores data instantiated from a given declarative template, and a vertical one composed of template lists. Molecule clusters are shaped after the definition of a declarative template, which is an abstraction of a triples pattern. The signature of such a template is subject-type, predicate-type, object-type, and is identified by a unique identifier. A declarative template is specified in terms of a given predicate and its frequent subject–object types. Figure 5.4(a) shows an example of some declarative templates for the running example. In Figure 5.4(b), we can observe two molecule clusters about the two bloggers in the running example. In this example, a template list would store all last names, thus providing an efficient method to identify clusters associated

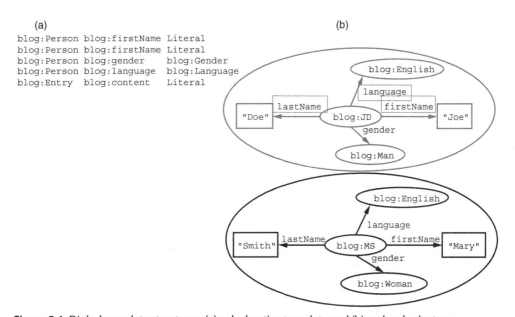

Figure 5.4 Diplodocus data structures: (a) a declarative template and (b) molecule clusters.

to a given last name value. The Diplodocus system uses the standard query processing approach detailed in Chapter 6 by using intensively the different hash tables and lists provided as index structures. By locating together all the data concerning a given object, the system limits the number of I/O operations.

The **gStore** system (Zou et al., 2011) considers RDF data sets from a graph perspective, more precisely as an edge-labeled one. The authors argue that a dedicated graph approach has to be designed for RDF graphs compared to existing graph databases (Angles and Gutierrez, 2008). The following three characteristics make a difference: RDF graphs are usually larger (i.e., number of triples), the number of occurrences of vertex and edge labels are larger, and the proportion of practical SPARQL queries taking the form of a star query is important (i.e., queries where a set of triples patterns form a start around, usually a variable subject and its neighbors). These specificities of RDF graphs, as well as the goals of gStore, motivate a particular storage organization.

The system has two main objectives: supporting update operations on RDF triples, and effective answering of SPARQL queries that are containing wildcards (i.e., with WHERE clauses composed of FILTER operations with partially defined regular expressions). Intuitively, the triples storage layout assigns to each resource a unique integer identifier and a signature. The signature, stored as a bit string, contains some information about the triples in which the resource plays the role of a subject. A structure, taking the form of a tree, denoted as a *vertex signature tree* (VS-tree for short), is designed to index signatures of all resources. This index corresponds to a balanced tree where a leaf is a resource's signature and internal nodes are signatures corresponding to bitwise OR of the children's signatures. This optimized tree structure enables us to efficiently locate, from its root, a certain resource signature. The support for effective processing of RDF queries with wildcards is the main motivation for the creation of this index.

The GRIN [Udrea et al., 2007] system was the first RDF indexing system to use graph partitioning. Its goal is to provide an index solution that is adapted to the graph matching approach of RDF query languages. The goal of this index structure is to keep together graph nodes that are close to each other in the graph. This is obtained by using notions of node centrality and distance between nodes in a graph to compute a radius from those center vertices. All the vertices within a given radius are stored in the same structure as the central node. Hence, a graph decomposition is performed in terms of n center nodes. The index structure corresponds to a binary tree where root node denotes the complete graph, intermediary nodes designate "center" triples and are storing a radius value. The leaf nodes contain triples and form a partition of the graph. The GRIN system also comprise a query processing component adapted to this index structure, i.e., it searches for the graph partitions that contain the query answer. An evaluation of the system emphasize that the index is relatively small and can be built faster than other solutions. Nevertheless, GRIN does not operate on disk and the size of the data that can be stored is relatively limited. DOGMA [Bröcheler et al., 2009] has been designed by part of the team behind GRIN. The index is graph-based and stored as a binary tree but is tuned for scalability by supporting to reside on disk.

5.2.1.2 Production-ready systems

In this section, we present systems that have or being used in production in industry or large academic projects. These systems can be either open-source or commercial. The commercial ones usually propose an entry product that can be used for free.

In Chapter 3, we presented Sesame as a Java framework for the Semantic Web. Here, we consider it on the RDF Store perspective. It is considered to be one of the earliest system to reach a production ready status. It was first developed by the Aduna company and later became an independent open source project under the name openRDF.org.

This RDF Store [Broekstra et al., 2002] proposes several physical storage approaches: in-memory, on disk as binary files and using an RDBMS. The in-memory configuration takes the form of a bipartite graph and proposes a parameter that enables to persist the data in a file before the system is being shut down. This enables to reload the data once the system is started again. Deactivating this parameter means that no data is automatically stored at the end of a session and thus each store initialization starts with an empty data set. Although fast since everything is kept in main memory, this approach does not support large data sets. The so-called native store is currently the default solution (thus motivating its placement in the native section), and preferred to the RDBMS based approach, for managing large RDF triple sets. It is based on on-disk indexes taking the form of B-trees. These indexes store quads and by default, two indexes are stored: spoc and posc, where c stands for the context. The end-user has the possibility to create multiple indexes by providing a list of 4-letter words containing the letters s, p, o and c, e.g., posc or psoc. The RDBMS back-end, supporting MySQL and PostgreSQL is deprecated. It is based on a triple table approach (See Section 5.3.1.1) that contains some additional columns, e.g., an RDF statement identifier and a boolean value indicating whether the triple has been deduced or not. Other tables for class, property, domain, range, subclassOf, instanceOf are being maintained to support reasoning services.

OWLIM (now GRAPHDB) corresponds to a family of RDF database systems that is implemented by the Ontotext Company. Three implementations are available: **OWLIM-Lite**, **OWLIM-SE** (Standard Edition), and **OWLIM-Enterprise**. The OWLIM systems are taking advantage of the Sesame libraries that provide APIs for storing, querying, and reasoning purposes. Using such libraries provides support for different RDF syntaxes, such as RDF/XML, N3, and Turtle, as well as query languages (including SPARQL). Therefore, it frees RDF store designers in developing their own parsers. The set of APIs provided by Sesame is named SAIL, standing for storage and inference layer, and is used by several other systems, such as BigData, Virtuoso, and Alle-grograph. The first system can be used free of charge while the last two are commercial products. In this section, we only consider OWLIM-Lite and OWLIM-SE solutions and leave the presentation of OWLIM-Enterprise to Chapter 7, which is devoted to distributed systems.

OWLIM-Lite thrives on small data sets that can be stored in the main memory (around 100 million statements for a server with 16 GB of RAM). Because all data-related operations like querying and inferencing are performed in memory, a basic (N-triples) file-based persistence is deemed sufficient. This aims to support data preservation and consistency between server startups. The main memory approach enables high through-put: it is considered to be three times faster than OWLIM-SE. Nevertheless, OWLIM-Lite does not propose any query optimization nor advanced features like full-text search.

OWLIM-SE provides a more advanced persistence layer that is based on binary data files and several indexes: POS and PSO. Additional data structures are supported but can-not be configured and are therefore not detailed by Ontotext. OWLIM-SE aims at data sets ranging around a billion triples even on a desktop machine. Just like in OWLIM-Lite, queries can be expressed in SPARQL or SeRQL (due to the use of SAIL), but OWLIM-SE provides some forms of query optimizations. Advanced features such as RDF rank, full-text search (integrated into SPARQL with a standalone or Lucene ap-proach), and geospatial extension are provided.

The OWLIM-Lite and -SE share many features. For instance, being implemented over the Sesame SAIL, repositories can be created, loaded, and queried through the user-friendly Sesame Workbench. Triples repositories can also be accessed with external editors, such as **TopBraid Composer**. Similarly, applications can be developed using either the Sesame or Jena APIs. The cornerstone of the OWLIM systems is the support for reasoning. This is handled by the *TRREE* (triples reasoning and rule entailment engine), which is being developed by Ontotext. Although more details will be provided in Chapter 8 about this component, we can highlight that inferences are based on forward-chaining of entailment rules. OWLIM-Lite performs all reasoning in-memory, while OWLIM-SE uses its set of data structures backed by the file system. To the best of our knowledge, no details on the indexing and storage approach of OWLIM have published.

Allegrograph is a commercial system produced by Franz Inc. It is among the earliest RDF stores, with a first version in 2004. **Franz Inc**. adopted a graph presentation and they therefore define the system as a NoSQL graph database. Nevertheless, because the system is designed over its own implementation of a NoSQL store, we consider that it belongs to the native RDF storage approach. Like other database systems in this category, such as **Neo4J**, full ACID transactions compatibility is implemented. The default set of seven indexes supported by Allegrograph are SPOGI, POSGI, OSPGI, GSPOI, GPOSI,

GOSPI, and I, where S, P, O are the standard subject, predicate, and object entries of a triple, and G stands for a URI-based named graph (which we have already seen in system storing quads). The newcomer here is I, standing for a unique triples identifier of the triples store.

The I index corresponds to a list of all triples organized by ID number. Its goal is to support fast triples deletion because such an identifier is able to identify a triple without requiring S, P, O, and G entries. The set of indexes is customizable—that is, one can add its own index and remove some of the seven default ones. The system is designed for maximum loading and query speed. Since its earlier versions, the system has produced evaluation emphasizing leadership in performance: Allegrograph was the first system to reach 1 billion (in 2004), 10 billion (in 2008), and 1 trillion (in 2011, in 338 hours on a cloud Intel-based high-performance computing cluster) statement data sets. Allegrograph provides a REST protocol architecture by using the Sesame HTTP client. Adapters for application development have been designed on top of these services for the following programming languages: Java (through Sesame and Jena APIs), Python, C#, Ruby, Clojure, Scala, Perl, and Lisp (which is the domain of expertise at **Franz Inc.**). Queries can be expressed in SPARQL but also Prolog (due to its nice integration with the Lisp implementation of Allegrograph).

Stardog is another commercial product and is developed by **Clark & Parsia**, which also well-known in the Semantic Web community for implementing the **Pellet OWL** reasoning system. The store is advertised as being "a graph database that uses RDF data, SPARQL for queries, OWL for reasoning, and pure Java for the enterprise." Two indexing modes are supported in Stardog, one based only on triples and another one for quads. In both cases, the indexes are stored on-disk, but an in-memory mode is available. No other details are provided in any publications. As a graph database, Stardog supports ACID transactions, SPARQL 1.1 (but some support for Gremlin for specific graph navigation is provided), and full-text search through the use of Lucene. Among the original features of Stardog, we can highlight the support for integrity constraint validation which adopts a closed-world assumption in a declarative and high-level manner by enabling integrity constraints to be defined in OWL, SWRL, or SPARQL. We will detail reasoning aspects in Chapter 8. Although having a shorter history (development started in 2010) than its direct commercial competitors, the system already has an impressive list of customers including some large companies.

BigData (**Systap, LLC**) is an open-source project the development of which started in 2006. Different distinct deployment models are supported: a standalone storage solution (so-called *journal*), a set of journals with replication, and a distributed approach using journals for the backend storage. In this section, we concentrate on journal and replication (a.k.a. scale-up or highly available [HA] journal) systems and leave the details on the distributed (a.k.a. scale-out or *federation*) approach for Chapter 7. The HA journal approach replicates the data on a set of nodes, therefore queries scale linearly in the size of the replication cluster (which is advised to be at least three machines to be efficient). The journal proposes several backing store models that differ on the ratio of reads and writes performed on the data. For instance, the so-called *WORM* (write once, read many) approach adopts an append-only file structure, while the RWStore (read–write store) expects higher write rates. The architecture is inspired by **Google**'s **Bigtable** approach. Depending on the approach—that is, triples, quads, or a special triples with provenance—three or six indexes are created: spoc, poc, ocs, csp, cp, and os for quads. The RDF store uses a standard dictionary approach with identifiers encoded into 64-bit identifiers. The index approach corresponds to the YARS approach. In the query optimizer, plans according to two different approaches are considered. In the default one, the join order optimization uses a standard approach using static analysis and fast cardinality estimation of access paths (see details in Chapter 6). In a second approach, which is quite original in the context of an RDF store, runtime sampling of join graphs is used. The journal is said to support data sets of up to 50 billion triples.

4Store was developed by **Garlik** (now **Experian**) and is one of the most established distributed triples stores. In this chapter, we are interested in the storage and indexing approach of this triples store and abstract away from its distribution strategy, which is detailed in Chapter 7. Thus, we concentrate on the so-called storage nodes that handle a segment of the quads data set. Each storage node consists of two indexes. A first one corresponds to a hash on predicates where the value points to two distinct structures. These structures are radix trees (a.k.a. compact prefix trees), where the key is the subject or the object. The leaves of the trees point to the remaining quad entries, the object and the named graph (respectively subject and named graph). This is analogous to some PSOG and POSG indexes, which makes this approach reminiscent to the non-native property table solution described later in this chapter. Radix trees are rarely used in indexing structures due to their $O(n)$ worst-case lookup performance compared to $O(\log n)$ for B-trees. Nevertheless, radix trees are motivated in Harris et al. (2009) by an efficient computation of keys that are kept short and evenly distributed, thus making the worst-case lookup conditions uncommon. The second index proposes some fast access to named graphs by using a hash table that points to a list of triples. A new version of 4Store, named **5Store**, is being developed but has been only used within Experian and is not yet published.

Apache's **Jena TDB** system is stated as being faster, more scalable, and better supported than the Jena SDB, which is a non-native system relying on an RDBMS. TDB is, for instance, the system supporting persistence in the **Fuseki SPARQL** server. The architecture is built around three concepts, namely a node table, triples/quads indexes, and a prefixes table. The node table serves to store the dictionary and follows the two mappings approach presented in Chapter 4. Practically, the string-to-id and id-to-string operations are respectively implemented using B+trees and a sequential file. A large cache is dedicated to ensure fast data retrieval during query processing.

Triples and quads indexes are stored in specialized structures and respectively store three and four identifiers from the node table. B+trees are used to persist these indexes. The system supports SPARQL update operations, which are handled using ACID transactions (with the serializable isolation level) through a *WAL* (write ahead logging) approach. This implies that write transactions are first written into a journal and then stored in the database when resources permit it. This approach presents the benefit of not requiring a locking solution for read transactions. Finally, Jena TDB supports a bulk-load solution that does not support transactions. The different features contained in Jena TDB, such as some security aspects as well as some APIs, make it a solution to consider in a production setting.

5.2.2 Highly compressed storage

We have presented some systems that give special attention to the memory footprint of the stored data, such as RDF-3X and Hexastore. With the increasing amount of produced RDF data and the emergence of the Big Data phenomenon, some systems are considering highly compressed storage approaches. We can consider two different approaches: systems based on multiple indexes, and systems based on data structures that enable self-indexing.

5.2.2.1 Multiple indexes

BitMat (Atre et al., 2009) is a main memory–based bit-matrix structure for representing a large set of RDF triples with the idea to make the representation compact. Each RDF triple is considered as a three-dimensional entity that conceptually gives rise to a single universal table holding all RDF triples. This table can be horizontally partitioned into multiple fragments based on the use requirements. BitMat can be viewed as a three-dimensional bit cube, in which each cell is a bit representing a unique triple and denoting the presence or absence of that triple. For representing the bit cube in memory, it is flattened in a two-dimensional bit matrix. There are six ways of flattening a bit cube into a BitMat. Each structure contributes to a more efficient particular set of single-join queries. To deal with the inherent sparsity of BitMat, these structures are maintained as an array of bit rows, where each row is a collection of all the triples having the same subject. The underlying goal is to represent large RDF triples sets with a compact in-memory representation and support a scalable multijoin query execution. These queries are processed using bitwise AND, OR operations on the BitMat rows, and the resulting triples are returned as another BitMat. BitMat is designed to be mainly a read-only RDF triples storing system.

 TripleBit (Yuan et al., 2013) is an RDF data management system based on a two-dimensional bit matrix storage structure. In this matrix, columns correspond to a clustering of predicates, and rows are subjects and objects. The matrix is composed of

Table 5.1 TripleBit Triples Matrix for the Running Example

	firstName		gender		isFollowing	language	lastName	
	t1	t6	t3	t8	t5	t4	t2	t7
JD	1	0	1	0	1	1	1	0
MS	0	1	0	1	1	0	0	1
Man	0	0	1	0	0	0	0	0
Woman	0	0	0	1	0	0	0	0
English	0	0	0	0	0	1	0	0
"Joe"	1	0	0	0	0	0	0	0
"Doe"	0	0	0	0	0	0	1	0
"Mary"	0	1	0	0	0	0	1	0
"Smith"	0	0	0	0	0	0	0	1

Boolean values with 1 specifying the presence of a subject–predicate or object–predicate pair. Therefore, two 1's can only be stored per column. Table 5.1 depicts the triples matrix corresponding to the running example.

A clever compression approach takes advantage of this data sparsity and enables a storage compactness. The system also introduces two indexing structures: ID-chunk and ID-predicate bit matrices. The former supports the fast search of pertinent chunks matching a given subject or object. The latter provides a mapping solution of a subject or object to the list of related properties. The system uses a dictionary approach that uses a prefix-compression method that is reminiscent to front coding.

5.2.2.2 Self-index engines
Recently, systems such as **HDT** (Header Dictionary Triple) and **WaterFowl** started to use high-compression *succinct data structures* (SDSs) (see Chapter 4).

The HDT system (Fernandez et al., 2010) mainly focuses on data exchange (and thus on data compression). Its former motivation was to support the exchange of large data sets highly compressed using SDS. Later, Martinez-Prieto and colleagues (2012) presented HDT FoQ, an extension of the structure of HDT that enables some simple data retrieving operations. Nevertheless, this last contribution was not allowing any form of reasoning nor was it providing methods to query the data sets.

The WaterFowl system brings the HDT FoQ approach further to its logical conclusion by using a pair of wavelet trees in the object layer (HDT FoQ uses an adjacency list for this layer) and by integrating a complete query processing solution with complete RDFS reasoning (i.e., handling any inference using RDFS expressiveness). This is made possible by an adaptation of both the dictionary and the triples structures. Note that this adaptation enables us to retain the nice compression properties of HDT FoQ. In this section, we consider the storage layer of WaterFowl, and query processing and reasoning are presented in later chapters.

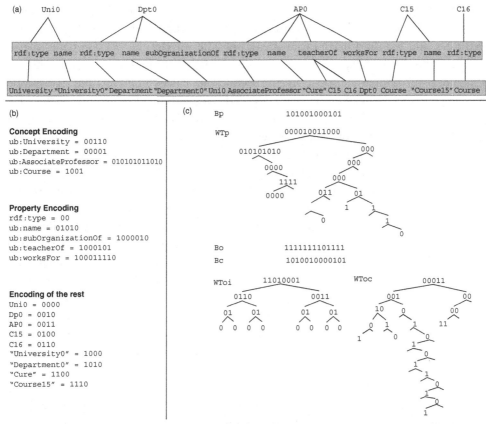

Figure 5.5 Overview of data structures in WaterFowl. (a) Forest representation of RDF triples, (b) Extract of concepts, properties and instances encoding. (c) WaterFowl two layers representation

WaterFowl's architecture is largely based on the use of SDS and enables the representation of triples in a self-indexed, compact manner without requiring decompression at query answering time. By self-indexed, we mean that this single index is sufficient to recreate the original document. This prevents storing any additional documents or indexes. The high-compression rate obtained from SDS enables the system to keep all the data in memory and limits latencies associated with I/O operations via an efficient serialization/deserialization solution.

We are using a LUBM (LeHigh University Benchmark) data set with its ontology for this example. The storage system is composed of two layers where the first layer encodes the relation between the subjects and the predicates—that is, the edges between the root of each tree and its children in Figure 5.5(a). The bitmap Bp is defined as follows. For each root of the trees in Figure 5.5(a) (i.e., each subject), the leftmost child is encoded as a 1, and the others as a 0. On the whole, Bp contains as many 1's as subjects in the data set and is of equal length to the number of predicates in the data set. In Figure 5.4(c), one obtains `101001000101` because there are five subjects with the last subject having one predicate, the first and fourth having two predicates, the second having three predicates, and the third having four predicates. The wavelet tree `WTp` encodes the sequence of predicates obtained from a preorder traversal in the forest (e.g., second row in Figure 5.4a). Unlike the first layer, the second one has two bitmaps and two wavelet trees. `Bo` encodes the relation between the predicates and the objects—that is, the edges between the leaves and their parents in the tree representation. Whereas the bitmap `Bc` encodes the positions of ontology concepts in the sequence of objects obtained from a preorder traversal in the forest (e.g., third row in Figure 5.4a). The bitmap `Bo` is defined in the same manner as `Bp`, but only considering the forest obtained by removing the first layer of the tree representation (i.e., the subjects). In Figure 5.4(a), one obtains `1111111101111`. The bitmap `Bc` stores a `1` at each position of an object that is a concept, and a `0` otherwise. This is processed using a predicate contextualization—that is, in the data set whenever a `rdf:type` appears, we know that the object corresponds to an ontology concept. Together with a high proportion of RDF triples contained in `rdf:type` properties in practical data sets, this contextualization aspect motivates a special encoding, with the `00` binary value, for this property. In Figure 5.5(a), considering that the predicate `rdf:type` is encoded by `00`, one obtains `1010010000101`. Finally, the sequence of `objects` obtained from a preorder traversal in the forest (e.g., third row in Figure 5.5a) is split into two disjoint subsequences, one for the concepts and one for the rest. Each of these sequences is encoded in a wavelet tree (`WToc` and `WToi` respectively). This architecture reduces the sparsity of identifiers and enables the management of very large data sets and ontologies while allowing time and space efficiency.

Consider the following simple SPARQL query:

```
PREFIX rdf: <http://www.w3.org/1999/02/22-rdf-syntax-ns#>
PREFIX lubm: <http://www.lehigh.edu/~zhp2/2004/0401/univ-bench.owl#>
SELECT ?x WHERE {
    ?x rdf:type lubm:AssociateProfessor
}
```

This query will be translated as the following set of SDS operations:

```
for (int i=1; i <= rankWToc('01 010 10 11 010',size(WToc)); i++) {
    // for each occurrence of the concept  Associate Professor
    posWToc= selectWToc('01 010 10 11 010',i);
    //retrieve its position in WToc
    posBc=selectBc(1,posWToc);
    posBo=rankBo(1,posBc);
    //retrieve the position of the corresponding predicate
    x=rankBp(1,posBo);
    // retrieve the index of the corresponding subject
}
```

5.3 NON-NATIVE STORAGE APPROACH

A set of techniques has been proposed for storing RDF data in relational databases. Currently, this is widely considered to be the best-performing approach for their persistent data store due to the great amount of work achieved in making it efficient, extremely scalable, and robust. Efficient storage of RDF data has already been discussed in the literature with different physical organization techniques such as the triples table, property table, and vertical-partitioning approaches. The strategy used by each tool depends on if the tool is concerned with query performance or with the performance of adding or updating knowledge to the database. We devote a section to the particular case of Ontology Based Data access which are mainly addressing data stored in RDBMS.

As emphasized by Figure 5.2, the last few years have seen the proliferation of RDF stores based on NoSQL systems. In Section 5.3.3, we present the systems belonging to this category.

5.3.1 Storage systems based on RDBMS

5.3.1.1 Triples table

The triples table approach is perhaps the most straightforward mapping of RDF into an RDBMS. Each RDF statement of the form [`subject`, `predicate`, `object`] is stored as a triple in one large table with a three-column schema (a column for the subject, predicate, and object respectively). Table 5.2 proposes a representation of the running example with a triples table with nonencoded triples elements.

To enable fast table lookups, several indexes can be added for each of the columns. This approach enables us to make joins less expensive. However, because the collection of triples is stored in one single RDF table, the queries may be very slow to execute. Indeed, when the number of triples scales, the RDF table may exceed the main memory

Table 5.2 Triples Table

Subject	Predicate	Object
`blog:JD`	`blog:firstName`	`"Joe"`
`blog:JD`	`blog:lastName`	`"Doe"`
`blog:JD`	`blog:gender`	`blog:Man`
`blog:JD`	`blog:language`	`blog:English`
`blog:JD`	`rdf:type`	`blog:User`
`blog:JD`	`blog:isFollowing`	`blog:MS`
`blog:MS`	`blog:firstName`	`"Mary"`
`blog:MS`	`blog:lastName`	`"Smith"`
`blog:MS`	`blog:gender`	`blog:Woman`
`blog:MS`	`rdf:type`	`blog:User`
`blog:isFollowing`	`rdf:type`	`rdf:Property`

size. Additionally, simple statement–based queries can be satisfactorily processed by such systems, although they do not represent the most important way of querying RDF data. Nevertheless, RDF triples store scales poorly, because complex queries with multiple triples patterns require many self-joins over this single large table as pointed out in Wilkinson et al. (2003), Weiss et al. (2008), and Kolas et al. (2009). The triples table approach has been used in systems like Oracle (Chong et al., 2005), **3Store** (Harris and Gibbins, 2003), **Redland** (Beckett, 2001), RDFStore (Reggiori, 2002), and **rdfDB** (Guha, 2000).

The **Jena SDB** system also adopts the triples table approach and basically corresponds to a Java Loader for multiple RDBMSs, such as **MySQL**, **PostgresSQL**, Oracle, **SQL Server**, and **DB2**. Either triples or quads can be loaded in respectively a triples or quads table. Intuitively, triples or quads stored with Jena SDB are stored in tables with respectively three or four columns. In the former, an SPO primary key is defined and additional PO and OS indexes are created. In the latter (i.e., quads), the primary key is GSPO (with G the named graph URI) and five additional indexes are created: GPO, GOS, SPO, OS, and PO. The official SDB web page states that this system is no longer maintained and that the Jena TDB should be preferred. Jena TDB is stated as being faster, more scalable, and better supported than Jena SDB. The bulk loader is not transactional and there is no support for nested transactions.

The **Virtuoso** system (Erling and Mikhailov, 2007) is produced by OpenLink. The database engine was first developed as an RDBMS and progressively evolved toward the XML and RDF data models. Given the maturity of the OpenLink RDBMS and efforts provided on the RDF, the system definitely has to be considered as a production-ready solution. Originally following a row-store approach, the system was recently extended to become a hybrid approach by supporting column-store features. Later in this section, we present the swStore system, which was in 2007 the first RDF engine to emphasize the adequacy and efficiency of a column-store type of data storage for RDF triples. Note that, as highlighted in Chapter 2, the column-store approach is also gaining popularity in the RDBMS markets of both OLAP and OLTP.

Virtuoso stores quads combining a graph identifier entry to each triple (s,p,o). Thus, it conceptually stores the quads in a triples table expanded by one column. The columns are g for graph, p for predicate, s for subject, and o for object. While technically rooted in an RDBMS, it closely follows the model of YARS but with fewer indexes. The quads are stored in two covering indexes, <g, s, p, o> and <o, g, p, s >, where the URIs are dictionary encoded. Several additional optimizations are added, including bitmap indexing. In this approach, the use of fewer indexes tips the balance slightly toward insertion performance from query performance, but still favors a query one. Being a popular production-ready system implies the existence of several features. Among them, we can highlight some security concerns as well as a rich set of data providers and drivers to access RDF data, such as ODBC, JDBC, ADO.Net, OLE

DB, and XMLA (XML for Analysis -- an industry standard for data access in analytical systems). The system also supports stored procedures and built-in function definitions that can be used from SPARQL queries. Finally, SPARQL extensions such as its own full-text search engine, geospatial queries (using a special type of index that is denoted R-tree), business analytics, and intelligence features and subqueries are supported.

Virtuoso proposes several kinds of licenses. For a single machine deployment, a GPL open-source solution is available. In Chapter 7, we will present some details on the commercial version of Virtuoso that enables an installation on a cluster of machines.

The **RDFJoin** project (McGlothlin and Khan, 2009a) provides several new features built on top of previous cutting-edge research, including vertical partitioning (Abadi et al., 2009) and sextuple indexing (Weiss et al., 2008), namely Hexastore. While Hexastore is a main memory solution, RDFJoin proposes a persistent column-store database storage for these tables with the primary goal to reduce the need and cost of joins and unions in query implementations. Indeed, it also uses the six possible indexes on s, p, o using three tables: PS-O, SO-P, and PO-S. These tables are indexed on both the first two columns so they provide all possible six indexes, while ensuring that only one copy of the third column is stored. By keeping three separate triples tables and normalizing the identification numbers, RDFJoin allows subject–object and object–object joins to be implemented as merge-joins as well.

RDFJoin uses conversion tables closely matching the dictionary encoding of the vertical partitioning and Hexastore projects and the auxiliary mappings tables of the BitMat project discussed previously. All the third-column tuples are stored in a bit vector, and a hash indexing based on the first two columns is provided. This reduces space and memory use and improves the performance of both joins and lookups. For example, the PS-O table has columns Property, Subject, and ObjectBit Vector, where ObjectBit Vector is a bit vector with the bits corresponding to all the object IDs that appear in a triple with the property and subject values appearing in respective columns. This also applies for the SO-P and PO-S tables. Thus, all of the RDF triples in the data set can be rendered from any of these tables.

Additionally, execution of subject–subject, subject–object, and object–object joins are done and stored as binary vectors into tables called *join tables*. This task is performed one time for any RDF data set during the preprocessing stage to avoid overhead. Then, the results are stored in the relational database where they are quickly accessible. Indeed, RDFJoin stores much of its data as binary vectors and implements joins and conditions as binary set operations. This implementation provides significant performance improvement over storing each triple as a unique tuple. RDFJoin supports insertion of new RDF triples but does not allow direct updates or deletions of triples in the database. Moreover, there is no support for inference in RDFJoin.

RDFKB (Resource Description Framework Knowledge Base) (McGlothlin and Khan, 2009b) is a relational database system for RDF data sets supporting OWL inference rules and knowledge management. The solution is implemented and tested using column-store and RDFJoin (McGlothlin and Khan, 2009a) technology. It supports inference at data storage time rather than as part of query processing. All known inference rules are applied to the data set to determine all possible knowledge. The core of the RDFKB design is that for each RDF triple, all possible additional RDF triples are inferred, stored, and made accessible to queries.

McGlothlin and Khan made the choice to store redundant information. At query execution time, there is information about any knowledge related to the query, and this can be used to limit the scope of the inference search. Queries against inferred data are simplified and performance is increased. However, inferring all possible knowledge may be very expensive and the performance penalty can be high as the vocabulary is increased because more triples are persisted and loaded into memory. Moreover, to handle a query that does not need inference, the architecture builds a second copy of all tables, including all triples from the data set but ignoring all triples added by the inference rules. The trade-offs of this approach are added storage time, increased storage space requirements, and increased memory consumption (McGlothlin and Khan, 2009b). Note that the architecture of RDFJoin tends to minimize the costs of these trade-offs. RDFKB provides support for adding new triples. Moreover, inference is computed once a triple is added with the effect of increasing the amount of time required to add and store new triples. On the other hand, it does not support transactions that delete or change triples in the data set.

5.3.1.2 Property table

The property table technique has been introduced for improving RDF data organization by allowing multiple triple patterns referencing the same subject to be retrieved without expensive join mechanisms. This model has two variants: the clustered property table and the property-class table. In the former, RDF tables are physically stored in a representation closer to traditional relational schemas to speed up the queries over the triples stores (Wilkinson, 2006; Chong et al., 2005). In this approach, each named table includes a subject and several fixed properties. The main idea is to discover clusters of subjects often appearing with the same set of properties. The triples that cannot be clustered in such tables are stored in a "leftover" triples table as presented in the previous section. Figure 5.6 presents an extract of the running example with the clustered property table where we consider that the `firstName`, `lastName`, and `gender` properties tend to appear together, and similarly for the `content`, `blogDate`, `category`, and `creator` properties. In the "leftover" triples table, we consider that only a few users provide information on their language and email address, therefore motivating the fact that it is not stored in the user property table.

The property-class table (Wilkinson, 2006; Broekstra et al., 2002) uses the `rdf:type` property of subjects to cluster similar sets of subjects together in the same table. Figure 5.7

User property table

subject	firstName	lastName	gender
blog:JD	Joe	Doe	blog:Male
blog:MS	Mary	Smith	blog:Female
blog:MD	Miles	Davis	Null

Blog property table

subject	content	blogdate	category	creator
blog:Blog1	Today…	10/13/2013	blog:Techno	blog:JD
blog:Blog2	Science is..	10/15/2013	blog:Science	blog:JD
blog:Blog3	My phone ...	10/15/2013	blog:Techno	blog:MS
blog:Blog4	Je suis ...	10/16/2013	Null	blog:MD

Leftover triples table

subject	property	object
blog:JD	language	English
blog:MD	email	milesd@sowhat.jazz.net

Figure 5.6 A clustered property modeling for the running blog example.

class: User type

subject	firstName	lastName	gender	language	email
blog:JD	Joe	Doe	Male	English	Null
blog:MS	Mary	Smith	Female	Null	Null
blog:MD	Miles	Davis	Null	Null	milesd@sowhat.jazz.net

class: Blog type

subject	content	blogdate	category	creator
blog:Blog1	Today ...	10/13/2013	blog:Techno	blog:JD
blog:Blog2	Science is	10/15/2013	blog:Science	blog:JD
blog:Blog3	...	10/15/2013	blog:Techno	blog:MS
blog:Blog4	My phone ...	10/16/2013	Null	blog:MD
	Je suis ...			

Figure 5.7 A property-class modeling for the running blog example.

provides an example of the running example. Note that it does not provide a leftover table, although it is accepted in that storage method due to the information attached to each object.

The immediate consequence is that self-joins on the `subject` column can be avoided. This is particularly useful since this join pattern is considered to be a frequent one, e.g., in star shaped queries. However, the property table technique has the drawback of generating many `null` values because, for a given cluster, not all properties will be defined for all subjects. This is due to the semi-structured aspect of RDF.

A second disadvantage of the property table is that multivalued attributes that are furthermore frequent in RDF data are hard to express. In a data model without a fixed schema like RDF, it's common to seek for all defined properties of a given subject, which, in the property table approach, requires scanning all tables. Note that, in this approach, adding properties requires also to add new tables, which is clearly a limitation for applications dealing with arbitrary RDF content. Thus, schema flexibility is lost and this approach limits the benefits of using RDF. Moreover, queries with triple patterns that involve multiple property tables are still expensive because they may require many union clauses and joins to combine data from several tables. This consequently complicates query translation and plan generation. In summary, property tables are rarely used due to their complexity and inability to handle multivalued attributes. This approach has nevertheless been used by tools like Sesame (Broekstra et al., 2002), Jena2 (Wilkinson et al., 2003), **RDFSuite** (Alexaki et al., 2001), and 4Store (Harris et al., 2009).

5.3.1.3 *Vertical partitioning*

The vertical-partitioning approach suggested in **swStore** (Abadi et al., 2007) is an alternative to the property table solution that speeds up queries over a triple store, providing similar performance while being easier to implement. In this approach, RDF data is vertically partitioned using a fully *decomposed storage model* (DSM) (Copeland and Khoshafian, 1985). Each triples table is divided into n two-column tables, where n is the number of unique properties in the data. In each of these tables, the first column contains the subject and the second column the object value of that subject. Figure 5.8 provides an example of the vertical partioning approach for our running example. The tables are stored, by using a column-oriented DBMS (Stonebraker et al., 2005) (i.e., a DBMS designed especially for the vertically partitioned case, as opposed to a row-oriented DBMS, gaining benefits of compressibility and performance) as collections of columns rather than collections of rows.

The goal is to avoid reading an entire row into memory from disk, like in row-oriented databases, if only a few attributes are accessed per query. Consequently, in column-oriented databases only those columns relevant to a query will be read. Note that the approach creates materialized views for frequent joins. Furthermore, the authors suggest that the object columns of tables in their scheme can also be optionally indexed (e.g.,

firstName

subject	object
blog:JD blog:MS blog:MD	Joe Mary Miles

lastName

subject	object
blog:JD blog:MSblog:MSD	Doe Smith Davis

gender

subject	object
blog:JD blog:MS	blog:Male blog:Female

Figure 5.8 Extract of the vertical-partitioning approach on the running blog example.

using an unclustered B+tree), or a second copy of the table can be created clustered on the object columns. One of the primary benefits of vertical partitioning is the support for rapid subject–subject joins. This benefit is achieved by sorting the tables by subject.

For the tables being sorted by subject, one has a way to use fast merge-joins to reconstruct information about multiple properties for subsets of subjects. Note that an index-all approach is a poor way to simulate a column store. The vertical-partitioning approach offers support for multivalued attributes. Indeed, if a subject has more than one object value for a given property, each distinct value is listed in a successive row in the table for that property. For a given query, only the properties involved in that query need to be read and no clustering algorithm is needed to divide the triples table into two-column tables.

Note that inserts can be slow in vertically partitioned tables because multiple tables need to be accessed for statements about the same subject. In Sidirourgos et al. (2008), an independent evaluation of the techniques presented in Abadi et al. (2007), the authors pointed out potential scalability problems for the vertical-partitioning approach when the number of properties in an RDF data set is high. With a larger number of properties, the triple store solution manages to outperform the vertical-partitioning approach.

Note that there is no inference support in swStore. As a first step to an efficient RDF storage roadmap, **roStore** (Curé et al., 2010) proposes an intermediate ontology-guided approach that extends the vertical-partitioning approach. Therefore, its approach outperforms swStore when reasoning over property hierarchies is necessary. The proposal is based on a set of semantic query rewriting rules to improve query performance by reasoning over the ontology schema of the RDF triples.

In this solution, there is a single table for each property hierarchy. Those tables have three columns (one for each element of the RDF triple). The rest of the tables are following the pattern design of the vertical-partitioning approach. A direct consequence of this design is to reduce the number of tables for ontologies containing several property hierarchies, such as ontologies in the medical domain like OpenGalen.

The reduction of the number of property tables has a big impact on the performance of queries requiring joins over properties of the same property hierarchy due to the generation and maintenance of fewer relations than in swStore. Therefore, performance of an important number of queries requiring inferences on property hierarchies are improved because fewer joins are needed. The aim of this approach is to try to analyze the efficiency of a compromise approach where fewer partitions are used. Intuitively, such physical organization will take benefits of requiring a less important number of joins in practical queries.

5.3.1.4 Other approaches
The **DB2RDF** (Bornea et al., 2013) approach is a recent extension to IBM's DB2 RDBMS to store RDF triples. One of the key ideas is that storing objects of the same predicate in the same relation column has many advantages in terms of data retrieval. The system is composed of two pairs of relations. The first pair proposes an SPO index approach where a first relation denoted *direct primary hash* (DPH) stores information related to a subject on a single tuple or multiple tuples. The data structure is composed of a tuple of the following form: (entry, spill, (pred,value)*), where spill is a Boolean value indicating if a subject's information is spread on a single tuple or several tuples. Another structure, namely *direct secondary hash* (DSH), is handling multivalued properties. Intuitively, it contains two columns: the first one corresponds to a pointer from some object value in DPH and the second one is its value. The second pair of relations supports an OPS index and is organized similarly to the first pair—that is, *reverse primary hash* (RPH) and *reverse secondary hash* (RSH). In RPH, rows correspond to triple objects and RSH follows the approach of DSH.

In both PDH and RPH, the idea is to place (for all tuples) the same property in the same column (pred$_i$, value$_i$). In Figure 5.9, the DPH table represents the information related to the person from the running example when a set of three pairs of

DPH

entry	spill	pred1	val1	pred2	val2	pred3	val3
blog:JD	0	firstName	Joe	lastName	Doe	gender	Male
blog:MS	1	firstName	Mary	lastName	Smith	gender	Female
blog:MS	1	language	lid1	null	null	null	null
blog:MD	0	firstName	Miles	lastName	Davis	null	null

DSH

l_id	value
lid1	English
lid1	French

RPH

entry	spill	pred1	val1	pred2	val2	pred3	val3
Joe	0	firstName	blog:JD	null	null	null	null
Doe	0	null	null	lastName	blog:JD	null	null
Male	0	null	null	null	null	gender	lid2
Mary	0	firstName	blog:JD	null	null	null	null
...							

RSH

l_id	value
lid2	blog:JD
lid2	blog:JC

Figure 5.9 Table organizations in the DB2RDF approach.

predicate values are stored for each row. Of course, in real cases, the number of pairs is supposed to be a lot bigger than this—for example, the maximum number of columns per rows in DB2 and Oracle are around 1,000. With four triples associated with the blog:MS subject, the data has to be stored on two rows, therefore the spill value is set to 1 to indicate that state. Moreover, the value for the language of blog:MS is multivalued and requires entries in DSH where the language values (English and French) require two rows. The RPH and RSH take the information contained in DPH but indexes it by object. We have introduced an additional blog user, blog:JC, to highlight the DSH table for the multivalued gender predicate on the Male object.

In Figure 5.9, we can note the high sparsity of the DPH and RPH tables. This implies that a naive handling of null values will impact storage efficiency as well as I/O operations for query processing. An important issue in this system is the predicate-to-column assignment. The system supports two methods depending on whether a data sample is available or not. Intuitively, if no such data is available, a hashing approach is adopted, otherwise a graph coloring mechanism is used. Considering this assignment, the current state of DB2RDF does not provide any information on data insertion and update performances.

5.3.2 Ontology-based data access

We dedicate a section to *ontology-based data access* (OBDA), which is a recent paradigm in data management that aims to exploit the semantic knowledge expressed in ontologies when querying data. This is motivated by the fact that ontologies can improve query answering by enriching the vocabulary of data sources, such as semantic query expansion. For example, it enables us to relate the vocabularies of different data sources during data integration or to palliate data incompleteness by allowing inference of new facts.

Most of the systems designed in the context of OBDA are using an RDBMS as the storage backend. This is mostly motivated by the robustness and good understanding of complexity issues related to query answering in the context of SQL. Through a detailed presentation, we will see that much of the results obtained on an RDBMS-based OBDA could be applied to other database management systems. Nevertheless, we do not know of any systems based on any of the NoSQL categories.

Of course, this approach implies that an ontology for the database domain is available and satisfies some constraints, such as expressivity. This is a main difference with the systems that we have presented in the previous section where the existence of an ontology is usually not required or not really restricting its expressive power. Another difference is that, in OBDA, the data is originally stored in a database management system, with all its standard features like schema, indexes, and triggers. The database may have served and may still be serving many applications directly through an approach like ODBC or JDBC. Usually for data integration reasons, an ontology is added on top of this database instance and will therefore permit us to perform new reasoning services. The dominant approach in OBDA is *description logics* (DL) based and the queries correspond to *conjunctive queries* (CQs), or existential conjunctive first-order formulas. CQs are the most commonly used queries in relational databases and can be translated to select-project-join (SPJ). The main OBDA reasoning task is CQ answering. It amounts to checking the entailment of the query (with free variables substituted with candidate answer tuples) from the first-order theory corresponding to the DL knowledge base.

In Chapter 3, DL was introduced as a family of knowledge representation languages mainly corresponding to a subset of first-order logic. Some of the languages underpin the logical aspects of the OWL languages, such as OWL Lite (SHIF(D)), DL (SHOIN(D)), OWL2EL (EL), and OWL2 DL (SROIQ(D)). All these DL names define a given language with a set of constructors, such as conjunctions, disjunctions, negations, quantifiers, cardinalities, etc. These languages are also characterized by complexities for a set of selected reasoning problems. For example, with DLs like ALC (considered the first DL of interest due to its set of constructors) or SHIQ, the combined complexities of CQ answering are respectively Exptime-complete and 2-ExpTime-complete and NP-complete for data complexity.

Besides these high complexities, some lightweight DLs have been identified with polynomial complexity for CQ answering. The DL-Lite family is one of them and it motivated the creation of the OWL2QL recommendation. The basic DL-Lite logic provides key conceptual modeling constructs like concept inclusion and disjointness, as well as domain and range constraints; other DL-Lite logics support functionality constraints, property inclusion and disjointness, and data types. A key characteristic of the DL-Lite family is first-order rewritability. Intuitively, first-order rewritability implies that CQ answering can be performed by substituting the input conjunctive query with a new first-order query that encodes the relevant information from the ontology, and evaluating this first-order query over the data using any standard RDBMS. This approach, called query rewriting, guarantees the same low data complexity as answering first-order queries in databases (precisely AC0). This important property motivated the design of several alternatives to compute a rewriting. One important issue these solutions are trying to address is the huge size of produced rewritings, out of which many may return an empty result set. Recently, solutions based on forward-chaining (see Chapter 8) provided some encouraging results but come at the cost of having to modify the source data. This ability is not adapted to data integration applications, the main playground of OBDA.

The DL-Lite family is not the only DL addressing OBDA; the EL DL family is another interesting candidate. As its name invokes, it is the logical underpinning of the OWL2EL W3C recommendation. Although relatively restricted in terms of expressivity, it is known to be practically used in popular biomedical ontologies such as Snomed CT and the Gene Ontology. The data complexity of CQ answering is known to be P-complete for this family. In this context, CQ answering is usually performed using a forward-chaining approach, which implies the data integration problem already highlighted with DL-Lite ontologies. Finally, more expressive DLs like Horn-SHIQ, which are a superset of both the DL-Lite and EL logics, also propose a polynomial data complexity for CQ answering. Nevertheless, to the best of our knowledge, no implementations of CQ answering algorithms are available to such logics.

OBDA is not limited to approaches based on the use of DLs. As suggested by our last example, Horn-SHIQ, rule-based approaches are also potential candidates. This follows from a long history in the database community to investigate inference mechanisms, such as deductive databases. The most popular language in this tradition is Datalog, which can express ontological knowledge using positive first-order rules. These rules are composed of a so-called head and body, both of which are conjunctions of atoms without functions. However, in such rules, all variables in the head necessarily have to occur in the body. This aims to prevent the generation of individuals not originally present in the data set. Note that this is particularly desired in a knowledge-base setting where open-world assumption is a key concept.

Starting from these interesting properties, research on Datalog-based OBDA intensified but these rule language extensions have to integrate existential quantification, such as existentially quantified variables that can appear in the rule head but not in the body, which is bound to undecidability in the general case. Due to these interesting properties, research work on different Datalog languages like Datalog+/− emerged in the context of OBDA. The goal is to identify a decidable fragment with an interesting tradeoff between complexity of query answering and expressivity. Most of the identified decidable fragments are based on properties of forward-chaining and backward-chaining or a combination of them. Note that they also share the same worst-case complexity of the DL solutions we have seen in this section. Precisely, linear Datalog+/− augmented with a restricted form of equality and negative constraints is polynomial in data complexity.

A state-of-the-art OBDA system using the DL approach is **Ontop** (Rodriguez-Muro et al., 2013). This system uses the Quest and OntoPro components. The former proposes an efficient SPARQL-to-SQL query rewriting solution that supports SPARQL 1.0 queries and RDFS, OWL2QL reasoning. OntoPro is a **Protégé** plugin providing mapping facilities as well as an integration with Quest.

5.3.3 NoSQL

More and more implementations of RDF engines are using NoSQL stores because some of them are gaining in terms of maturity and features. Most of these engines are using systems corresponding to the column-family category, such as Apache's **HBase, Cassandra,** and **Accumulo**.

5.3.3.1 Key-value store

The popular key-value store systems, such as **Redis, Riak, DynamoDB,** and **Aerospike**, are using a data model that seems too simple to address the issues associated to the RDF data model. As such, it is not a surprise to struggle to find RDF stores based on these systems.

The **AWETO** system (hash-based two-tier RDF storage) (Pu et al., 2011) is one of those stores and uses **Tokyo Cabinet** (an open-source key-value store) as the B+tree implementation of the different indexes. The system uses four different index orders: S-PO, P-SO, P-OS, and O-PS. The notation introduces a separation between elements of a triple: a single atom and a two-atom tuple—for example, in P-OS, P is a single atom and OS is a two-atom tuple. This separation enables us to store the two components in two different indexes, respectively the atom position (AP) index and the binary tuple (BT) index. The AP index is a key-value store in a disk implemented using a B+tree. The key of that index is a pair of numerical values. Using a dedicated encoding, the first value indicates the role of the atom as well as the BT index—for example, P-SO is encoded as 0, 1 for P-OS, etc. The second value of the key corresponds to the dictionary identifier of the atom. The value of the AP index contains pointers to all the BT entries associated to that key. The BT index is persisted on disk and takes the form of a standard file used in an RDBMS. The authors of AWETO claim that the efficiency of their system, demonstrated over different evaluations, is due to their indexing approach, as well as their implementation relying on the Tokyo Cabinet's B+tree.

5.3.3.2 Document stores

We know of at least three solutions based on document stores. Two of them are using the popular **MongoDB** system, namely **D-SPARQ** and **Tripod**, and the other one is based on **CouchBase**. Due to lack of information, we do not present the Tripod system here. The CouchBase solution does not correspond to a complete system implementation but was rather created in the context of an evaluation of the ability of NoSQL systems to store and query RDF data (Cudré-Mauroux et al., 2013). The CouchBase system is a document-oriented, schemaless distributed system that makes intensive use of the **Membase** system (i.e., a key-value store) and of Apache's **CouchDB** system (i.e., a document store that uses JSON as a document format). CouchBase adopts an in-memory approach where a data set is distributed on the main memory of the cluster's nodes. To ensure good performance, the system contains a built-in cache solution to speed up random reads and writes.

The storage of RDF triples is based on a mapping to JSON documents. This mapping supports the distribution of RDF triples over a set of documents identified by subjects. That is, one document is created per subject, using that value as its key, and that document contains two JSON arrays, one for property values and another one for object values. In CouchBase, query expression is supported by JavaScript MapReduce views. Intuitively, the map function is executed over every stored document and emits a certain number of key-value pairs. Following a shuffling operation that sends pairs with the same key to a given reduce node, the reduce function aggregates the pair according to the specified code to provide a given result.

Executing such map and reduce functions enables us to create materialized views that can be used as any other documents. In this system, three views complement the primary structure. They address the patterns where only the property or object are known, and the pattern where both the property and object are known. Together with the primary index on the subject, they constitute a set of four indexes, one on S, P, O and OP. In this context, a translation from SPARQL to map and reduce functions needs to be performed. This implementation uses the Jena framework and a set of heuristics to use relevantly the available indexes.

The **D-SPARQ** (Mutharaju et al., 2013) system emerged from a collaboration between different universities. It aims at using the MongoDB system and MapReduce processing. A main benefit of using the document-oriented MongoDB over its competitors remains in its support for secondary and compound indexes. Intuitively, compound indexes enable us to answer queries on any prefix of the index. It also comes with support for complex queries and interesting performances for random write and read operations. Just like CouchDB, MongoDB uses the JSON document format and stores it in a compressed, binary form named BSON (Binary SON). The storage schema of D-SPARQ is quite similar to the one proposed in the previously presented CouchBase system. A document, identified with a subject URI, stores all triples information for this given subject. Therefore, as many documents are created as there are distinct subjects in the data set. The system also proposes a compound index on a predicate–object pair. Note that such a compound index handles data retrieval given a predicate–object pair or a predicate alone. This approach is motivated by its ability to reply efficiently to star-shaped queries because they are mainly driven by subject values and are easily retrieved with this storage layout. Although quite frequent in practical querying of RDF data, other forms of queries, such as snowflake or long chains, cannot be forgotten. We will come back to this system in Chapter 7 because one of its key aspects is to address data distribution.

Finally, **MarkLogic** is an enterprise-ready system—that is, it features many tools enabling the implementation of applications and is known to be used by paying clients—that was first designed to store and query XML documents (in the early 2000s) and then evolved to handle JSON, RDF, and SPARQL. The system is now advertised to be a NoSQL database with a document-oriented approach. The main features or the system are ACID transactions with recovery, auto-sharding, and automated failover management over a shared-nothing architecture, and integration with the Hadoop ecosystem. The system provides some master–slave replication, many facilities for a deployment on a cloud environment (e.g., Amazon's EC2), full-text search, and support for geospatial indexes. The RDF store based on MarkLogic benefits from all these features and claims to ease reification and provenance by adding metadata to the triples.

5.3.3.3 Column family

The column-family NoSQL category has motivated the design of an important number of RDF stores. A main advantage over the other categories is its ability to support data distribution over a cluster of commodity hardware as well as its integration with MapReduce frameworks. We will come back to the distribution aspects in Chapter 7. We start our investigation with approaches proposed in Cudré-Mauroux et al. (2013) and then present complete systems that have been implemented in different contexts, such as cloud computing.

Two popular and open-source column-family systems are Apache's HBase and Cassandra. They both can be used to store RDF triples or quads using an index structure that is reminiscent of the YARS system (Harth et al., 2005). We consider that each triple element is encoded using a standard dictionary. Then, in the case of triples, the following three indexes are sufficient to ensure efficient index scans: SPO, POS, and OSP. The same organization is used for these indexes: row keys of column families corresponds to the concatenation of triple identifiers, such as S, P, and O, and column values are left empty. This approach leverages lexicographical sorting of the row keys, enabling the coverage of multiple triples patterns with the same structure—for example, SPO covers patterns such as S?? and SP? in addition to SPO. This compact representation possesses the advantage of minimizing network and disk I/O and therefore supports fast joins for query processing.

Another data organization is proposed in Cudré-Mauroux et al. (2013) that is based on both Apache's HBase and **Hive**, a SQL-like data warehouse that offers interactions with Hadoop. The schema is described as adapting a property table approach on the HBase store. A compressed subject value serves as the row key and all triples for that subject value are stored in a column family, with a column consisting of a predicate as a key and an object as a value. The timestamps (cell in HBase) support multivalued attributes. The Hive system is used for the query tasks. In fact, SPARQL is translated into HiveQL, which is creating temporary tables to perform joins between patterns of the query's BGP.

CumulusRDF is an RDF engine that uses Cassandra, a column family NoSQL store, as a storage backend. Therefore, this RDF store benefits from the whole Cassandra machinery providing a decentralized, highly available, scalable storage solution with failure tolerance through replication and failover mechanisms using a no single point of failure approach. The storage of RDF triples supports the notion of a named graph (i.e., it stores quads), and aims to cover all six possible RDF triple patterns with indexes and to exploit prefix lookups to reduce the number of materialized indexes.

In Ladwig and Harth (2011), the authors describe two storage layouts that are denoted as hierarchical and flat. In the hierarchical layout, an important use of Cassandra's supercolumn supports the overall storage organization. Intuitively, a *supercolumn* is an additional layer of key-value pairs that occurs in a column family. With that solution, the subject, predicate, and object of a triple are respectively stored in the key, supercolumn, and column, and the value is left unspecified. Therefore, there are multiple supercolumns (i.e., predicates) for each row key (i.e., subject), and for each predicate, there are multiple possible columns, each of them storing a single object value. This provides an efficient SPO index. Two similar indexes are constructed for POS and OSP—motivating the distribution over row keys, supercolumns, and columns. These three indexes are considered sufficient to support the six possible triples patterns. Note that, at the time of writing this chapter, in the latest versions of Cassandra, this option is not supported anymore and matches the HBase and BigTable approaches that provide only the notions of key spaces, column families, and columns. Therefore, this hierarchical storage layout is not adapted to recent Cassandra releases.

The flat layout makes intensive use of Cassandra's secondary index solution. In that solution, a standard key-value model is adopted where the row key is a triples element and the column key and value correspond to the remaining triples pair. For instance, considering the SPO pattern, the subject is stored as the row key, the predicate is a column key, and the object pair is the column's value. Because columns are stored in a given sorted order, this approach enables us to perform both range scans and prefix lookups on column keys in an efficient manner. Just like in the hierarchical layout, two other indexes are needed, namely POS and OSP, to cover all possible triple patterns. The POS requires special attention due to the distributed approach of Cassandra. The goal is to prevent data skew caused by the inequitable distribution of triples over predicates—for example, rdf:type usually represents an important fraction of the entire data set. Therefore, in the case of POS, setting P as the unique row key is not an efficient approach, because some very large rows will emerge and be stored on some given nodes, possibly exceeding node capacity for some data sets and preventing efficient load balancing. The proposed solution is based on Cassandra's secondary indexes. That is, PO is used as the row key for the POS pattern and the remaining S is stored as the column key. In each row, a special column stores the predicate with a p key. This, through the use of a secondary index on p, enables us to retrieve all values for a given predicate. Note that this flat layout does not use supercolumns. Recently, CumulusRDF has been extended with a fourth index to support RDF named graphs (i.e., storing quads instead of triples) with a CSPO index. Curiously, CumulusRDF does not make any use of dictionaries but prefers to store URIs, literals, and blank nodes as column keys and values.

The **Rya** engine enables us to store large RDF data sets (i.e., billions of triples) on the cloud and as such concentrates on scalability. It uses Apache's Accumulo, an open-source variant of Google's Bigtable, characterized by distributing the data on commodity hardware, automatic load balancing, and partitioning a column-oriented model that integrates data compression. The data model resembles HBase, a distributed key-value store with a sorting of keys in lexicographic order on row IDs. A key is composed of a row identifier, a column, and a timestamp. Note that the notion of column is different from the ones encountered in Cassandra and HBase, although it also corresponds to a triple. Here a column is composed of a family, qualifier, and visibility, and supports different sorts. Also just like HBase, it leverages on the Hadoop ecosystem that is its distributed file system (HDFS), Zookeeper (for distributed coordination), and Hadoop (for distributed computing).

The adoption of Accumulo is motivated by the following features. First, by using a server side iterator model, it supports the execution of large computing tasks directly on the servers and not on the client machine. This approach improves the performance of many operations by limiting the transfer of large amounts of data across the network. The second motivation consists in a so-called batch scanner client API that allows us to reduce multiple range scans into one merged client request. The bulk importing feature is another element that is quite efficient when importing a large number of RDF triples. This method uses Hadoop to dispatch rows to identified servers and perform local imports. Finally, similar to Cassandra, Accumulo natively integrates bloom filters to accelerate row-based lookups. The storage layout of RDF triples takes advantage of these features. In a nutshell, it uses a similar approach to CumulusRDF by only implementing three indexes, namely `SPO`, `POS`, and `OPS`. For each of them, it benefits from the fact that all key-value pairs are sorted and partitioned on the row identifier of the key. For instance, in the case of the `SPO` index, the three elements of a triple are all stored in the row ID, leaving the column and value empty. This approach supports direct-range scans on the literals and provides fast importing and querying operations through simple serialization and deserialization of the row IDs.

The next two systems are evolving in a cloud infrastructure using the available data stores. They have been implemented in the Amazon Web Service (AWS) cloud but are using different database solutions.

Amada is defined by its authors as a Web data repository in the cloud. Its architecture belongs to the software as a service (SaaS) category, which natively provides scalability and elastic resource allocation. The system aims at providing a storage solution for Web data formats of the W3C, namely XML and RDF, and is based on the AWS cloud infrastructure. As such, it uses two of its data storage solutions: Amazon's Simple Storage Service (S3) is responsible for storing the data (i.e., RDF triples), while the column family SimpleDB, one of Amazon's proprietary stores, takes care of data indexes. Note that in the AWS ecosystem, SimpleDB is frequently used to index objects stored in S3, as well as to collect metadata about these objects. With this approach, S3 is extended with query functionalities generally met in database management systems. Amada benefits from the automatic indexing facility provided by SimpleDB. Finally, Amada also uses Amazon's Simple Queue Service (SQS) to handle the asynchronous message-based communication between the different components. Several indexing strategies have been designed and evaluated using SimpleDB. In the so-called attribute-based strategy, three indexes are created, one for each element of a triple, and each index is stored in a different SimpleDB domain (a collection of items).

Stratustore is an RDF store that uses SimpleDB as an RDF store with a single index backend. It uses the API of the Jena framework for its different parsing and querying operations. It uses a single index, `SPO`, where subjects, predicates, and objects are respectively stored in SimpleDB's items, as attribute names, and as values for these attributes. The main drawback of this approach is its inability to handle patterns with a variable at the predicate position. To prevent this, the system can be enriched with one additional entry per triple. This entry consists of a `SOP` index where objects are stored as attributes and predicates as values. Of course, this comes at the cost of an important increase of the storage space. Concerning query processing, the solution is not considered to be very efficient because the joins need to be computed at the client side. The main benefit of the system is its high throughput when the data is distributed over a large number of nodes.

5.3.3.4 Graph databases
We have already described several RDF stores that are adopting a graph perspective to store and query RDF triples. Allegrograph has been described due to its history and position in the RDF database management systems market and for the fact that it is based

on its own NoSQL store. The other example is gStore, which does not use a standard graph database system but has rather implemented its own storage backend.

In general, graph databases have the ability to store different types of graphs, such as unlabeled, undirected, weighted, hypergraphs, etc. The graph perspective also supports a navigational querying method that is more intuitive and can also be more efficient than the SQL-like SPARQL approach. But the RDF ecosystem possesses some assets such as established standards recommended by the W3C, including ontology languages to support reasoning services. For instance, there isn't any standard for querying graph databases—for example, Cypher is a proprietary language used in Neo4J and Gremlin, although used by several systems, it is only a blueprint.

Considering the leading NoSQL graph system, namely Neo4J, we can observe that its data model is more expressive than what RDF allows, such as Neo4J permits properties to have attributes. Therefore, Neo4J can be adapted to store RDF graphs and even supports SPARQL in addition to Cypher and Gremlin, and can easily be adapted to store RDF graphs. The **HypergraphDB** system uses an even richer data model corresponding to a hypergraph—it allows *n*-ary relationships. This system has some extension for the support of RDF (through Sesame's SAIL) and OWL 2.

The **Trinity.RDF** system is a distributed, in-memory RDF storage system. The system is based on Microsoft's Trinity database, which corresponds to a key-value store on Microsoft's Azure cloud. Therefore, modeling is based on a key-value representation. The data structure is made of an atomic key (e.g., subject) and two adjacency lists in the value. Each adjacency list is composed of a pair of entities, such as predicate and object. An adjacency list structure stores incoming links and the other outgoing links. This structure is used for indexing subjects and objects. A third index is created for predicates. For each predicate a list of subjects and objects is stored. Default distribution of triples is hashing on the node IDs—that is they are randomly partitioned. Other partitioning methods can be used. The power law distribution is taken into account to model RDF data with the main objective of preventing communication between cluster nodes at query time. Because the data is modeled as a graph, the query processing uses graph navigation rather than joins. The project is relatively new and a first research paper has only been published in 2013 (Zeng et al., 2013).

5.4 COMPLEMENTARY SURVEYS

Although we have presented a complete overview of existing RDF store systems, it seems fair to emphasize several comparable surveys of this active domain. Some of these surveys date back to the early 2000s and it is interesting to follow the evolution in terms of provided features and maturity of the systems since then. A chronological analysis also highlights the need to distribute data sets over a cluster of machines. During the last few years, this has motivated the emergence of architectures using NoSQL data stores. These aspects are highlighted in the timeline shown in Figure 5.2.

In Magkanaraki et al. (2002), the authors describe a wide range of tools in terms of storing, accessing, and querying ontologies. The tools and query languages are described across a variety of features with performance figures, based on those provided by the tools. This survey defines and uses similar criteria to ours, such as query languages, implementation languages, inference support, APIs, export data formats, and scalability/performance properties (some of which are investigated in upcoming chapters). The survey considers how the tools are appropriate for ontological applications rather than for more simpler Semantic Web ones. In Beckett (2002), the author considers open-source RDF storage systems and defines a set of criteria such as programming languages and systems, APIs, capacity/performance, query languages, and inferencing. Despite the quality of this survey, first, the standards and the solutions have evolved quite significantly since 2002 and, moreover, other frameworks like multiple indexing and compliant RDF storage approaches have appeared. In Barstow (2001), the author uses a similar set of criteria. Nevertheless, information about these criteria are given for some storing systems, but no real comparisons have been performed.

Beckett and Grant (2003) extensively studied the use of RDBMS for Semantic Web storage and its related issues and the schemas used. In 2004 and in the SIMILE research project, a survey of open-source RDF storing systems was done by Lee (2004). It provides a complete performance evaluation for a set of chosen tools but does not clearly define additional criteria for the evaluation. In Stegmaier et al. (2009), the authors evaluated a selected set of RDF databases that support the SPARQL query language through general features such as details about the software producer and license information, and an architectural and efficiency comparison of the interpretation of SPARQL queries on a scalable test data set.

5.5 SUMMARY

- Many types of storage and indexing for RDF documents are available. They can be categorized by being native or non-native, whether they depend on an existing management system or not.
- Native systems are based on an approach specifically designed for RDF triples. They principally correspond to multiple indexing approaches. The most efficient systems are considered to be in this category (e.g., RDF-3X), but they are not always ready for production because of the lack of some important components, such as a set of APIs to support application development, e.g., this is missing to the RDF-3X framework, or the handling of security issues. Some highly compressed, main memory single indexing approaches are emerging but are quite recent and cannot be considered as mature.
- Non-native systems are using an existing database management system that has not been originally developed for the RDF data model. These systems mainly concern

RDBMS, and more recently stores based on NoSQL systems are emerging and are tackling the cloud computing market. Several commercial RDF engines belong to these two categories.

- The fact that Oracle, IBM, and Microsoft are releasing components in their environment (i.e., RDBMS and/or cloud solutions) is an interesting feature toward the future of RDF data management. The fact that such companies are entering this market means that some commercial activities are emerging.

- A survey of the RDF store market clearly emphasizes the following group of production-ready systems (in alphabetic order): Sesame, 4Store, Allegrograph, BigData, Oracle, OWLIM, Stardog, and Virtuoso. The IBM DB2-based and Microsoft (Trinity.RDF) systems described in this chapter should clearly become contenders in their respective companies, but are quite new and may lack some maturity at the time of writing this book (2014).

CHAPTER SIX

Query Processing

6.1 INTRODUCTION

In the previous chapter, we presented the main physical organization and indexing approaches available in open-source and commercial RDF stores. This enables us to present the query processing aspects of the systems. Here, we only consider the SPARQL query language. This is motivated by the official W3C recommendation status of this technology, something that other query languages such as RDQL (a query language that served as an inspiration for SPARQL and which was developed in the context of the Jena framework) and SeRQL (which is still being used in **Aduna's Sesame**) do not possess.

The set DBMS components responsible for answering queries is named a *query processor*. Its main objective is to provide a correct and complete (at least in a nonreasoning setting; see Chapter 8) answer to a given query. But most of the time, this may not be considered sufficient, and in the era of Big Data, performance is a major factor. Thus, one is expecting the delivery of the answer set almost instantly or at least with a minimum of latency (usually in the range of a few milliseconds). This is only attainable if one does not propose a naive execution of the SPARQL query. For example, executing the query as provided by the end-user rarely guarantees the most efficient execution. One may obtain better performances by executing an optimized version of the original query. Such an optimization is automatically generated and executed by a query optimizer component. To define such an optimized rewriting, the system performs an in-depth analysis of the original query, as well as the database instance including its metadata. In terms of metadata, the generally assumed absence of a schema associated to an RDF data set renders this optimization task more involved. This is not the case for a relational database context, where a schema is inevitably provided. Nevertheless, in the presence of an RDFS or OWL ontology, some optimizations may be performed. Additionally, we have seen that multiple data structures, most of them associated to indexes, are available in the systems presented in Chapter 5 and are intensively investigated by the RDF store to perform this rewriting.

Being a declarative language (like SQL), SPARQL enables the definition of queries at a very high level. That is, the end-user does not express or specify the kind of algorithms that will be used to scan and/or join the data. Rather, he or she expresses what the query should return and from which part of the store it can be retrieved. The machinery of accessing, filtering, joining, and constructing the answer set is the responsibility of the query processor, which does its best in optimizing each of these stages. These optimizations steps imply, naming just a couple, the utilization in the most efficient way of the system's index possibilities and the reordering of the triples execution. Query optimizers are generally obsessed with the minimization of the number of input and output operations, and the limitation of the main memory footprint. Clearly, this can only be guaranteed by considering the peculiarities of the underlying system. For example, a main memory database will not be concerned with secondary memory issues, and a system built over a multiple indexing approach will need to design an efficient index selection policy to optimize the queries.

To fulfill these properties, a query processor is generally composed of various components. In an RDF store, they correspond to the ones presented in Figure 2.3 in Chapter 2. In the remainder of this chapter, we present the principal ones and their associated techniques—that is, the parsing, rewriting, optimization, and execution tasks that are generally encountered in both native and non-native systems. Note that these components are present in most database management systems, and in the case of an RDBMS, are the result of years of research and development. Most of the solutions we are presenting in the following sections are directly inspired by the methods and technologies that have emerged from research conducted toward the development of RDBMSs. A majority of them have been adapted to the peculiarities of RDF triples—for example, dealing with a graph model and handling a possibly much larger number of joins. A smaller portion of them are either not considered or used in some restricted forms because they are not amenable to the graph approach, such as cost selectivity based on data statistics.

Moreover, if the RDF data set is associated to an RDFS or OWL ontology, then the possibility of cleverly handling query processing is increased. In this chapter, we do not consider deep reasoning mechanisms, but defer that presentation to Chapter 8. Nonetheless, the expressivity of Semantic Web ontologies supports some query simplifications that cannot be performed using the metadata contained in a relational database schema. For instance, we present a semantic simplification of a SPARQL *basic graph pattern* (BGP), a set of triples in a WHERE clause, that can be integrated in the rewriting component.

Most of the queries we are dealing with in this chapter involve selections, or SPARQL queries with SELECT, ASK, DESCRIBE, or CONSTRUCT clauses. The tasks required for these different SPARQL query forms are more or less the same and are concerned with the four previously cited components. Among them, the query optimizer is frequently considered of key importance to obtain an efficient query execution. This is mainly due to the large join order search space associated to SPARQL queries. That is, the triples pattern–matching approach of the SPARQL query language implies that practical queries involve many joins—for example, in the scientific domain, some queries can contain more than 50 joins. Therefore, the ordering of these joins has a preponderant impact on the performance of query processing. These SPARQL queries generally

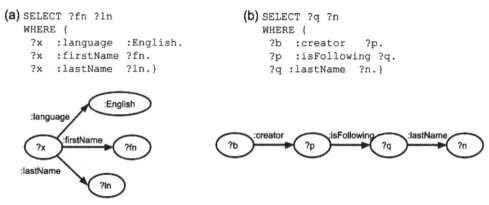

```
(a) SELECT ?fn ?ln
     WHERE {
        ?x  :language   :English.
        ?x  :firstName ?fn.
        ?x  :lastName   ?ln.}
```

```
(b) SELECT ?q ?n
     WHERE {
        ?b :creator    ?p.
        ?p :isFollowing ?q.
        ?q :lastName   ?n.}
```

Figure 6.1 (a) Star and (b) path (chain) SPARQL queries.

follow two main patterns: *star* and *path* (a.k.a. *chain*) queries. With a star query pattern, the BGP of a SPARQL query can be represented as a graph where an important number of relations are directly connected to a central node. A path or chain query pattern has a linear shape. In analyzing both cases, nodes can be variables, URIs, or blank nodes. Figure 6.1 presents two examples of such queries for the blog running example. Associating one of these query shapes to a BGP enables us to apply some specific optimization heuristics that can have a major impact on the query execution performance.

Section 6.6 discusses SPARQL queries that are concerned with updating RDF data sets. Little work is devoted to the implementation of their efficient processing. This can be justified by the recent appearance of DELETE and INSERT statements, which suffice to perform update operations, in the latest SPARQL 1.1 W3C recommendation.

6.2 QUERY PARSING

Query parsing is the first task performed in any database management system when a query needs to be processed. In most systems, the main goals of this task are the same and aim to ensure that the query is correctly specified—that is, it's well formed according to the query language syntax—and to convert the query into an internal format that may be specific to each system. The objective of this internal format is to facilitate the manipulation of the query by the other components of the query processor, such as the query optimizer.

Depending on the underlying data model of the database management system, the internal formats can take different forms. For example, in the context of an RDBMS, implementations are frequently inspired by so-called relational algebra. The query is converted into a parse tree that contains expressions of the relational algebra. This so-called logical query plan is then improved using a set of rules, such as algebraic transformations or groupings of certain operators. Of course, several logical query plans can be generated out of these rules. An accurate evaluation enables us to identify the most efficient logical plan among a set of possible ones. The heuristics used to evaluate logical plans are a main differentiator of available RDF stores. The internal format of many RDF stores is directly inspired by the relational algebra. This is a direct consequence of the proof, provided in Angles and Gutierrez (2008), that SPARQL under bag semantics (a variation of set semantics where duplicates are allowed) and the relational algebra have the same expressive power.

A query parser is required on both native and non-native storage approaches. Even in the case of a non-native system relying on an RDBMS, the SPARQL queries need to be parsed before being translated to SQL queries. This is mainly to detect ill-formed SPARQL queries. The resulting SQL query is then handled by the RDBMS query processing system and is again going through parsing, rewriting, optimization, and execution phases that are handled by the RDBMS.

The implementation of a SPARQL parser is time demanding, especially if optimizations are required to ensure good performances. This required effort is a principal reason why many available systems rely on existing parsers. The most popular parsers are components of frameworks and systems that we have already presented in previous chapters: Jena and Sesame. Intuitively, they propose a set of APIs for the Java programming language considering these two frameworks, and therefore provide access to many useful functionalities.

In Chapter 3, we presented Apache's Jena framework as a popular and open-source set of APIs and tools to build Semantic Web applications. Among them, the *Jena ARQ* is defined as a SPARQL processor for Jena and proposes features such as the parsing of SPARQL 1.0 and 1.1 queries (including aggregation and updates), where the triples found in the triples patterns can be described in different formats (e.g., turtle, N-triples, and RDF/XML). It also proposes an extendable SPARQL algebra (i.e., a relational algebra counterpart for SPARQL) that can serve as an internal language for operations such as query optimization. Jena ARQ is used in the storage systems of the Jena framework, namely TDB and SDB, but also in systems such as **Hexastore** and **RDFMatView**.

We have already presented Aduna's Sesame as one of the first historic RDF database systems, made available in 2002. Similar to Jena, Sesame is an RDF data framework and includes facilities for parsing, storing, inferencing, and querying over RDF data. As such, it supports both recommendations of SPARQL in the most popular formats. Due to its so-called stackable interface, which abstracts the storage engine from the query interface, the Sesame framework is widely adopted by both open-source and commercial RDF stores, such as **GraphDB**, **Bigdata**, **4Store**, or **Virtuoso**.

Considering other programming languages, we can mention RDFLib (a Python library), Rasqal (a C library, implemented as a package of the Redland RDF library), and ARC (a PHP library).

```
SELECT                                                                ?name
WHERE                                                                     {
  ?user1    rdf:type          blog:Person;
            ex:firstName      ?name;
            blog:isFollowing ?user2 .
  ?user2    rdf:type          blog:Person.
}
```

Figure 6.2 A simplifiable SPARQL query.

6.3 QUERY REWRITING

We now present the different steps of SPARQL query rewriting. This comprises simplification, encoding and translation operations.

6.3.1 Query simplification

The principal idea of query simplification is to reduce the number of triples patterns in a SPARQL's BGP. This can be performed by finding those triples patterns that can be deduced from inferences at the ontology level, such as RDFS or OWL Tboxes. To provide a concrete example, let's consider the query example of Figure 6.2 together with the RDFS ontology extract of Figure 6.3. Note that the removal of the two `rdf:type` triples would still produce a semantically equivalent rewriting of the original query. This is due to the domain and range of the `isFollowing` property, which already specifies that `?user1` and `?user2` must be of type `Person`. Similar simplifications can be discovered from over RDFS, RDFS +, or OWL axioms, such as with functional and inverse functional properties.

Performing such a reduction of triples patterns in the BGP has several advantages. First, it diminishes the number of joins to be taken into account during the query optimization and execution steps. Therefore, it can have a major impact on query answering performance. Second, the cut-down query is more amenable to human reading. That is, by removing some unnecessary triples patterns, the query is more easily understood and analyzed, and may be modified by the end-user.

The reasoning aspect in this query simplification implies a set of triples patterns and an ontology, but does require access to the Abox. Its goal is to remove superfluous triples patterns of a BGP, and it has nothing to do with the completeness of the computed result set. This is quite different from the inference services we cover in Chapter 8, where the

```
blog:isFollowing              rdfs:domain    blog:Person ;
                              rdfs:range     blog:Person .
```

Figure 6.3 Extract of the RDFS blog ontology.

Tbox and the Abox are required to achieve the completeness of the query answer set. We will see that this can be performed in one of two different ways:

1. Materializing implicit Abox facts.
2. Adding new triple patterns to a BGP.

Finally, this simplification step is generally performed before the SPARQL encoding phase for efficiency reasons—that is, concepts, properties, and ontology axioms are generally not encoded within the dictionary. Some of the more advanced work that we know of in this form of encoding are Rodriguez-Muro et al. (2012) and Curé et al. (2014), which provide an efficient encoding of the concept and property subsumption relationships in dictionaries. These two approaches have already been detailed in the Chapter 4.

6.3.2 Query encoding and decoding

Encoding and decoding a query concern systems that are using dictionaries as presented in Chapter 4. Encoding is an early step of query processing, generally executed after parsing and once validation is ensured. This operation consists in transforming each triples pattern in a SPARQL query BGP, such as URIs, literals, and possibly blank nodes, into corresponding identifiers of the dictionary. In general, this is performed using one of the different data structures presented in Chapter 4. For example, a hashing structure takes the triples entry as key and the identifier as value. In dictionary-dependent systems, all remaining query processing operations can be performed using this representation. Because providing the query results into this representation does not provide any value to the end-user, a decoding approach is necessary. It translates the query answer tuples into URIs and literals (rarely blank nodes). Usually this step requires another data structure where key is the identifier and value is the triples entry—that is, it exactly contains the same set of identifiers and triples entries but reverses the roles of keys and values.

Of course, the cost of these operations has to be negligible compared to the overall cost of the query execution. Therefore, one has to give particular attention to the data structures used to support the encoding and decoding operations. The query processing also benefits from handling integer-based versions of the query—that is, the memory footprint of the query and the intermediate result sets consume less and are less important than with a nonencoded approach.

6.3.3 Query translation

A query translation is required in non-native RDF triples stores that are using an RDBMS system (directly or through an OBDA approach) or a NoSQL store. This translation amounts to transforming a SPARQL query into a target query language, such as SQL for RDBMS and OBDA. This mainly involves the exploitation of a set of mapping axioms that propose correspondences between elements present in BGP triples and relations/attributes in the underlying relational database or entities in a NoSQL database, such as documents/keys in a document store.

In the case of a physical organization using an RDBMS, the translation operation is relatively straightforward due to the equivalence of SPARQL and SQL queries, which can both be viewed as conjunctive ones. The case of OBDA is more involved because it's supposed to encompass data deduction through the query rewriting approach. This is performed through the rewriting of a SPARQL query, together with the mapping axioms and the ontology into a set of SQL queries. There is a detailed presentation of OBDA in Chapter 8.

The DB2RDF store we presented in Chapter 5 claims that performance gains can be achieved when the SPARQL and the SPARQL-to-SQL translations are independently optimized. In this system, the SPARQL query optimizer basically follows the standard approach detailed in Section 6.4—that is, an optimal data flow tree identified from a data flow graph enables the design of an execution tree. This execution tree is then passed to an SQL builder component that performs its translation. The operations performed by the query translator consist of:

1. Translating the execution tree into an equivalent query plan. This takes into account the specificities of the storage layer.
2. Generating an SQL query from this query plan. This step is performed using some SQL templates that are predefined in the system.

Situations where a NoSQL database are used are more involved because there is no accepted standard for any of the four categories of NoSQL stores, except to some extent with Gremlin, a graph traversal language that is part of so-called blueprints (a form of *Java Database Connectivity* (JDBC) for graph databases) that the following databases have adopted: **Neo4J**, **TinkerGraph**, **Titan**, **OrientDB**, **DEX**, **Rexster**, and Bigdata. Here we provide some examples of translation to NoSQL-based RDF stores. Nevertheless, query execution is quite different in graph databases. Instead of performing expensive joins, graph-oriented query languages navigate nodes following edges. This prevents managing large temporary results and their joins because only the nodes matching query filters are accessed.

In the context of column family stores, for the **CumulusRDF** system (which uses **Cassandra** as a storage backend) no translation to *CQL* (Cassandra Query Language) is performed. Instead, SPARQL queries are processed (using Sesame's query processor) to generate index lookups over the different Cassandra indexes. Because these index lookups are defined procedurally, we can consider that any forms of optimization are quite difficult to process. This implies that the generated index lookups need to be optimal to ensure efficient query answering.

We saw in Chapter 5 that many systems are using a MapReduce approach to benefit from a parallel-processing, fault-tolerant environment. PigSPARQL, presented in Schätzle et al. (2013), is a system that maps SPARQL queries to Pig Latin queries. In a nutshell, Pig is a data analysis platform developed by **Yahoo!** that runs on top of the Hadoop processing framework, and Latin is its query language that abstracts the creation of the `map` and `reduce` functions using a relational algebra–like approach. Therefore, Pig Latin is used as an intermediate layer between SPARQL and Hadoop. In the

PigSPARQL project, SPARQL queries are transformed into a tree algebra that is optimized and used toward the generation of the Pig Latin programs. Using the Pig machinery, these programs are translated into MapReduce jobs. Some simple optimizations are performed over the internal format trees.

6.4 OPTIMIZATION

Query optimization is necessary in almost all database management systems and is most amenable when these systems rely on a declarative query language, such as SPARQL. In general, a query can be optimized in different manners. The one that we would like to pursue is the one that has the minimal cost. This cost aspect may be characterized by different factors, the number of triples to process being an important one. The cost of an optimization can either be exact or approximated. Exact ones require very fast plan enumeration and cost estimation, which is generally not obtainable with query languages where the order join space can be large. Therefore, an approximated approach, relying on some heuristics, is used most of the time.

In this section, we consider optimization required in native systems. For systems based on an RDBMS (including those corresponding to OBDA), the optimization is handled by the database management system. That is, the SQL query obtained from the translation of the SPARQL query is following the standard query processing approach of an RDBMS: parsing, name and reference resolving, conversion into relation algebra, and optimization. We will not provide any details about the optimization in the relational context, but we can just highlight that many aspects are shared with the current state of the art in RDF stores.

The case of triples being stored in a NoSQL system is harder to apprehend and mainly depends on the features of the system. In stores proposing a dedicated declarative query language (e.g., *Cypher* for Neo4J unQL for CouchDB or CQL for Cassandra), an approach similar to those found in most RDBMSs is generally implemented. For the other NoSQL systems, those relying on a procedural, API-based approach, automatic optimization is generally very complex or not possible to implement. This leaves the query execution performance issue to the developer of the query. In situations where a SPARQL needs a translation into such a program, we can consider that either an optimization phase is first performed or not at all. In the latter, poor performances can be expected even for relatively simple queries.

The query execution performance is a priority in most query processing implementations. Due to the graph characteristic of RDF data, SPARQL queries generally have a higher number of joins compared to SQL queries. In that situation, providing an efficient join ordering (i.e., defining the order of a triples pattern execution) has a key impact on the overall execution time of the query. Of course, the mechanisms associated to the discovery of this efficient order have to be as fast as possible and require the smallest memory footprint. We need to keep in mind that the time imposed by the optimization

```
1)    ?user1    rdf:type              blog:Person.
2)    ?cat      rdf:type              blog:Science.
3)    ?user2    rdf:type              blog:Person.
4)    ?user2    blog:isFollowing ?user1.
5)    ?blog     cat:category          ?cat.
6)    ?blog     blog:owner            ?user1.
```

Figure 6.4 BGP of SPARQL query asking for all followers of bloggers writing about science.

step is included into the overall query processing. In that context, one at least expects that the execution of any optimized query is performed faster than the nonoptimized version of this query. Note that just being able to identify such a situation is already a really complex task. Therefore, the approach of most query optimization components aims at providing a best effort.

Considering a BGP with N triples patterns, $N!$ different pattern orderings are possible, corresponding to $N!$ different query plans. In the context of the six triples patterns of Figure 6.4, the 720 different plans certainly have different execution performances. The main objective of the query optimizer consists in discovering at least one of the most efficient plans in the shortest amount of time, because that discovery time is included in the overall perceived query execution duration. In most cases, this time constraint does not allow us to evaluate the cost of all query plans. Heuristics come to the rescue and provide a rule of the thumb to discover one of the most efficient plans in a relatively short time. One problem is that these heuristics generally provide a plan that is a local optimum with no guarantees of being a global optimum. Nevertheless, for the sake of performance, this optimization approach is considered satisfactory.

In the remainder of this section, we present some popular heuristics in the context of RDF data. Different forms of heuristics are frequently used in a query optimizer. An important group of them tackle the join order execution of SPARQL BGP triples. This is known to have a substantial impact on the overall performance of query execution. Therefore, it's generally considered that determining the best join ordering is a crucial issue in SPARQL query optimization. Note that this is also true for SQL queries, but it's exacerbated in a SPARQL context where it's known that the number of joins can be a lot more important—that is, queries with more than a dozen joins are common in SPARQL, while this is relatively rare in an RDBMS context. Then we present some of the most popular solutions implemented in commercial or academic state-of-the-art systems.

6.4.1 SPARQL graphs

Most query optimization techniques for SPARQL are using a BGP abstraction, which takes the form of a graph. The analysis of this graph enables the definition of the execution order of the triples patterns. In the literature, we encounter three kinds of graphs that

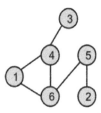

Figure 6.5 SPARQL join graph for Figure 6.4.

differ by what graph abstraction they consider as a node and an edge. These graphs are not to be confused with the kind of graphs we can depict from RDF data.

SPARQL join graph

The most obvious form abstracted from a SPARQL BGP is usually referred as a *SPARQL join graph*. It corresponds to the approach presented in RDF-3X (Neumann et al. 2008) and Hexastore (Stocker et al., 2008) and serves for a static optimization of SPARQL BGP. In this graph, nodes correspond to triples in the BGP and are labeled with distinct identifiers. The edges relate nodes that are sharing a common variable. Note that triples patterns sharing a constant are not related. Let's consider the BGP of Figure 6.4 and its corresponding join graph depicted in Figure 6.5.

We can see that as a first step, the graph is not directed nor are its edges labeled. The six nodes correspond to the six triples patterns, and nodes (1) and (6) are related because they share the `?user1` variable. Therefore, this graph supports a representation of triples pattern joins. Note that if the SPARQL join graph is not connected, then the Cartesian product of the result of each subgraph is needed to compute the overall answer set. This is usually associated to a high memory footprint and slow query execution.

Transforming this graph into a *directed acyclic graph* (DAG) permits the definition of an execution plan but does not specify the order in which the triples have to be executed. For example, a DAG induced from Figure 6.5 is proposed in Figure 6.6. From this DAG, several query plans (i.e., join orders) can be extracted: 3, 4, 1, 6, 5, 2 or 3, 4, 6, 1, 5, 2. In Sections 6.4.2 and 6.4.3, we present additional heuristics that can help in identifying efficient join orders.

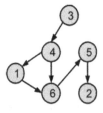

Figure 6.6 A DAG from the graph in Figure 6.4.

SPARQL variable graph

Another way to represent a graph out of the BGP of a SPARQL query is to consider that nodes correspond to variables and two nodes are related by an edge when they appear together in the same triples pattern. This SPARQL graph version has been denoted *SPARQL variable graph* in Tsialiamanis et al. (2012), and proposes several interesting characteristics. First, the variable-to–graph node relationship corresponds to a bijection. Therefore, each node is labeled with its associated variable name. Comparatively, in a join graph, a variable may "appear" (through edges) as many times as the number of joins it's participating in. Nevertheless, the number of occurrences of each variable in the BGP is stored in its corresponding node. Second, the edges correspond to BGP triples and not to join relationships. Together with SPARQL's frequent high number of joins, these characteristics ensure that a variable graph is smaller than its join counterpart.

Based on this graph form, Tsialiamanis and colleagues (2012) consider SPARQL query optimization through a reduction to the *maximum-weight independent sets* problem (Gibbons, 1985). This work was first introduced in the context of the *Heuristic SPARQL Planner* (HSP), Interestingly, HSP is the first query optimizer for SPARQL that only exploits the syntactic and structural aspects of triples of a BGP to select an execution plan. That is, no form of statistics is used to optimize query execution. The notion of independent sets is reminiscent to graph theory and consists of a set of nodes, no two of which share an edge. When the nodes of a graph are annotated with weights, the maximum-weight independent sets problem corresponds to the search for the independent set of the maximum total weight. This problem is known to be NP-hard, even under restrictions in the forms given to the graph.

Nonetheless, the limited size of real-world SPARQL queries makes the computation of this problem practical for SPARQL variable graphs in terms of milliseconds on modern hardware, as noted in Tsialiamanis et al. (2012). The approach adopted in HSP considers an independent set as a block of merge joins. These blocks can then be connected by some other join algorithms, such as hash or nested loop joins. Figure 6.7 presents the variable graph (we have omitted the ? symbol in the Figure) of Figure 6.4's query, where each node contains the variable name and the number of occurrences in the query's BGP—that is, the `?user1` variable is present in three triples patterns in the query, thus its weight of three. Because of triples 4 and 6, the `?user1` node is related to respectively the nodes `?user2` and `?blog`.

The algorithm for finding the maximum-weight independent sets works as follows. Only variables that are involved in more than one join are considered—that is, graph nodes with a weight greater than two. In the running example, only the `?user1` node

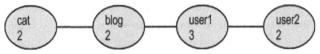

Figure 6.7 SPARQL variable graph for Figure 6.4.

satisfies this constraint and the obtained maximum-weight independent set is {?user1, ?cat}, which has a total weight of five. Note that the sets {?blog, ?user2} and {?user2, ?cat} are also independent sets, but their totals are not the maximum because they equal five. For graphs containing more nodes satisfying this weight constraint, several algorithms, such as Bourgeois and colleagues' (2010), are able to compute a maximum independent set. The method also works for nodes with a weight equal to two but makes less sense in terms of optimization using merge sorts.

In the running example, a single maximum-weight independent set is discovered. But in some cases, several sets can coexist and the system needs to select one among them. A set of heuristics can help in performing this selection. In the HSP method, only triples pattern–based heuristics are being used. We present the most important ones in Section 6.4.2 because they generally can be used in other systems. If none of the heuristics enables us to select one maximum independent set, one is selected randomly.

The variables of the selected set are stored in a variable set V, and all triples from the BGP containing any of these variables are removed from the original BGP. The removed BGP is used as the starting triples set for a new iteration of the algorithm. In the running example, this corresponds to triples 1, 2, 4, 5, and 6 of the SPARQL query in Figure 6.4—that is, the triples patterns containing the variables ?cat and ?user1. The idea now is to execute each of these triples patterns against the database containing the facts. However, to perform an efficient execution, the system needs to find a relevant order, which consists in ordering the triples associated to each variable present in the set V. For example, for the ?user1 variable, which order of the triples patterns 1, 4, and 6 is the most efficient? The same question applies to the ?cat variable: Is performing 2 then 5 more efficient than executing 5 then 2? This is performed using a hash table, where the key is the triples pattern number of the BGP and the value is a pair constituted by an access triples pattern (e.g., spo) and a variable. The access triples pattern corresponds to one of the six triples indexes available for the RDF store: spo, sop, pso, pos, ops, or osp. The heuristic here is the triples pattern order presented in the next section. Intuitively, the fewer variables in the triples pattern, the better.

In addition, variable positions also play an important role. For ?user1, the triples pattern 1 will be executed first and then 4 and 6 (or 6 then 4 because they have the same pattern, ?p? that is variables at the subject and object positions and a known predicate). For the ?cat variable, the order is 2 then 5. So this step terminates by providing a join order and an access path for all BGP triples. The triples patterns are executed in the computed order, retrieving some data bindings for involved variables, including ?user2 in the example. This approach ensures that merge joins are the most efficient forms of joins we can get in this situation. The set of triples patterns of the maximum-weight independent sets are run to completion—that is, they are all being executed. Finally, the remaining triples patterns of the original BGP, just number 3 in the running example, need to be executed to provide the final answer set. The data bindings obtained

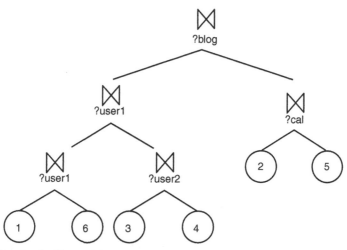

Figure 6.8 Bushy plan for Figure 6.4.

in the previous step are used for the execution of these last triples patterns. That is, the values obtained for the `?user2` variable are joined in a certain way, such as a nested loop or hash, with triples pattern number 3.

The whole process generates the bushy plan shown in Figure 6.8. All joins, except the last two upper ones, correspond to merge joins. As specified earlier, the triples patterns 1 and 2 are the starting points of execution. Note that in the query for Figure 6.4, we did not specify the distinguished variables—that is, the variables present in the SE-LECT clause of the query. The variables are necessarily a subset of the variable set displayed at the top of Figure 6.8.

SPARQL hybrid graph

Another SPARQL graph, proposed in the context of the BitMat RDF store (Atre et al., 2010), is denoted as a *constraint graph* (in reference to the constraint satisfaction domain). It can be considered to mix the variable and join graphs seen earlier. This graph contains two kinds of nodes: one node per triples pattern (denoted `tp` node), and one node per joined variable (denoted `jvar` node). Two `tp` nodes are connected when they share a variable, and this undirected edge is labeled with possibly several labels that correspond to the type of join between the two triples over the same variable. A join type corresponds to a pair of letters in {`S`,`P`,`O`}, which correspond respectively to the subject, property, and object positions in a triple (e.g., `SS` for a subject-to-subject link). Each letter in that pair corresponds to the position of the shared variable in respectively the first and second triple.

Figure 6.9 shows the constraint graph for the BGP in Figure 6.4. The nodes labeled with integer values between 1 and 6 correspond to the `tp` nodes, and the other nodes

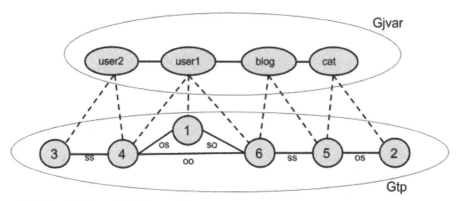

Figure 6.9 Constraint graph for Figure 6.4.

(those with alphabetical labels) are the `jvar` nodes. Between the `tp` nodes 3 and 4, the edge label is `SS` because the only shared variable is `?user2`, which appears in both triples at the subject position. In this constraint graph, multiple labels can exist for an edge when more than one variable is shared between two given triples patterns. Other kinds of edges exist in that graph: undirected and unlabeled edges between `jvar` nodes (when they appear together in the same triple) and between `jvar` nodes and `tp` nodes. Defined as such, the constraint is a hybrid of the join and variable graph. In fact, we can even decompose the constraint graph into `Gjvar` and `Gtp` subgraphs (see Figure 6.8).

 The use of the hybrid graph in the BitMat system can be generalized as follows. The method starts with an initialization step that associates a data structure to each `tp` node. These data structures, denoted `Dtp` with subscripts, contain the data corresponding to the triples pattern. That is, for `tp` node 3 (i.e., `?user2 rdf:type blog:Person`), a single row containing all instances of type `Person` is stored. Then the system is composed of two main steps, a pruning step and a final result generation step. The pruning step starts from the `Gjvar` subgraph and transforms it into a tree if it corresponds to a cyclic graph. Given this tree, a walk over the `jvar` nodes from the root (selected as the variable with the least number of associated `tp` nodes) and back in breadth-first search order is performed. For each `jvar` node walked through, the system computes the intersection on the `jvar` variable bindings retrieved from the data structures associated to the corresponding `tp` nodes. Once this intersection is computed, it helps in removing all values in each `Dtp` that are not in the intersection.

 Let's consider that `jvar` node `?user2` is the root. It's associated to `tp` nodes 3 and 4, which respectively have `Dtp3` and `Dtp4`. Let's assume that an extract of `Dtp3` is the set of persons $\{a,b,c,d,e,f\}$, and `Dtp4` is the set of pairs of persons following each other, $\{(a,b),(b,a),(d,e),(e,d)\}$. The intersection on the `?user2` variable is the set $\{a,b,d,e\}$. And the new `Dtp3` and `Dtp4` are cleaned to respectively become $\{a,b,d,e\}$ and $\{(a,b),(b,a),(d,e),(e,d)\}$. Then the walkover continues, possibly modifying Dtp4 because it can be impacted by the ?user1 variable. On the walk back, Dtp3 can also be modified.

At the end of the tree walk over, all Dtp sets are cleaned of nonquery-relevant values. Then comes the second step, which aims at the reconstruction of the final result from the Dtp sets. In a nutshell, this step can be considered a multiway join between the Dtp structures. Intuitively, the method starts with the Dtp structure with the least triples. It generates bindings for variables in that triple. Next, the system selects another triples pattern that shares a join variable with any of the previously selected triples patterns. It checks if it can generate the same bindings for the shared join variable and generate bindings for the other variables. This process goes on until all triples patterns are processed and all variables have consistent bindings.

6.4.2 Heuristics-based query optimization

In the previous section, we presented three different graph representations that are used to navigate through the joins and/or the variables of a SPARQL query. The descriptions of algorithms using these graphs emphasized that heuristics are needed to select the most cost-effective triples join order. This section presents the most popular heuristics in current RDF stores. Throughout this presentation, the notion of a selectivity condition will appear multiple times. In the context of SPARQL query processing, it amounts to the fraction of triples matching the pattern of a BGP triple. To understand the importance of this notion, consider the BGP in Figure 6.10.

We can easily imagine that there is much more binding for ?x on the first name "John" (let's say 100,000 binding) than there is on the last name "Doe" (let's say 2,000 binding). Therefore, the second triple is more selective than the first one. Considering the execution of the BGP in the order 1. then 2., 100,000 values for ?x will be stored in the main memory to only retain those out of the 2,000 possible ones that have a "Doe" last name. With the order 2. then 1., 2,000 values for ?x will be stored in the main memory and the system will retain only those that have a "John" first name. This simple triples reordering has a big impact on query execution—mainly, the memory footprint required in the second one is way less important (50 times in this example) than the first one. The number of scanned data entries is also less important in the second one.

Next, we distinguish between two forms of heuristics. A first one, based on statistics, is heavily influenced by similar systems in RDBMS. We will see that in the context of RDF

```
1. ?x blog:firstName "John".
2. ?x blog:lastName "Doe".
```

Figure 6.10 Simple BGP example.

triples, it has its limits, but can nevertheless be useful in several situations. The second one is dedicated to triples patterns and their possible occurrences in the context of a BGP.

Statistics-based approaches

The simple triples ordering of the BGP in Figure 6.10 was already influenced by some forms of statistics: we assumed that 100,000 triples were concerned with a "John" first name and 2,000 with a "Doe" last name. Heuristics requiring some precomputed statistics are very common in RDBMSs, and they are usually referred to as *histograms*. Such histograms are hard to compute for RDF graphs due to the absence of a schema. This induces a high join-hit ratio, which requires a complex form of correlated join statistics.

The simplest form of statistics is computed for RDF data sets and does not consider the notion of the joined triples pattern. The statistics are usually denoted as the size of bound triples elements, such as bound subjects, predicates, and objects, and correspond to the average number of RDF triples for an RDF resource. Practically, they are computed as the approximation of the ratio of the number of subjects, respectively predicates or objects, on the total number of triples. Of course, these simple statistics only consider one element at a time, therefore they may be useful for BGP with two variables—that is, only one SPARQL triples pattern is a constant and its statistics are sufficient for a relevant estimation of the selectivity of triples. The selectivity estimation is more complex to compute for SPARQL triples with one variable because the statistics involving the two constants are the most accurate but would also imply an important number of precomputations.

Consider the following example: `s1 p1 ?o`, where `s1` and `p1` are some URIs and `?o` is a variable. Both the `s1` and `p1` statistics do not provide a precise selectivity estimation. For instance, some statistics on the co-occurrence of `s1` and `p1` in the RDF data sets would provide a better one. Having these statistics available at query time implies the precomputation of all combinations of subject/predicate pairs, but also of subject/object and predicate/object pairs. With data sets ranging over millions or billions of triples, this is not a realistic solution due to memory space consumption and precomputation duration. In the presence of an OWL ontology, some of these computations can be avoided. For example, if a property `P` is specified as functional, then we know that for each distinct subject, the maximal number of individuals for that property is one. Note that this implies the existence of a single URI for that instance due to possible `owl:sameAs` assertions for that object. A structure storing equivalences between URIs identifying the same individual could be used to prevent costly joins at query answering time. Nevertheless, for many RDF data sets, either ontologies are not sufficiently defined or they are not available at all.

The Jena TDB system proposes a number of strategies for query optimization. The simplest consists in preventing any triples patterns from reordering—that is, the query is executed as provided by the user or application. It presents an interest where the application queries are known to be optimized by the end-user, and it ensures that no time is lost trying to optimize something that is already optimal. Another one uses a built-in reordering based on the number of variables in a triples pattern (see the next subsection). The most advanced one is based on statistics and has the originality of being tunable per database. In fact, the TDB optimizer exploits a set of rules, stored in a dedicated file, for approximate matching counts of triples patterns. Although a default set of rules can be generated, the end-user has the ability to add, modify, and remove rules. This enables a fine-tuning of the statistics computed for a given database and thus adapts its optimizations to a given domain. The description of the *Statistics Rule Language* enabling the definition of these rules is outside the scope of this book but interested readers can find more details at `http://jena.apache.org/documentation/tdb/optimizer.html`.

The RDF-3X system uses two kinds of statistics. The first approach resembles those of an RDBMS and is based on histograms. To obtain an accurate estimation of join selectivity, the associated structures are quite detailed and compressed to ensure storage in the main memory. All these statistics are computed during the creation of indexes and therefore come at a price of an important time for data preparation and overhead of space consumption. Although the join-size predictions are relatively accurate, the approach requires the assumption of independence between predicates.

The second statistics approach aims at overcoming this independence assumption. Intuitively, a precomputation of frequent paths in the data set is performed and retains exact join statistics. Again, particular attention is given to keep this information in the main memory to prevent additional I/O exchanges during query processing. The general policy of the RDF-3X query optimizer uses join-path cardinalities as a default; when they are not available, the policy is to assume predicate independence and use histograms. Nevertheless, they are both combined to optimize composite queries, involving all kinds of triples patterns.

This statistics-based approach provides sufficient precision for data sets ranging in the millions of triples, but it does not scale to the hundreds of millions or billions of data sets encountered today. To reply to this limitation, the selectivity estimation of RDF-3X was extended with an approach defined in Neumann and Weikum (2009). This approach aims at computing "exact" result cardinalities for single triples patterns that contain at least one variable. This operation is performed at query compile time and is considered to be part of the overall query optimization process. The structures enabling this computation are mainly based on B+trees for which special attention is given to keep them as small as possible through the use of high compression methods. Their creation is performed at the data preparation time, and both their space utilization and processing time are considered to be marginal compared to the overall duration and size required. Therefore, the selectivity estimation only requires at most two lookups in these B+trees.

Graph pattern–based approaches

In Tsialiamanis et al. (2012), a query optimization approach tailored for SPARQL and a storage model corresponding to a single triples table are proposed. The originality of this work consists in not relying on any statistics and solely on heuristics based on the syntactic and structural variations of the query—that is, its set of graph patterns. The algorithm's goal consists in reducing the memory footprint, by minimizing the size of the intermediate results required by the query execution, by maximizing the number of merge joins.

Five optimization heuristics are proposed and can be used in combination or separately. They are using the usual s, p, o, and $?$ symbols to respectively denote subjects, properties, objects, and variables. A first heuristic, denoted *triples pattern order*, is based on the following selectivity-based (i.e., based on the potential number of triples being returned) order of possible BGPs:

$$(s,p,o) \prec (s,?,o) \prec (?,p,o) \prec (s,p,?) \prec (?,?,o) \prec (s,?,?) \prec (?,p,?) \prec (?,?,?)$$

This states that the less variables a graph pattern contains the more selective it is. This is quite obvious because a graph pattern with no variables returns a single triple, while others can generate many triples, all of them in the case with three variables. The ordering of the six inner triples patterns requires some knowledge of RDF data sets. For instance, a graph pattern with a single variable at the property position is more selective than graph patterns with a variable at the subject or object positions. In fact, although possible, it's rarely the case that different properties relate the same subject and object. The order of the graph patterns with two variables considers that less triples are being accessed if one provides the object then the subject then the property. Note that this heuristic matches with other research work on SPARQL query optimization, for example, Stocker et al. (2008).

While the first heuristic concentrates on single triples patterns, a second one considers sets of graph patterns (i.e., a whole BGP) through the combination of their variables. That is, it concentrates on the selectivity of a combination of a pair of graph patterns in the case of variable co-occurrence. The following order can be defined:

$$p \bowtie o \prec s \bowtie p \prec s \bowtie o \prec o \bowtie o \prec s \bowtie s \prec p \bowtie p$$

The most selective pattern denotes two graph patterns such as $(s,?x,o)$ and $(s,p,?x)$—that is, the same variable is present at the property and object positions in two graph patterns in the same query. Obviously this pattern is rarely encountered in real-case queries, as is the $s\bowtie p$. The last four patterns are more suggestive but represent a certain interpretation of practical data sets.

The last three heuristics give more attention on the kind of information encountered in a graph pattern. Intuitively, a literal, necessarily at the object position, is more selective than a URI because it cannot have outgoing edges. Moreover, the more bound components in a graph pattern, the more selective it is. Finally, graph patterns containing nondistinguished variables (i.e., not present in the SELECT clause) should be executed early in the process of query processing.

6.4.3 Access path selection

The last step of the query optimizer we are studying is related to the specification of the access paths to the structures containing the data. In this context, an access path specifies the method for retrieving the data. It could be an expensive sequential scan, or a more efficient index scan when an index matching of the selection conditions of SPARQL BGP exists. The proliferation of indexes in RDF systems presented in Chapter 5 were justified by the efficiency of the index scan (e.g., 15 indexes in RDF-3X). Determining relevant access paths requires a complete overview of the different data structures, logical query plan, and kinds of join algorithms that can ensure an effective query execution.

Concerning join algorithms, the three most popular implementations in RDBMS and RDF stores are nested loop joins, hash joins, and merge joins. For reasons common to RDBMS, merge joins are considered the most efficient ones in a triples context. Therefore, join ordering and access paths try to maximize their occurrences in the physical query plan. For example, due to its high index materialization (i.e., a total of 15 indexes) and adapted join ordering policy, RDF-3X is able to favor fast merge joins. Recall that RDF-3X is storing six clustered indexes on all (S, P, O) permutations— that is, a given data set is persisted in tables SPO, SOP, OSP, OPS, PSO, and POS, together with nine other indexes. Needless to say that the system is equipped with clever strategy is required to identify which clustered index is the most selective.

Nevertheless, this may not always be possible to rely solely on merge joins. In such cases, the order of the result set of previously executed joins may not match the next join to perform. This is either handled by reordering the two entries of this next join (which may be very expensive due its possibly very large size), or by a hash join algorithm or a nested loop one.

As in an RDBMS context, the different joins can be executed in different manners: principally left-deep or bushy joins. The former supports a small memory footprint because intermediary results are extended through the chain of joins. This organization only supports pipeline parallelism. On the other hand, bushy joins may require a larger memory footprint but come with a more important capacity to support join execution parallelism. In Figure 6.8, we provided a representation of a bushy plan for the BGP of Figure 6.4. In Figure 6.11, we present a possible left-deep plan for that same BGP.

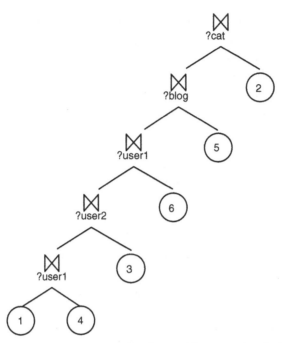

Figure 6.11 Left-deep plan for Figure 6.4 (Note that the variable supporting the join is indicated under the join symbol)

6.5 QUERY EXECUTION

The query execution component applies the physical plan generated by the query optimizer. That plan should ensure a minimal memory footprint and I/O operations, as well as a fast execution time.

Some optimization can be implemented by this component. In Neumann and Weikum (2009), the RDF-3X was extended with a runtime technique aiming at accelerating the execution of queries. This technique, named *sideways information passing* (SIP), is inspired by its equivalent mechanisms encountered in the relational and deductive database ecosystem, but is here adapted to the RDF data model. At the time of its presentation, the designers of this technique highlighted that it could be integrated relatively easily in RDF systems. This has been proven to be true and, since then, several other RDF systems, such as the **IBM** DB2RDF store, have implemented this efficient method.

The full potential of SIP is met in the following situations. Queries implying large index scans are tackling very large RDF graphs. Moreover, the query processing system is supposed to perform index scans and merge joins in parallel—that is, in a pipelined manner. SIP aims at minimizing these index scans and merge joins while enabling communication between operators running in parallel over the same attributes. For example, consider three index scans I1, I2, and I3 with joins between I1 and I2 the result of which is joined to I3. All scans are permitted to obtain the subjects of the triples and run in parallel. If all subjects are retrieved in the same order, then passing information between a selective I3 scan and a nonselective I1 scan can prevent the latter from scanning many values. Moreover, I2 and I3 can also communicate about information on their respective subject values to reduce the amount of data to be read or merged during query execution. Information exchanged concern gaps on considered values. For example, in an extract of subject values (1, 3, 4, 8, 43, 52), it's worth noticing the I1 index scans of the 8 to 43 gaps. Intuitively, it's not necessary for I1 to read subject values in that interval because they will never be joined. Note that this efficient approach only requires the evaluation of operators that can benefit from value-gap information and maintain bookkeeping of relevant gaps in a sorted value list encountered during scans and merges. The former is performed at query compile time and the latter during query runtime.

6.6 QUERY PROCESSING FOR UPDATE QUERIES

In this section, we consider some approaches that are handling update operations—that is, the insertion, deletion, and updates (which can be performed with a DELETE and INSERT statement sequence) of triples—of RDF data in the absence of an underlying ontology. This setting already poses some issues due to the multiple indexing approaches adopted in the most efficient RDF engines contemplated in Chapter 5. For instance, RDF-3X, considered one of the most efficient implementations, has a total of 15 indexes without counting additional structures to handle dictionaries and to provide accurate selectivity estimations. Although demonstrated through evaluations to be very efficient for queries retrieving data, we can ask ourselves how these systems are handling update operations. This question is legitimate due to the maintenance cost that is required on index structures whenever data is modified. Therefore, update operations are rather complex to handle efficiently because they involve writing on the triples storage structure and may also impact many indexes, dictionary maps, and structures supporting data statistics. For example, RDF-3X generally requires the modification of six clustered B+tree-based indexes in the presence of update operations.

In any database management system, the support for update operations considers concurrency control and transactions. These aspects add up to the implementation complexity of a system even for nondistributed engines. As a consequence, very few systems propose an efficient support for updates. We can also consider that the March 2013 SPARQL 1.1 W3C recommendation, which is the first version to address update features in this language, is a justification of the lack of implementations on this important issue. Of course, one can handle an update operation by naively recomputing a set of the storing structures. This approach is highly inefficient and is not adapted to online updates. For example, in the clustered property table proposal, updates over properties in the RDF triples imply to recompute the property clustering and reconstruct the property tables. In the swStore system (Abadi et al., 2009), to prevent inefficient writes to many columns following a data insertion, the following solution is proposed. Online updates are stored in an overflow table that is being periodically scanned to serve materialization of the updates. Obviously, in this context, one cannot expect real-time access to information because no one can guarantee when recently updated data can be retrieved from the query processing engine.

Curiously, the most detailed research and implementation approach is the one supporting the largest number of indexes and additional structures, namely RDF-3X, through its X-RDF-3X extension. This work considers that the kind of updates performed in most RDF engines do not correspond to classic OLTP transactions but can nevertheless pose some consistency problems. In the original RDF-3X system, a deferred-indexing method with no support for transaction processing handles data updates. In a nutshell, all updates are performed in a private program execution workspace. Once that program terminates or issues a save point, the updates are merged into differential indexes shared by all running programs. Finally, each differential index is periodically stored into its corresponding main index by a background process. Of course, this mechanism implies some performance limitations that motivate the design of an extended version. This new method is presented in Neumann and Weikum (2010) and is based on an online maintenance algorithm.

In the presence of an underlying ontology, the support for update operations is even more involved because it has to deal with inferences. That is, in the popular case of inference materialization, an insertion (or deletion) of a single triple may actually impact a large number of triples. The identification of these triples may require interactions with a reasoner. Complete coverage of these issues is contemplated in Chapter 8.

6.7 SUMMARY

- Query processing in RDF stores leverages from the research and development in the field of RDBMS. All non-native RDF engines directly benefit from RDBMS query processing facilities.
- Due to the absence of standards for NoSQL systems, non-native RDF systems using one of these approaches have an entry effort to provide. The lack of stability and maturity of some NoSQL stores may slow the adoption of these technologies for RDF stores.

- With the emergence of very large RDF data sets (several billions of triples), distribution over a cluster of commodity hardware will be more and more frequent. Given a partitioning method, this imposes the consideration of novel query processing methods that will enable us to perform some of the associated tasks in parallel without requiring too much data exchange over a network.

- With the release of the SPARQL 1.1 W3C recommendation and its introduction of the DELETE and INSERT statements, RDF systems are facing important challenges for the efficient management of triples updates. We consider that due to the lack of an efficient implementation, this problem is still open.

- Because many systems are based on multiple indexes, a trade-off will be needed between the efficiency of data retrieving and the cost of updating triples and all associated indexes. This is mainly motivated by the need to maintain indexes when data is updated. In the case of multiple indexes, this can have a dramatic impact on the overall store performance.

- In Chapter 8 we will see that the popular materialization of inferences has an important impact for update operations. Intuitively, inferred data may need to be removed when some new data is deleted from the database, and many new triples may be generated from the insertion of a single triple.

- It seems that in the presence of ontologies, many optimizations can be considered for query processing. Research should be conducted by a collaboration of teams originating from the database and Artificial Intelligence/Semantic Web domains.

CHAPTER SEVEN

Distribution and Query Federation

7.1 INTRODUCTION

The RDF database management systems we have studied so far are characterized as centralized, which means that storage and processing are taken over by a single machine. While being adapted to certain situations, this type of system architecture suffers from many limitations—for example, with Big Data workloads that generally address very large data volumes through distribution and replication. Data and associated processing, such as query answering, are distributed over a set of machines and a lot of benefits are obtained by replicating those data fragments over some of these nodes.

Therefore, for applications facing data deluge constraints, a *distributed database management system* (DDBMS) is required. A DDBMS can be defined as a system where data management is distributed over several computers in a computer network. This field has long research and development histories in the relational data model with systems such as **Ingres** (http://www.actian.com/products/operational-databases) and **System R** (http://www.mcjones.org/System_R/) being designed as early as the beginning of the 1980s. Mainly due to advances in network computing, such as the emergence of the Internet and computer clusters, these systems' features and capacities have evolved since then. This has led to the development of novel distribution approaches and new DDBMS categories like peer-to-peer (P2P) and federated databases.

Being an integral part of the Big Data ecosystems, RDF is totally concerned with the distribution phenomena. Distributed RDF stores have benefited from the experience and results obtained in the relational DDBMS context. Therefore, it's not surprising to more or less observe the same system categories even if the schemaless characteristic of RDF imposes some peculiarities. Figure 7.1 presents a taxonomy of distributed RDF stores.

In homogeneous DDBMS, the nodes that are managing the distributed databases correspond to similar systems. The main architectures for homogeneous DDBMSs are based on P2P or client-server approaches. In contrast, the nodes of a heterogeneous system are supposed to exploit different types of DBMS. We can identify two main kinds of RDF heterogeneous distributed systems depending on the presence of a global schema to mediate the different databases. The mediator-based approach corresponds to the OBDA systems we have already discussed in previous chapters. The solutions that are not

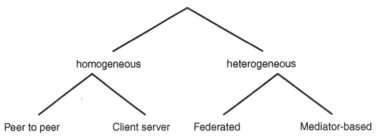

Figure 7.1 Taxonomy of the distributed RDF stores.

requiring a global schema are denoted as *federated* RDF stores. These systems respond to different use cases that we present in the context of our running example.

We consider that the blog web application from our running example has been very successful and now has users all around the world. To ensure good application performances, the RDF blog database is now stored over a cluster of machines that are geographically distributed in Beijing, San Francisco, New York, and Paris. Each of these sites has their own local database which we consider are of the same type. In a first query, we assume that some employees at the headquarters in San Francisco need to retrieve the number of distinct blogs for each category. In the same context, in a second query, someone wants to perform some recommendations over blog entries of the Movie category using the linked movie database (LinkedMDb), which publishes linked open data that can be accessed with SPARQL.

The first query is a typical scenario using a DDBMS. Intuitively, the query has to access the data stored at each location to return the correct result. In Section 7.2, we present the different types of architectures that are used to develop such systems. The second query uses a federated approach. In a nutshell, while some of the data can be locally retrieved from the application nodes, the remaining data is stored on a distant node accessible through a SPARQL endpoint. This form of federated query processing is a main feature of SPARQL 1.1 and is detailed in Section 7.3.

Before delving into the details of these solutions, it's important to stress some of the properties, advantages, and limitations of RDF distributed systems.

7.1.1 Properties

One aspect that is common to the homogeneous and heterogeneous approaches is the notion of transparency, which can take different forms. The most important one from an end-user or application developer point of view is the query transparency. This is expected from the homogeneous and the mediated RDF distributed systems. Intuitively, one writes queries as if the database is centralized—that is, the end user or developer does not need to know that the database is distributed, on which nodes of the cluster some data is stored, etc. In both the homogeneous and mediated systems, the presence of a global schema supports this property. The query processing is thus entrusted with the tasks of translating the original query into a set of queries sent to some of the cluster nodes. This transparency form does not apply to a federated approach, which is characterized by the absence of a global schema. Therefore, the end user has to specify the SPARQL endpoint that can serve some of the triple patterns.

Another form of transparency operates at the schema level—that is, the distributed systems autonomously decide on which node of the cluster to place some data. This mainly concerns the homogeneous system category because, in general, one does not really control that aspect with heterogeneous systems. This property gives the database administrator (DBA) the impression that he or she is administering a centralized database because most of the distribution aspects are taken care of by the software. Anyhow, it's usually preferred, for performance reasons, to give some control on the distribution aspect to the DBA.

Some other forms of transparency have been the subject of a lot of works for the relational model but do not concern, at least for the moment, RDF stores. Take the case of update transparency, which allows database updates to be specified without assuming the distribution aspects. Very few distributed RDF stores are addressing this transparency efficiently. We have already seen in Chapter 5 that very few centralized RDF stores are handling update operations efficiently, especially in a reasoning context. As a consequence, one can understand that transaction transparency has not been the subject of many research projects for RDF stores. This form of transaction aims at ensuring that all distributed transactions maintain the integrity and consistency of the database.

Distributing data over a set of interconnected nodes has many advantages but also comes with limitations that are mainly related to the complexity to implement these systems. We discuss these advantages and limitations next.

7.1.2 Advantages

Many usage improvements can be obtained using a distributed database system reliability, high availability and performance, scalability and data integration. We have stressed that data distribution frequently goes with replication. The benefits that one can obtain with such an approach is an improved *reliability* of the system. For our blog running example, consider that the data fragment containing all the blog categories is stored in all four nodes. That data is still available to the New York, San Francisco, and Beijing nodes even if the Paris node fails. In another scenario, we decide to store the category data at the Paris node only. Then in case that nodes breaks down, neither the New York, San Francisco, nor Beijing nodes can access the categories. A consequence of increased reliability is a *higher availability*, especially compared to a centralized system. In case of a failure, the latter is unable to operate while a distributed system, may still be able to perform some or all operations. That aspect is part of the design of a distributed system.

High performance is obtained due to the following reasons. With a clever data distribution, one can ensure that the data needed for certain queries is stored at nodes that are geographically closer to the emission of those queries. For instance, the French-speaking blog entries are stored at the Paris node, the chinese ones in Beijing. Note that the English speaking blogs are obviously stored at the San Francisco and New York nodes but it may be interesting to persist some of them in Paris (for people from the UK) and Beijing (for people from Australia). Thus sharding the data sets may require more attention than first expected. Thus, all operations emanating from French-speaking countries like France, Belgium, or Switzerland will communicate with the Paris node. This will guarantee faster query answering as a result of fewer network communications. Some queries can also be executed in parallel—that is, the query workload can be distributed to several nodes, each one executing a portion of the total operations. Finally, distributed database systems undertake efficient load balancing of the query operations. Consider that the French-speaking blogs are replicated on several machines at the Paris location. Then all operations at that location should be evenly distributed over the different machines, which will avoid overloading any of the machines.

Load scalability is an important quality of a distributed system. It's known that it's easier to expand a distributed architecture by adding new nodes (i.e., scale out) than to expand a given server with some disks, CPU, or memory (*i.e.*, scale up). It's also financially advantageous to scale out with commodity hardware than to scale up an originally expensive server that is going to constrain the kind of possible expansions to proprietary costly hardware.

Finally, *data integration* is the forte of distributed databases. It's particularly easy to integrate novel data in the case of heterogeneous databases, as one needs to enrich mapping assertions in the mediated approach and write queries that are tackling the right SPARQL endpoint in the federated approach. The effort is more important for homogeneous systems if the data to integrate is not compliant with the target data model but, given the advantages previously cited, it's still easier than in most centralized systems.

7.1.3 Limitations

On the end-user and DBA side, the main limitation is the database *design effort* that requires to address the distribution and replication aspect. That is, deciding how to distribute and replicate the data over a cluster of nodes that could be geographically distant requires a very good understanding of the applications that will invoke the databases and of the query workload (for instance, consider where to store the English speaking blogs in our example).

On the developer of the DDBMS side, the advantages that have just been presented require some major efforts. This complexity implies *security* as well as *consistency* issues when data replication is used.

Finally, the financial advantages have to be contrasted with the *cost* of handling the complexity of the implementation and maintenance level, as well as the cost of hiring experienced developers and DBAs. This justifies that some production-ready systems propose a centralized free version and a commercial distributed one.

7.2 HOMOGENEOUS SYSTEMS

As noted before, in a homogeneous distributed system, all the machines of the cluster are using the same DBMS software. In fact, a homogeneous DDBMS can be considered a centralized database where a set of interconnected machines would transparently handle data storage as well as processing tasks. This characteristic makes the design and management of such systems much easier compared to the heterogeneous systems. This assessment has the following important consequences: it's less demanding to guarantee load scalability by adding new nodes that are running the same system; and one can improve overall system performance by benefiting from parallel processing capacity. Note that, due to a lack of standards, such benefits cannot easily be obtained if different DDBMSs were installed at different nodes.

In a homogeneous system, the distributed processing is generally managed by the DDBMS. Therefore, one has to concentrate on data distribution. A proper design of this distribution has a major impact on the overall performance of the system. This design is impacted by two main factors, fragmentation and allocation, the characteristics of which are detailed in the following sections. Different system architectures can also be adopted for a homogeneous DBMS. In this section, we focus on P2P and client-server (when several clients and servers can be used) architectures, which are particularly popular in distributed RDF stores.

7.2.1 Data fragmentation

Intuitively, data fragmentation concerns the methods used to split the data. In the relational model, horizontal and vertical fragmentations can be used. In the former, the split is performed at the tuple level (i.e., a set of n tuples is stored on each machine), while in the latter, the split is performed at the column level (i.e., a set of m columns is stored on each machine). Some systems also permit a hybrid fragmentation approach that mixes both the horizontal and vertical fragmentations—that is, for a subset of tuples only a subset of the columns are stored at one node of the cluster. Of course, to define an efficient fragmentation strategy, one has to possess a precise understanding of both the database domain and the application(s) (and its query workload) that will access it. Clearly, more applications are accessing the database (possible with different query workloads), the more complex an efficient fragmentation. We can consider that the finer grained the fragmentation (i.e., going into the hybrid one), the more precise the understanding of these parameters. Obviously the manner in which one decides to regroup the tuples or columns has an impact on the overall performance of the system. It's generally assumed that a fragmentation solution is lossless—that is, no data should be lost during the decomposition process and a reconstruction of the original data should be permitted.

In the context of the schemaless RDF data model, we can easily demonstrate that the vertical fragmentation, and jointly the hybrid one, is not an efficient option. The most intuitive form of vertical fragmentation would store the subjects, predicates, and objects of a set of triples at distinct nodes. We can also think of different permutations, such as subjects and predicates on one machine and objects on another one. Similarly, a hybrid fragmentation would imply to store independent subsets of the subjects (respectively predicates and objects) on distinct nodes. Such fragmentations are impractical because they would require joins within a triples pattern as well as joins between triples patterns. All these joins would require communication between nodes of the cluster, which we already stressed is a major performance bottleneck of distributed systems.

It remains that the only viable fragmentation approach for RDF triples is the horizontal one. This corresponds to slicing RDF triples into fragments that will be stored on different machines. In the next section, we present different manners to allocate these triples to different machines.

7.2.2 Data allocation

Data allocation is responsible for the placement of fragments at different nodes of the cluster. Evidently, one can expect this allocation to be optimal in terms of system performance. The allocated data may be replicated at different nodes to improve the reliability and performance of read-only queries but will come at the price of slow query writes or consistency trade-offs (see Chapter 2).

In the context of a distributed RDF store, data allocation can be performed using one of the following practical methods:

- *Random allocation.* Each fragment is randomly stored on one of the cluster machines. In terms of query processing, this approach imposes to send queries to all machines and implies high throughput over the network to compute the queries' final result. Obviously, this is far from ideal because the query processing is highly inefficient in terms of the workload of each node and network communication.
- *Hash-based allocation.* A hash function identifies the machine on which the fragment is to be stored. The hash function operates over a so-called sharding key, which is in many cases the subject of RDF triples; this ensures that all triples with a given subject are stored on the same machine. This approach enables the direct lookup to machines where the triples or quads are stored with a globally known hash function. It's recognized as being efficient for simple index loop queries but not for complex ones, because too many network communications are needed. This approach is used in systems such as YARS2, SHARD, and Virtuoso.
- *Range-based allocation.* This type of allocation stores data entries the sharding keys of which belong to a given range on one particular machine. For example, the sharding key could be the triples subjects and one may decide to store all URIs starting with letters from A to M on machine M1 and those from N to Z on machine M2. This approach supports direct lookups via a global data structure, but is generally associated with data skew because we may end up with a lot more triples on one machine than on another one.

- *Graph partitioning.* This method uses a graph function to split the graph into sub-graphs and stores them on different machines. The main idea is to keep triples that are close to each other in the graph on the same machine. This should limit, at least for certain query classes, the network communication between nodes at query answering time. Graph partitioning is known to be a hard problem that usually requires heuristics and approximation algorithms. Nevertheless, research works such as Huang et al. (2011) and D–SPARQ have tackled this problem for RDF data and have encouraging evaluation results.
- *Query load-based allocation.* This type of allocation considers that one has the typical query workload of the distributed database to model. Given a set of queries, an optimal allocation can be defined—that is, keeping triples that are going to be accessed together at the same nodes to ensure that joins are performed locally. This approach is reminiscent of the denormalization approach we presented in Chapter 2 for RDBMS and NoSQL systems. This method raises several issues, such as the ability to efficiently update the allocation strategy when some new queries are appearing. Moreover, one can ask whether RDF stores are really the kind of DBMS for which the query workload is precisely identified beforehand. **Partout** (Galarraga et al., 2012) is one of the first systems to adopt this approach.

Finally, replication implies that the system stores several copies of the same fragment on different machines. This enables us to increase the availability of the data (because the same fragment can be accessed from different machines) and to support faster query evaluation for simple read queries requiring an access to a fragment stored at the same location or when a parallel query processing is developed. In cases where triples updates are supported, which is rarely the case, the replicas have to be maintained. This can be performed through different approaches that can be categorized as synchronous or asynchronous.

Synchronous replication is considered to be very costly because it generally requires one to obtain exclusive locks on all copies of the modified fragment. This introduces some latencies and can even prevent some transactions to run to completion. For these reasons, asynchronous replication is used more often in recent database management systems like **NoSQL** and **NewSQL**. It can, nevertheless, bring some temporary inconsistencies among fragments stored at different machines. For example, a fragment stored on machines M1 and M2 may have different states for a short period of time, known as the *inconsistency window*.

7.2.3 Architectures

In this section, we present the two most common types of architecture for homogeneous distributed RDF stores: peer-to-peer and client-server.

7.2.3.1 Peer-to-peer (P2P)

In P2P systems, there is no centralized control or hierarchical organization. Therefore, the systems running at each node are all equivalent. Compared to a client-server system, we can consider that each P2P node acts as both a client and server because it's able to both send a request to another node and respond to a request. In general, a P2P network implements a kind of virtual overlay network on top of a physical network. Via a logical overlay connection, peers are able to communicate between each other, and the real data exchanges are being performed on the underlying physical network.

There exists several forms of P2P networks that are differentiated according to the kind of possible peer links and the method used to index and locate resources. In *unstructured P2P networks*, such as **Napster**, **Gnutella**, and **Gossip**, no particular structures are imposed to the overlay network. This permits us to easily build and maintain such networks, but it also comes with poor query performances because queries must be flooded through the network to search for a given resource. *Structured P2P networks*, such as **Chord**, **Can**, and **Pastry**, impose a specific topology to the overlay network and guarantee efficient searches of resources. The most common approach of structured P2P networks is to implement a distributed hash table (DHT) to identify and locate nodes and resources. This approach supports efficient query facilities but comes at the price of the DHT maintenance, such as to discover and advertise resources, and difficulties in providing efficient load balance.

Given this definition, we can state that in a P2P RDF data management system, both RDF triples and indexes are distributed and maintained over a P2P network. A cooperation among the peers is required to build a distributed index. The efficiency of this cooperation has a major impact on the overall performance of the system. The system also aims to load balance both the data storage and processing tasks in the most optimal manner.

The first P2P-based RDF stores were defined using unstructured P2P networks. This is the case of **Edutella** (Nejdl et al., 2001), which is based on Gnutella. The system suffers from the absence of a centralized index and does not possess a method to locate RDF triples over the network. Therefore, its only query solution is to send a given query (expressed in RDF-QEL in the case of that system) to all the nodes. Each node locally processes the query, possibly with no results, and the final answer set is computed from each node's result. It has been demonstrated that this large query flooding prevents Edutella from scaling to a large number of nodes.

Nejdl et al. (2003) is a successor to Edutella that overcomes some of the scalability issues. Better performances are obtained by introducing the storage of metadata about the content present at each node. This approach is denoted as a schema-based P2P network because the metadata are used for routing purposes. To prevent sending queries to unnecessary peers and overwhelming consumption of the network, a superpeer topology for the schema-based networks is proposed. There, each peer connects to a single superpeer, and they are all interrelated to create a superpeer network. Thus, these superpeers determine the peers and superpeers that will receive queries. Two limitations are the need for an upfront definition of schemas and the identification of superpeers.

RDFPeers (Cai and Frank, 2004) is the first distributed RDF store that uses a structured P2P network. It provides storing, indexing, and querying using RDQL since SPARQL was only in the early draft stages at the W3C. The system stores each triple at three different places in a *multi-attribute addressable network* (MAAN) by using several globally known hash functions to retrieve respectively the subject, predicate, and object entries of RDF triples. In a nutshell, MAAN (Cai et al., 2003) extends the P2P DHT Chord protocol (Stoica et al., 2001) to support range and multi-attribute queries. RD-FPeers has several limitations: load balancing is not guaranteed because nodes storing popular entries will rapidly be overwhelmed; each triple is replicated three times due to the three-way indexing approach; and queries with low selectivity may suffer suboptimal performances.

MIDAS-RDF (Tsatsanifos et al., 2011a) is a recent P2P RDF store that addresses some of the drawbacks of Edutella and RDFPeers and supports some novel features. For instance, it does not store duplicates of RDF triples and provides an effective routing solution. Through a distributed multidimension index structure, it's able to support an efficient range search over the overlay network. It also implements reasoning services for the RDFS entailment regime.

7.2.3.2 Client-server

Client-server architectures (a.k.a. master–slave) are based on communication protocols that enable one node, the client (slave), to send requests to another node, the server (master), which returns a response to that client. In the rest of this chapter, we respectively use server and client interchangeably with master and slave.

It's possible to implement many variants based on this architecture. In a strict master–slave system, every node of the network has a fixed role and nodes of the same type do not interact (e.g., no communications between clients). This enables us to designate a particular node as the master, given its processing and memory capacity, to manage appropriately the expected workload. Note that most commercial RDBMSs use a strict client-server architecture. Other architectures may permit to have more than one master or allow interclient communications. Among the RDF stores adopting a client-server architecture, several recent ones are using the MapReduce framework. The master corresponds to the so-called *job tracker*, which runs on a single server, and the slaves are task trackers that run on the remaining nodes of the cluster. In short, when a job is submitted to the MapReduce framework, the master breaks the job into several tasks that are run by the slaves.

In this chapter we focus on systems either using an RDF store for the storage layer, such as Huang et al. (2011), or on approaches based on MapReduce together with a *distributed file system* (DFS), such as Hadoop DFS. Moreover, we provide some additional information on some of the systems that were presented in Chapter 5, such as Trinity.RDF and Virtuoso.

Yars2 (Harth et al., 2007) is based on the **Yars** system, introduced in Chapter 5 as a native system. It provides distributed indexing methods and parallel query evaluation methods. The cluster is made up of commodity hardware and a shared-nothing architecture. Based on the fact that it stores quads, the system proposes three different forms of indexes:

1. A keyword index that uses **Apache Lucene** as an inverted index to map terms occurring in RDF objects to subjects.
2. Six quad indexes (motivated by the use of prefix lookups) based on sparse indexes (indexes are in-memory and six sorted files are stored on disk and Huffman encoded).
3. Join indexes to speed up queries containing combinations of values or paths in the graph. The partitioning method is hash based. The distributed query processor uses lookup requests performed in parallel.

The data model of **4Store** (Harris et al., 2009) has already been presented in Chapter 5. This distributed system is based on shared-nothing master–slave architecture. It constitutes processing and storage nodes that persist data fragments in a nonoverlapping manner (called segments in the paper but that correspond to our notion of fragments). Each machine of the cluster can store one or more fragments. The method for computing fragments is kept simple and is based on the integer value attributed to each subject, denoted RID, modulo the number of fragments. Of course, this solution does not prevent data skew. The problem is known by the designers of the system, but they claim that for commonly encountered data sets, the distribution among fragments is acceptable.

For SPARQL triples patterns where the subject is not known, the fragmentation approach forces us to send the query to all storage nodes. The allocation method is also based on a simple modulo operation. The system supports replication of fragments of several storage nodes. In terms of communication, 4Store permits an exchange between processing and storage nodes via TCP/IP with a single connection established per segments between processing and storage nodes. This enables us to process some queries in parallel because several requests can be sent to different segments at the same time. In such a situation, the performance bottleneck is the slowest storage node. Note that no direct communication is allowed between storage nodes. Query processing is coordinated by a single processing node. The joins of a SPARQL BGP are executed on this node exploiting access paths reading data on storage nodes. To assemble the results, the system disposes of two operations: bind (to perform binding on several nodes) and resolve (to map an RID to attribute RIDs and the lexical value of the RID). The query processor is inspired by the standard relational algebra with specific optimizations related to the selectivity of the bind operations. Currently, 4Store does not support update operations efficiently but it proposes reasoning services (see Chapter 8) and full text search.

The approach adopted in Huang et al. (2011) is based on a master–slave architecture. The master handles the fragmentation and allocation tasks and also supervises query processing. Each slave is composed of the following components: an RDF store system (e.g., RDF-3X) and a data replicator component. Compared to the other systems presented in this chapter, the main originality is to propose a fragmentation approach that is based on a graph partitioning algorithm. That is, the RDF data set is analyzed as a graph and the partitions are defined according to the graph's topology. The main motivation against a hash-based partitioning is to allow nodes of the RDF graph that are close together to be stored on the same machine of the cluster. This is aimed at limiting the amount of network communication between nodes of the cluster when answering a query. While this approach enables us to execute some queries in parallel without any internode communication, some more complex queries require such network exchanges.

The identification of such queries is performed by the master and the execution is performed through some Hadoop jobs. Of course, this dramatically slows down the execution time due to the inherent starting time of the Hadoop framework. To limit the number of queries requiring this approach, a data replication approach is used. The principle is to replicate nodes at the boundary of graph partitions on each partition. This approach is denoted as the *n-hop guarantee*. The higher the *n* value, the higher the replication rate. So, selecting the *n* value amounts to finding a trade-off between communication and storage overhead. The paper experiments with *n* values of 1 and 2. The computation of the *n*-hop guarantee is also performed through MapReduce jobs, but the allocation overload is not considered to be a critical performance bottleneck because it's performed once when loading the data set. Note that the paper does not consider update operations.

Some information on **Trinity.RDF** (Zeng et al., 2013) has already been provided in Chapter 5. The system's architecture is composed of three types of computing nodes: a so-called string server (corresponding to a dictionary as presented in Chapter 4), a query proxy, and a set of Trinity machines. The query proxy receives the SPARQL queries, generates a query plan that is sent to the Trinity machines, and receives the intermediary results that are gathered together to produce the final answer. Efficient query plans are generated from statistics and indexes information possessed by the query proxy. This component is also aware of the status of each Trinity machine during the query processing phase. A Trinity machine corresponds to a key-value store and is responsible for storing a set of RDF triples, executing the query plans it receives on its own data set, and sending its results to the query proxy.

Trinity machines can also communicate between each other regarding intermediary results. The method used for such communications is based on a message-passing approach that is built in Trinity. The graph model is designed on top of the key-value store and makes an intensive use of adjacency lists. Intuitively, the string server component provides a unique identifier to each RDF triples subject and object that correspond to a graph node. The default approach uses these identifiers as a key and places two adjacency lists in the value position. The first one corresponds to the incoming pairs—that is, a pair composed of the predicate and subject identifiers of a triple—while the second list corresponds to outgoing pairs—that is, a pair composed of predicate and object identifiers of a triple. Based on this approach, a random partitioning approach is achieved by Trinity.

The main limitation with this solution is related to a possible data skew that may occur if some nodes have a high connection degree while some others have low ones. A second graph model and another partitioning method is then proposed. In terms of the graph model, the adjacency lists of the previous model are decomposed in such a way that pairs are associated to some keys. These keys are themselves stored as the key for the subject and object keys. The partitioning idea is to store the incoming keys and nodes of the adjacency node list on the same machine. The storage cost of the second model is more important than the first one but prevents data skew and limits communication between Trinity machines. A threshold approach has been defined to automatically select between the two approaches. The adopted graph perspective enables a navigation approach to query answering. That is, instead of relying on join algorithms, the system exploits some graph methods such as checking if a path exists between a set of nodes. This approach is also motivated by the ability to support novel query operations, such as to compute similarity between nodes, random walks, and community detection.

The Enterprise edition is the most complete system version of the **GraphDB** family, formerly OWLIM. It aims at managing and synchronizing multiple GraphDB instances, namely the GraphDB standard edition, in a resilient and scalable cluster configuration. By doing so, it permits the design of parallel query processing. The architecture is based on a master–slave approach but permits several masters that can control several workers nodes. The multiple masters' configuration prevents the issues related to a single point of failure. The masters do not store any data, they just route queries to the set of workers they manage. Nevertheless, they maintain the state of their worker nodes. Updates are also handled by masters. Given an update operation, the master will communicate with the worker possessing the data to be modified. If that worker is not available, then that situation can be resolved thanks to two distinct replication strategies: incremental or full replication. In both cases, once the worker is available again, the master will try to synchronize its state with the worker replicating its data. This can be performed incrementally by running some missing transactions or by running a full state copy from one machine to the other. In that case, both workers cannot be accessed for other update operations. Considering worker nodes, failover and load balancing are processed automatically.

The journal version of **Bigdata** was presented in Chapter 5. In a nutshell, it's a key-value store with a RDF graph abstraction on top of it. The graph data uses a similar indexing approach to the YARS project. It's announced to scale up to 50 billion on a single machine. Two other versions of the system exist: highly available replication cluster (**HAJournalServer**) and horizontally sharded cluster (**BigdataFederation**). The

HAJournalServer follows a high-availability architecture where all the data is kept on all nodes. This permits the server to answer queries using a single node and therefore to perform efficient load balancing. When data needs to be updated, the data is replicated using a low-level write replication that uses a two-phase commit approach. The cluster uses a quorum-based replica control protocol. It's used to ensure that two copies of the same data item cannot be read or written by two concurrent transactions. When some nodes are rejoining the cluster, a playback of committed transactions, from an elected quorum leader, of that data set are executed to ensure that the node's state is up to date.

For data sets exceeding this volume, the BigdataFederation is considered the best choice. It enables us to distribute the workload and the data over a cluster of machines. This is obtained using a sharding approach based on dynamic key-range partitioning, which supports incremental growth and easier rebalancing. Intuitively, the indexes are split into shards at runtime. First, they are place on some nodes but can then move across nodes to improve load balancing. As shards get bigger, they are broken automatically and distributed over the cluster. A shard locator service supports clients to locate the needed data and therefore to send queries to the nodes possessing the right data. Just like in the HAJournalServer version, it uses a two-phase commit and requires all nodes to be available. In case a given node fails, the remaining nodes can still serve reads but writes will not be accepted.

In Chapter 5 we presented the open-source single-machine version of **Virtuoso**, but **OpenLink** also produces a commercial version that permits the distribution over a machine cluster. Two partitioning strategies are proposed. The first one consists of a data replication and therefore enables high availability. Considering that first aspect, Virtuoso is quite flexible and proposes several replication solutions. A common one is transactional replication, i.e., replicating transaction data, which can be performed either in a one way (from publisher to subscribers) or in a bi-directional manner. A two way synchronization to non Virtuoso servers, e.g. Oracle, MS SQL Server, IBM DB2, is also supported. These two mechanisms come with support for conflict resolution, i.e., detect whether an update has been correctly replicated to a subscriber. The second strategy is based on partitioning that is specified at the index level using a hash function on key parts. Each partition is replicated on different physical machines to ensure load balancing and fault tolerance. When triple updates are being performed, all copies are updated within the same transaction.

The clustering approach of the **Mark Logic** system distinguishes between two kinds of nodes: data managers (denoted as D-nodes) and evaluators (denoted as E-nodes). The D-nodes are responsible for the management of a data subset, while the E-nodes handle the access to data and the query processing. A load balancer component distributes queries across E-nodes. Both the set of D-nodes and E-nodes are handled dynamically to ensure high availability and query answering performance. That is, if more data needs to be stored, more D-nodes are added to the cluster, and if the query load increases, more

E-nodes are introduced in the infrastructure. The same physical machine can act as both kind of nodes; in fact, this corresponds to a single-host environment. In the situation where an E-node fails, the load balancer just needs to send the query to another running E-node. In case of a D-node failure, the data is still needed to answer the query. This can be resolved via a replication approach (the data fragment stored by the failing system is also stored on some other known D-nodes) or with a clustered file system. Finally, note that Mark Logic uses MapReduce to ingest, transform, and export large volumes of data in a bulk processing manner.

SHARD (Scalable High-Performance, Robust, and Distributed; Rohloff and Schantz, 2010) is a triple store designed on top of Hadoop. It relies on this framework for both the data persistence and query processing aspects. Considering data storage, RDF triples are stored in flat files in the HDFS file system. Each line of these flat files is organized as a single key-value pair where the key is the subject of any triple and the value is a set of predicate/object pairs associated to that subject. This approach is similar to the way **HBase** stores its data on disk. This flat file organization is adapted to the MapReduce approach, which expects key-value pairs as entries. Nevertheless, it's inefficient in terms of data redundancy (because some subjects frequently appear as the object of other triples), and it provides a single index on the subject. That second aspect is supposed to be taken care of by parallel query processing, which uses the Hadoop framework. Intuitively, each triples pattern of a SPARQL query is handled by an iteration of a MapReduce operation. The variable binding obtained at one iteration is assigned to the SPARQL triples patterns that have not yet been executed. A final MapReduce set is performed to filter the distinguished variables (those present in the SELECT clause) and to remove duplicates.

The **D-SPARQ** system (Mutharaju et al., 2013b) also uses MapReduce to distribute triples over a cluster of MongoDB instances. Like in Huang et al. (2011), some triples in the boundary of fragments are replicated. The fragmentation approach is based on subject values, ensuring that all triples of a given subject value are stored in the same document. This enables very efficient processing of star queries where the subject is the central node. To support effectively the other query patterns, compound indexes are created on subject–predicate and predicate–object pairs. Like all other systems, query optimization concentrates on triples pattern join ordering. Intuitively, after parsing a SPARQL query, it tries to identify triples patterns, such as star or pipeline shaped. Given the identified patterns, it tries to parallelize the retrieval of data from the different nodes using some specific strategies for efficient triples join ordering.

Other systems developed in an academic context include **HadoopRDF** and **PigSPARQL** (Schätzle et al., 2013). In HadoopRDF, most of the database jobs are performed by the Hadoop using some internal rules. For instance, this is responsible for storing the RDF triples in slave nodes, which correspond to RDF stores, instead of HDFS. With PigSPARQL, the data is stored in HDFS and the SPARQL queries are translated to PigLatin, which can then be executed in parallel by the Hadoop framework.

7.3 HETEROGENEOUS SYSTEMS

7.3.1 Query federation

RDF is the cornerstone of the Web of Data movement. This is an information space where certain queries can only be answered by retrieving results stored across different data sources. This is motivated by the fact that data is often owned and controlled by external independent providers that did not consent on a data schemata and/or may not provide access to raw data. This requires a new approach, denoted as query federation, where a query processor permits us to access data that may be stored on heterogeneous DBMSs. For example, the data needed to answer a query is present on a local DBMS produced by a given vendor as well as on some distant, possibly different, DBMSs. Note that in theory, these DBMSs may accept different query languages, forcing the federation query engine to go through some query translations.

In the case of RDF stores, this is rarely the case, and most systems support SPARQL. In this context, different types of query federation can be defined that differ on the access mechanism at the sources. In the most popular one, the data is accessed through SPARQL endpoints—this is the case for the **FedX, LHD, Splendid, Anapsid,** and **DARQ** systems. These systems are generally associated with time-efficient query federation solutions but depend on the availability of those SPARQL endpoints (see Aranda et al., 2013 for an evaluation of this aspect). Another solution is based on the Linked Data movement; **LDQP** (Ladwig and Tran, 2010) and **WoDQA** (Akar et al., 2012) are such systems, and they only require that the Linked Data principles (`http://esw.w3.org/SweoIG/TaskForces/CommunityProjects/LinkingOpenData`) are respected. Intuitively, four rules have to be addressed: (i) use IRIs to name things, (ii) use HTTP IRIs to support the ability to dereference, (iii) provide metadata about those things, leveraging from RDF and SPARQL standards, and (iv) enrich with links to other things. This approach complements the previous solution but is considered to be slower due to URI lookups. Finally, some systems enable access to data stored in DHTs, such as the **Atlas** system (Kaoudi et al., 2010). While being space and bandwidth consumption efficient, very few RDF data sets are being proposed with this kind of architecture.

Query federation provides two main benefits: it scales easily and makes data management simpler. That is, as long as our federation query engine supports one or all previously cited access methods, we can still refer to new data sources in the submitted queries. Data management cannot be easier because most of the time we do not have to manage the data we are accessing through our queries. Query federation also comes with other advantages. By providing a natural mechanism to put together heterogeneous triples stores, it allows us to load data in a parallel fashion on multiple CPUs and combine them at query time. Thus, it scales easily on demand. Moreover, by virtually combining heterogeneous data into a single store, it makes it easy to connect multiple stores together. It allows the user to explore the data without worrying about the origin of the triples. Even more interesting, it allows the user to store different kinds of data separately and combine them on demand when needed.

7.3.1.1 Challenges
Even though there are many advantages, there are still challenges when considering federated query processing. First, a query federation system should involve only relevant data sources when answering a given query to avoid subqueries being sent to all data sources. Next, for performance purposes, subquery joins should be done as close as possible to the data to avoid a unique set of joins in a nested loop manner from the query processor. Finally, a federation system should reduce as much as possible unnecessary data transfer between the mediator and the data sources. Note that the first two challenges already contribute to the last one.

To identify suitable data sources for a given subquery and optimize the query execution, several types of federated systems have been defined that can be classified as indexed-assisted and index-free. With an index-assisted system, the federated engine maintains a set of indexes that will be used for the sources selection. In an index-free system, other mechanisms can be used. For instance, sending ASK queries or retrieving, just before query federation, information just as data set statistics and bandwidth availability of involved SPARQL endpoints.

In index-assisted systems, data sources are supposed to provide some statistics on the data, such as the number of occurrences of each triples entity. The query federation system needs to aggregate all these statistics into a federation index that will coordinate the interactions between the data sources. Note that this approach is quite reminiscent of the statistics we were talking about in Chapter 6. There, we were arguing that complete statistics (histograms like in RDBMSs) are too eager in terms of computation time and space required to be stored. In a query federation context, the statistics are computed and maintained on different servers. Such servers provide an access to these information through a service. Nevertheless, a compromise between accuracy and index size is needed. Indeed, the more detailed the data statistics, the better the query optimization results can be achieved. Although the increasing amount of statistics implies storing a larger index structure, federation systems have to find the right trade-off between efficiency and resource consumption. Moreover, the aggregation of statistics implies that it should be updated regularly to take into account data sources changing over time. Such update processes should be guided by the data sources or derived on-the-fly by data extracted from query results.

The statistics are also intensively used to optimize query execution. As stated in Chapter 6, the execution order of query operators has a huge influence on overall query execution time. But this is not specific to query federation systems. Query optimization in a federation context includes aspects related to the distribution of the data. First, a federation system should minimize communication cost. This is directly related to the number of contacted data sources that may lead to communication overhead. However, minimizing data sources may induce incompleteness of results, and, yet again, a trade-off should be found by the federation system. Next, considering subqueries, most of the data sources are not capable of answering queries on other data than their own. Thus, as already mentioned, join operations are usually handled by the query issuer (i.e., the mediator). A better strategy would be to do some of the join operations in parallel in the data sources. Finally, considering large results that, despite an efficient query execution, may take a while to be retrieved, a better strategy may be to return the results as soon as they become available and apply a streaming strategy for the mediator.

7.3.3.2 SPARQL and query federation

A query federation system refers to any system providing a unique interface to multiple data sources. SPARQL is considered a multidatabase query language that requires the data sources to be explicitly specified. As previously observed, at a query level, techniques allowing us to obtain efficient query computation in a distributed setting have to be developed. In SPARQL 1.1, merging queries can be done through the SERVICE and VALUES keywords. While the SERVICE keyword allows us to invoke a specific SPARQL endpoint for a subquery, the VALUES keyword allows us to transfer the result of a subquery to an outer query. Even if the SPARQL recommendation does not specify how, query federation is needed for the virtual integration of RDF data sets. Indeed, in addition to a possible overhead in network traffic, loading all RDF graphs to a local machine may not even be possible for legal and technical reasons—for example, it may not be allowed to create copies of the data due to copyright issues, and up-to-date data may not even be available, such as data with a high modification rate or data created on-the-fly.

In Chapter 3, we presented the difference between the FROM and SERVICE keywords. Remember that the FROM keyword allows us to identify a data set to query, which may be a local or remote file to query. The corresponding query or subquery retrieves data from the local or remote location and then applies a query to it. The SERVICE keyword, instead of pointing at an RDF file, points at a SPARQL endpoint. Therefore, the SERVICE keyword asks to transfer the corresponding query to the specified SPARQL endpoint service, which will run it and return the result.

The use of the SERVICE keyword may result in an execution failure for multiple reasons. First, the corresponding SPARQL endpoint may be down. Then, the corresponding URI may not be dereferenceable. Finally, the SPARQL endpoint may return an error concerning the query itself. In any of these cases, the whole query corresponding to the SERVICE pattern will fail. In order not to spread the error to the encapsulating query, one can explicitly allow the failure of the SERVICE request by using the

SILENT keyword. The SILENT keyword indicates to the endpoint that related errors should be ignored while processing the full query. The SERVICE subquery results in a single empty solution without bindings.

For example, considering the following query with the SILENT keyword, in case of an error, the SERVICE request will return a solution sequence of one empty solution mapping. If the SILENT keyword is not present, the query will stop and return the error.

```
PREFIX blog: <http://example.com/Blog#>
PREFIX ex:   <http://example.com/terms#>
SELECT DISTINCT ?name (COUNT(?blog) AS ?nbBlog)
WHERE {
  SERVICE SILENT <http://someSPARQLendpoint.com> {
    ?user     ex:firstName     ?name ;
              ex:lastName      "Doe" ;
              blog:isFollowing ?user2 ;
    ?blog     blog:owner       ?user .
  }
}
```

7.3.3.3 Components

As pointed out in Görlitz and Staab (2011), a federation system is based on basic components: a declarative query language, a data catalog, a query optimizer, and a data protocol. The declarative query language, SPARQL, allows us to formulate concisely complex queries by providing a flexible way to express constraints on data entities and relations between them. The data catalog aims at mapping query expression to data sources and vocabularies for detection of similar terms. The query optimizer is needed to minimize processing and communication costs when retrieving data from different sources. Finally, the data protocol defines how information (queries and results) is exchanged between the sources.

7.3.2 Systems

Splendid (Gorlitz and Staab, 2011) tackles SPARQL endpoints but combines an index-assisted system with ASK queries, therefore it can be considered a hybrid approach, to provide optimal source selection and query routing efficiency. Both the source selection and query optimization are automatically processed and rely on statistical information provided by VoID (vocabulary of interlinked data sets) descriptions. VoID takes the form of an RDF schema that supports the description of metadata about RDF data sets. It's targeting applications aiming for the discovery, archiving, and cataloging of RDF data sets, and can thus assist end users willing to design such applications. Some of these statistics correspond to the number of triples; the number of entities; the number of distinct subjects, predicates, and objects; and the number of triples per predicate.

In the Index Manager, a component of Splendid, the statistics from VoID are aggregated in a local index. The local index takes the form of two inverted indexes, one for predicates and another one for types. Both these indexes have the same structure: they store the predicate or type as a key and contain a pair consisting of data source and number of occurrences as a value. Therefore, one can easily find how many times a given predicate appears in a given data source. Splendid's local index may not be precise enough to determine which data source to use. In that case, ASK queries are submitted to potential targets, usually by including the triple pattern of the original SPARQL query. Because ASK queries return a Boolean result, the system can easily make decisions about which data source to submit subqueries to. Two join execution strategies have been implemented. In a first one, results obtained from different data sources on the same variable binding are joined locally at the federation query engine. This approach is valuable for small intermediate results. The second one substitutes unbound variables with values obtained from previous triples patterns with the same variables. This approach limits network communications because only variable values are sent over the network.

FedX (Schwarte et al., 2011; `http://www.fluidops.com/fedx/`) is a framework developed by **FluidOps** for transparent access to sources through a query federation and available as an open-source software. FedX extends the **Sesame** SAIL (Sesame's storage and inference layer) API with a query federation layer enabling efficient query processing on distributed sources. FedX adopts an index-free approach that works as follows. It parses the global query and splits it into local subqueries that can be answered by individual data sources. That global query is optimized taking into account the distribution aspect. More specifically, it's split into local subqueries that are going to be answered by identified SPARQL endpoints. The obtained results are later merged by the FedX system and returned in aggregated form. The reduction of the number of intermediate results is guaranteed by the combination of an applied join-order optimization and grouped subqueries. It does not rely on precomputed statistics for query optimization and uses ASK queries and the maintenance of ASK histories to select sources. Some of the optimizations are as follows:

- To push SPARQL filter expressions that are placed in the execution list to permit early evaluations.
- All SPARQL statements are examined for their relevant data sources to avoid unnecessary communication during query processing.
- Heuristics are used to estimate the cost of each join.
- Statements with common pertinent data sources are executed together in a single SPARQL query to push joins to the particular endpoint.
- Joins are computed in a block nested loop join.

The **DARQ** system (Quilitz and Leser, 2008) is a full-featured query federation engine that is index-assisted and therefore maintains its own set of statistics and does not rely on any online mechanisms to select the sources. The source selection, query decomposition, and optimization tasks are supported by so-called service descriptions. It's defined using an RDF formalism and aims at declaring data available at endpoints in the form of capabilities. These capabilities specify what kind of triples patterns can be answered at a data source. They are only defined in terms of predicates and constraints on subjects and objects. The constraints correspond to SPARQL filter expressions and help in selecting sources more accurately. Service descriptions also permit the definition of access pattern limitations. This takes the form of patterns that must be included in a query and a pair of predicate sets that have to be bound to a subject (respectively, an object). The query optimization task benefits from statistics harvested from the sources. The statistics do not exploit VoID and are kept simple to simplify the processing and limit the size of stored information.

Along basic triples and entity counts, DARQ also provides average selectivity estimates for combinations of subject, predicate, and object. Moreover, it integrates restrictions on satisfiable access patterns on all three types of triples entities. Performing source selection implies matching the triples patterns of a query with capabilities of the sources. The DARQ approach assumes that the predicates of the SPARQL triples patterns are also specified—that is, variables appear solely at the subject and object positions. Given discovered matchings, subqueries are generated and sent to the corresponding data sources. These subqueries are optimized with the same perspective as the previously presented systems—that is, by minimizing the size of intermediate results—and reduce the amount of data transferred over the network.

The **DAW** (Duplicate Aware Federated Query Processing) system (Saleem et al., 2013) is motivated by the fact that very few federated query processing solutions evaluate the data duplication rate among candidate sources. Performing such an evaluation would enable us to avoid querying certain sources. Therefore, less sources would be required to answer a query. That would have the effect of improving query execution time as well as reducing the network bandwidth usage. Proposing such an approach is exactly the purpose of DAW, which is not a complete federated query processor but rather a system that runs on top of an existing one (the system has been evaluated on top of Splendid, DARQ, and FedX). Two main tasks are composing DAW. First it is ranking sources considering their contribution to the new query results. Second it is skipping sources whose contributions to the query is considered insufficient. This performed by computing the minimum percentage of new results a source contributes to. If that percentage is below an automatically and dynamically computed threshold, the source is skipped. Note that the skipping step assumes that the query answer set may be incomplete. Nevertheless, DAW evaluations emphasized that with a proper threshold, good query recall can be obtained. The ranking and skipping steps are based on indexes maintained by the DAW system. This uses the min-wise independent permutation (MIP) statistical synopsis approach. Intuitively, for each property of a data set source, some information is computed and stored using compact data structures that can support efficient union and intersection operations.

Another optimization level can be performed by detecting the sources that could contribute to a triple pattern but that will later be discarded due to joins with other triple patterns from the same query. Several systems have tackled this issue, which can be qualified as join-aware, in opposition to the triple pattern–wise source selection approach. It's obvious that efficient join-aware solutions can help to reach a new level of query execution performances and reduce the amount of network communications when answering a federated query. The **Anapsid** system (Acosta et al., 2011) was one of the first solutions to address that problem through the development of an extension that was evaluating namespaces and sending ASK queries to data sources at runtime. Recently, the **HiBISCuS** system (Saleem and Ngomo, 2014) showed better overall results by relying on stored indexes. Its approach is based on modeling SPARQL queries as directed-labeled hypergraphs. Based on this representation, algorithms have been designed to support discarding nonrelevant sources based on the types of joins present in the query. Just like DAW, HiBISCuS is an approach that can be used on top of existing federated query engines.

TopBraid Insight (`http://www.topquadrant.com/products/topbraid-insight/`) is defined as a "semantic virtual data warehouse with federated query capabilities." Its features make a production-ready system that eases the discovery of valuable information across a set of data sources. End users first exploit the graphical user interface (GUI) to gather data sources of interest in so-called ConnectSets, which can then be queried to create ExploreSpaces. These ExploreSpaces are stored and can be shared among users to reply to novel queries. This discovery aspect is generally considered as the main difficulty when one starts to use query federation in a given application domain. At the core of the TopBraid Insight system are the RDF and SPARQL technologies, which are transparent to the GUI end users but can be used through APIs by developers.

7.3.3 Mediator-based

Mediator-based information systems are another solution to provide a single interface to several data sources. In this type of system, an integrated schema is assumed to integrate the schema of the different data sources. The queries are then defined in a query language supported by the mediator system and are expressed in terms of entities of the integrated schema.

This kind of system corresponds to the OBDA approach we have already encountered in previous chapters. In these systems, the data sources generally correspond to RDBMSs, but some research has been conducted to also tackle XML and NoSQL stores. The integrated schema is represented as an ontology, usually expressed in the OWL2QL fragment, which has especially been defined for this purpose. Of course, OBDA makes sense in this chapter if distinct data sources can be integrated in the mediated schema and if queries combining several of these data sources can be efficiently computed. A crucial aspect of OBDA is the query answering, which is generally performed using rewriting techniques. A state-of-the-art system that has been identified in Chapter 5 is Ontop. It supports a mediator-based federation approach by using the **Teeid** (`http://teiid.jboss.org/`) data virtualization system allowing applications to use data from multiple, heterogenous data stores. To the best of our knowledge, this functionality is not considered to be production ready.

7.4 SUMMARY

- Distributing RDF data enables to increase data reliability and availability, and improve system performance and scalability. It also gives new perspective in terms of data integration.
- This also comes at the cost of a complex system that requires extra effort in terms of configuration and administration.
- We have identified two main categories of distributed RDF stores: those where the systems managing the distributed data are all the same, denoted homogeneous, and those where the systems managing the distributed data can be different.
- Among homogeneous systems, two main architecture types can be used: peer-to-peer and client-server. Both of these approaches can be implemented with different characteristics, such as whether the P2P system is structured or not and whether several masters can coexist.
- Heterogeneous systems can correspond to a federation query engine or a mediator-based system. Due to the high potential of SPARQL endpoints and the Linked Data movement, as well as the popularity of the SPARQL query language, the query federation approach has attracted a lot of attention. Mediator-based systems mainly correspond to OBDA systems and few of them are able to tackle different data sources.

CHAPTER EIGHT

Reasoning

8.1 INTRODUCTION

RDF stores are the database management systems of the Semantic Web. From a logical point of view, this implies that they may be equipped with access to some form of semantics—that is, predefined in ontologies and on the entities they are managing, such as concepts and properties. Properly processed, the semantics enable a system to interpret these entities. Such interpretations are performed through reasoning services, which are bridging the gap between raw data represented in the store and what the system knows about related entities. In Section 3.6 we presented different categories of services: those involving only the Tbox and those also relying on the Abox. This chapter focuses on the kind of inferences that are supported by RDF stores. Therefore, we can assume that such inferences will deal with both the Abox and the Tbox, such as the retrieval service that retrieves all instances of a given concept or instance checking. Nevertheless, services relying only on the Tbox may also be needed, such as the classification of the concept hierarchy.

In general, these services tend to derive implicit knowledge from explicitly stored knowledge. The set of relevant services may depend on the underlying ontology, which is usually expressed in one of the W3C ontology languages like RDFS and OWL 2 or one of its profiles. Recall that these languages mainly differ in their expressive power—that is, the kind of deductions they can perform—and that a trade-off between expressiveness and the complexity of reasoning problems motivates their existence. Intuitively, the more expressive the language, the more complex the processing of inferences, therefore the longer one has to wait to obtain the results of the deductions. The gathering of a set of ontologies (Tbox) together with some of its instances (Abox) is generally denoted as a *knowledge base*. Note that in the literature, this may also be denoted as an ontology, but here we reserve this term to the Tbox.

Until recently the SPARQL query language was not addressing the reasoning capabilities to handle RDFS and OWL vocabularies. The SPARQL 1.1 recommendation remedies this absence by including different entailment regimes. This notion is quite important to qualify the completeness of an answer set from a given query. The W3C document specifies the following entailment regimes: RDF, RDFS, OWL Direct, RDF-based semantics, and RIF Core. For each of these regimes, the recommendation specifies the valid entailment relation and how it's used, which graphs and queries are well formed, and what kind of errors can occur.

(1)	blog:JD	blog:isFollowing	blog:MS
(2)	blog:MS	rdf:type	blog:Person
(3)	blog:MD	rdf:type	blog:Man
(4)	blog:Man	rdfs:subClassOf	blog:Person
(5)	blog:isFollowing	rdfs:domain	blog:Person

Figure 8.1 RDF data set extract.

To illustrate the use of an entailment regime, let's consider the example shown in Figure 8.1, which is graphically represented in Figure 8.2.

Let's consider the two following queries over the data in Figure 8.1:

| (Q1) | SELECT ?p WHERE {?p rdf:type rdf:Property} |
| (Q2) | SELECT ?s WHERE {?s rdf:type blog:Person} |

In this context, we now consider the Simple, RDF, and RDFS entailment regimes where plain arrows represent explicit information and dotted arrows correspond to deduced facts. The Simple entailment regimes evaluates the basic graph pattern of a query using the RDF graph without any additional inferred triples. RDF and RDFS entailment regimes enrich the RDF graph with triples that can be deduced from their entailment rules (defined in Section 8.4.1). In the case of (Q1), the Simple entailment regime returns an empty answer set, while the RDF entailment rules enable the deduction of the following triple:

| (6) | blog:isFollowing | rdf:type | rdf:Property |

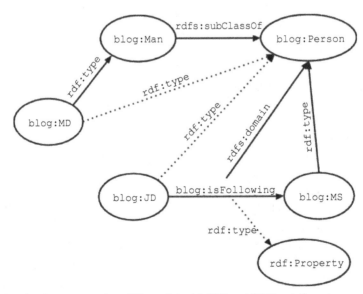

Figure 8.2 Graphical representation of Figure 8.1 with RDF and RDFS entailment.

The answer set of (Q1) for the RDFS entailment regime matches the RDF one.

Concerning query (Q2), in the case of Simple and RDF entailments, the answer set obviously contains triple {blog:MS}, obtained from triple (2). The RDFS entailment regime enriches this answer set with {blog:JD, blog:MD} according to the deduced following triples:

```
(7)    blog:MD     rdf:type     blog:Person
(8)    blog:JD     rdf:type     blog:Person
```

Therefore, with these entailment regimes, one can clearly appreciate the completeness of a query answer set and identify the kind of inferences that will be performed according to the underlying deduction rules.

Different aspects have to be considered in our presentation of reasoning with RDF stores. The first one deals with the methods used to process the inferences. Two main solutions can be envisaged. A first one consists in materializing in the store all the information that can be deduced. This ensures that all submitted queries will have access without additional efforts at query execution time to all inferred data. A second solution is based on performing the inferences at query execution time, usually by rewriting the submitted query, to retrieve all deductible data. In Section 8.2 we present the advantages and limits of these two approaches. Section 8.3 provides some details on existing processing methods. Finally, the last two sections provide details on implementations available on RDF stores: for systems based on a single machine approach in Section 8.4 and for distributed systems in Section 8.5.

Before delving into these different sections, we first present some background on the integration of a reasoning system within data and knowledge management systems.

8.2 REASONING AND DATABASE MANAGEMENT SYSTEMS

To apprehend the importance of reasoning in the context of a data and knowledge management system, we need to clarify what we mean with this notion. First, given the size of available data sets, we are interested in automated reasoning—that is, processed relatively autonomously by a machine. An agreed-on definition of reasoning is provided in Brachman and Levesque (2004): "it is the formal manipulation of symbols representing a collection of believed propositions to produce the representation of new ones" (p. 4). Some of the terms used in this definition need some explanation. The term *formal manipulation* implies the notion of some logic mechanism, such as a logical consequence or *entailment*. This is clearly the case in the Semantic Web where ontology languages like OWL are based on DLs (i.e., a subset of first-order logic), and inference services are based on an associated given semantics. The notion of a *representation* of some symbols is mentioned twice in the definition. Symbols are everywhere in this setting. They are either logical (e.g., conjunction, negation, qualifiers) or nonlogical (e.g., concepts, properties, instances, and literals). When organized in a manner that satisfies a well-defined syntax, these symbols enable the representation of a given domain, such as a blog or a biology application. Of course, for deductions to be of any interest, such a model only represents the facts and the knowledge that are believed to be true (more on this later in this chapter).

The capacity of appropriately using some knowledge in certain situations is a foundation for defining "intelligent" behaviors. This may be useful to complete the answer set of a query, to improve the performances of a system by understanding the impact of some parameters, or to design intelligent systems.

With these notions clarified, we can ask ourselves what is the state of intelligence support in current database management systems. An expert in database internal aspects would argue that there is already a lot of intelligence in an RDBMS, for instance, within the buffer management component to support fast query processing. But these smart mechanisms are not really made concrete to the end user; they just come in a global, opaque package and no one gives much attention to the mechanisms that make these systems so efficient. For example, these components generally do not have any direct impact with users' interactions, such as by extending the answer set of a query with some inferences.

Deductive databases, which are based on the relational model, are one of the few attempts to make intelligent behavior "visible" to the end user. This takes the form of a specialized query language, namely *Datalog*, and its execution environment. Through the definition of recursion-enabled queries, also called programs, composed of a set of rules, Datalog enables the system to deduce new information from stored data. Thus, a rule set forms a repository of domain knowledge that is used to extend the answer set of a given query. Although full of potential, this approach, on which research started in the late 1970s, has not been implemented natively by leading RDBMS vendors. Nevertheless, a new enthusiasm is surrounding this query language, mainly due to distribution workload concerns.

The system that manages knowledge bases, namely a *knowledge base management system* (KBMS), also referred to as a *knowledge-based system* (KBS) in the literature, is a good example of intelligent applications. These systems have evolved tremendously since their inception in the 1970s within the context of *artificial intelligence*. Early versions were mainly storing all the knowledge and facts in the main memory, which at the time was in the range of kilobytes to megabytes. That is, they were persisted in files and loaded into the main memory when starting the KBMS. Rapidly, the memory footprint required by the knowledge and/or the facts surpassed the capacity of the available main memory and efficient persistent approaches were needed. With the emergence of Big

Data, this phenomenon is amplified and it's now required to distribute the facts and possibly the ontologies over a cluster of machines, using both their primary and secondary memories. We have seen in the last few chapters that RDF stores are addressing each of these issues, and in Section 8.5 we present how the reasoning mechanisms have been adapted to these new architectures.

Just like its database counterpart, a KBMS is concerned with a set of tasks. The main prominent one has been defined within the *functional view* proposed by Levesque (Levesque, 1984). It consists of a so-called Tell & Ask interface and intuitively provides operations to construct and query a knowledge base. The main difference between standard databases and KBMSs is the support for reasoning services in the latter. While the classic query processing operations of Chapter 6 provide an efficient way to retrieve the answers of a query using data that is explicitly stored in the database, inference services aim at the completion of the answer set with implicit data. That is, through the formal manipulation of symbols representing a set of adopted propositions, a reasoning system is able to produce representations of new information and/or knowledge.

This difference between the two management systems is due to some intrinsic characteristics. For instance, a database represents exactly one interpretation, the one that is stored in the database instance. When one queries such an instance, the database is generally assumed to be complete, and this implies that the absence of a fact is interpreted as its falsity; for example, if someone cannot find a Delta Airlines flight between Paris and San Francisco at a certain date and time, he or she assumes that such a flight does not exist. This is generally denoted as the *Closed World Assumption* (CWA). Comparatively, a knowledge base represents many different interpretations, namely all its models. Therefore, the absence of information in the Abox only indicates a lack of knowledge. This is denoted as the *Open World Assumption* (OWA) and concerns the incompleteness of the Abox.

In the context of the blog running example, consider that the only assertion on the `isFollowing` property for Joe Doe states that he is following the blog of Mary Smith—that is, `isFollowing(blog:JD, blog:MS)`. Then, within CWA, this is understood as a representation of the fact that Joe Doe follows only one blog. Comparatively, within the OWA, the assertion only states that the system only knows of one blog that is followed by Joe Doe and it does not imply that Joe is not following any other blogs. To precisely state that Joe Doe is following a single blog requires us to make it explicit in the Abox, such as `(<=1 isFollowing)(blog:JD)` in a DL formalism.

The differences between CWA and OWA justify two distinct approaches to answering queries. In CWA, the system computes the answer set of a query using the only model that it can access, i.e., the current state of the database instance. In contrast, in OWA, the system has to consider all possible models to compute the answer set and this can be performed using a form of entailment.

Another difference between the two management systems relates to their respect of the *unique name assumption* (UNA). It states that two distinct names refer to two different real-world objects. RDBMSs respect UNA because any resource, such as a tuple in a table, is identified by values assigned to a set of columns (usually forming its primary key). It's assumed that this resource does not have another identifier or that no other resource has the same identifier. At the scale of the Web, this assumption does not hold. For example, a large portion of people using the Web have several email addresses, accounts on different social networks, or URLs that are associated to them, such as a professional web page, a blog, etc. Therefore, OWL knowledge bases do not assume UNA and this has an impact on reasoning. Moreover, in OWL 2, one can explicitly state that two individuals are the same or are different with respectively the `owl:sameIndividual` and `owl:differentIndividual` properties.

In the blog running example, suppose that one wants to store parent relationships. The ontology would state that a person has two parents, one male and one female. Consider that we assert that `Mary Smith` has `Will Smith` (typed as a `Male`), `Elizabeth Smith`, and `Liz Smith` (both typed as `Female`) as parents. In a UNA setting, such assertions would not even be allowed in the database because it would raise an integrity constraint violation—that is, only two parents are allowed and the recording of the third one would be rejected. In a non-UNA setting, this would be permitted and the system would use that information to infer that `Elizabeth Smith` and `Liz Smith` are the same person, because they are both females, and a single female parent is specified in the definition of a person.

Another difference between an RDBMS and a KBMS lies in the expressivity of their associated schema. In an RDBMS, a table is described in terms of some columns that have a type and may have some properties, such as a primary and foreign key, a unique value, a value comprised in a defined range or interval, and that it allows null values. In the case of an *object-oriented RDBMS* (OORDBMS), a special form of RDBMS, complex types can be defined and subsumption relationships between tables are allowed but no semantics is attributed to them. In both cases, the expressivity of the supported schema is very low and does not enable us to perform valuable deductions. In fact, the constraints expressed are considered as integrity constraints that should not be violated to keep the database instance in a consistent state.

In a KBMS, the ontology language used to define the Tbox can be of different expressivity. Even ontologies specified with RDFS are more expressive than the RDBMS schema and support the computation of interesting inferences (based on a predefined set of less than 20 rules). Of course, more constraints can be specified with ontologies of the OWL 2 family. This gain in expressivity comes at the price of a higher computation complexity. Just to give an idea about the languages involved in the Semantic Web, the very expressive OWL 2 Full is undecidable due to its unrestricted syntax, while the OWL 1 and OWL 2 DL are respectively NExponential and 2NExponential Time.

The OWL 2 profiles (OWL2 EL, RL, and QL) have been designed specifically to provide low complexities that correspond to polynomial time. Note that none of the constraints supported by these ontology languages are natively considered as integrity constraints but are used to entail new facts—that is, supernumerary and missing triples are not a violation.

8.3 REASONING METHODS

In this section, we present the advantages and drawbacks, as well as provide an example on the two main reasoning solutions adopted in RDF stores: materialization and query rewriting. We start with an introduction of some background knowledge on the possible methods to process RDF stores. They are emanating from research in artificial intelligence and can be organized in two categories: rule-based and object-based representations. The former is most frequently used for the less-expressive ontologies (e.g., RDFS, OWL Horst, and OWL 2 RL profiles), while the latter is tackling the more expressive ones (e.g., the DL versions of OWL and OWL 2).

8.3.1 Materialization versus query rewriting

A popular solution to extend query answering with inferences corresponds to the materialization approach, but terms such as *saturation* or *inference closure* are also frequent, which imply a preprocessing of the original data set. Intuitively, the materialization approach produces all implicit information that can be derived from the explicit knowledge and persists it in the system.

A second strategy consists in deriving the complete answer set at query processing time. This approach involves a rewriting (a.k.a. *reformulation*) of the original query according to the knowledge contained in the Tbox.

To present the advantages and limitations of both the saturation and reformulation approaches, we consider an example in the blog application. Table 8.1 proposes an extract of an RDF data set that contains raw data only—that is, it does not contain any inferred statements. To this data set, we associate an ontology, expressed in RDFS, from which Figure 8.3 proposes an extract of a concept hierarchy and that specifies a subsumption

Table 8.1 Extract of an RDF Data Set (No Materialization)

Subject	Predicate	Object
blog:Blog1	blog:category	Blog:Running
blog:Blog1	blog:creator	blog:JD
blog:Blog1	blog:content	"Yesterday .."
blog:Blog1	blog:language	blog:English
blog:Blog1	rdf:type	blog:Blog
blog:MS	blog:isFollowing	blog:JD

Running ⊑ OutDoorActivity ⊑ PhysicalActivity ⊑ Activity

Figure 8.3 Extract of an RDFS ontology.

chain between the `Running`, `OutDoorActivity`, `PhysicalActivity`, and `Activity` concepts.

We now consider answering the query retrieving all blog entries that are categorized with one of the concepts of the `Activity` hierarchy—that is, precisely, the set of concepts of Figure 8.3. This query can be represented using SPARQL as follows:

```
(Q3) SELECT ?blog WHERE { ?blog blog:category blog:Activity}
```

In a materialization approach, the required preprocessing of Table 8.1's data set would produce the data set of Table 8.2 where the bold triples are the results emerging from deductions. As a consequence, the materialization approach ensures fast query responses because no inferences are required at query processing time. But it implies a performance and storage overhead when loading the original data because it implies to derive all possible information.

With query rewriting reasoning, only the query would be modified and (Q4) would be transformed into (Q4) where we adopt a `UNION` approach. Note that among others the reformulation can also take the form of a set of queries and, in that case, the application would be responsible for merging the answer sets.

```
(Q4) SELECT ?blog WHERE {{ ?blog blog:category blog:Running}
        UNION { ?blog blog:category blog:OutDoorActivity}
        UNION { ?blog blog:category blog:PhysicalActivity}
        UNION { ?blog blog:category blog:Activity} }
```

Because the query is executed on the original set, there is not any extra cost associated to data loading. But query answering is costly due to the reformulation of the query

Table 8.2 Extract of an RDF Data Set (No Materialization)

Subject	Predicate	Object
blog:Blog1	blog:category	blog:Running
blog:Blog1	**blog:category**	**blog:OutDoorActivity**
blog:Blog1	**blog:category**	**blog:PhysicalActivity**
blog:Blog1	**blog:category**	**blog:Activity**
blog:Blog1	blog:creator	blog:JD
blog:Blog1	blog:content	"Yesterday .."
blog:Blog1	blog:language	blog:English
blog:Blog1	rdf:type	blog:Blog
blog:MS	blog:isFollowing	blog:JD

as it's required to communicate with a reasoner to find all subconcepts (queries with subproperties are less frequent but also possible), to rewrite the query, and to execute it (which may be costly in the presence of a large number of UNIONs). It's clear that this approach can lead to the generation of very large queries where an important number of UNIONs can be unsatisfiable and redundant is created in a naive way.

Another difference between these two methods occurs when dealing with Abox or Tbox updates. For the query rewriting approach, updates at the Abox level do not have any impact on the generated query, while updates at the Tbox level would only lead to the generation of a different query reformulation. The case of materialization is more involved in both the Abox and Tbox situations and leads to a problem known as *truth maintenance*. That is, the state of a materialized data set has to remain consistent after an update. The case of an insertion is relatively straightforward because it requires us to add some explicit and implicit triples. The case of removal is more complex because one has to identify all triples that have to be removed and also make sure that they are not entailed without the removed assertions. For example, modifying the category of blog:Blog1 in Table 8.1 to blog:Programming would lead to the removal of the first four lines of that Table 8.2. Anyhow, if blog:Programming is a subclass of blog:Activity, then the triple blog:Blog1 blog:category blog:Activity has to remain in the materialized data set.

The truth maintenance can be handled in different ways. Some solutions consist in (i) removing all the triples and recomputing the materialization, (ii) removing the inferred triples and recomputing the closure of all remaining statements, or (iii) an additional structure is maintained and is used to confirm the deletion operation. The first two solutions are far from being efficient—for example, imagine the operations that would be performed for a database with thousands of transactions per second. Even the last approach is not ideal due to the cost of maintaining the additional structure. Nevertheless, we will show in Section 8.4 that several existing systems are adopting this materialization approach, but generally they assume that updates are rarely occurring.

8.3.2 Rule-based approach

A large portion of RDF stores enabling some forms of reasoning are addressing ontology languages that can be processed with a rule-based approach. This is the case for the RDFS, RDFS+, OWL Horst, OWL 2 RL and EL, and to some extent OWL 2 QL. A well-known inference pattern corresponds to *modus ponens* which is generally expressed as follows: if A $\rightarrow$ B and A therefore B. The rule-based approach supports inference by resolution or some of its extensions. The resolution principle, introduced by Robinson (1965), is a generalization of modus ponens and arose in the area of automated theorem proving where it was used to prove that a theorem can be derived from a set of axioms. This approach underpins the logic programming and production rules paradigms. The main inference rule, in the context of propositional logic, used in this principle is the following: from the axioms X $\lor$ Y and $\neg$X $\lor$ Z, one can deduce Y $\lor$ Z (denoted a *resolvent*), where X, Y, and Z are atomic formulas or literals, $\lor$ denotes the logical OR operation, and $\neg$ denotes a negation.

We now present the resolution principle in the context of a simple example. Consider that from the axioms $\neg$A $\lor$ B $\lor$ C, A $\lor$ C $\lor$ D, and $\neg$A $\lor$ $\neg$B one would like to deduce C $\lor$ D, where A, B, C, and D are atomic formulas or literals. The main steps of the method are as follows:

1. Insert the negation of the axiom to be deduced into the set of original axioms.
2. Transform the axiom set into a so-called clausal form (a.k.a. conjunctive normal form), which relates atomic formulas with an OR operator.
3. Take the whole set of axioms and apply the inference rule and obtain some new axioms corresponding to intermediate resolvents.
4. Halt the procedure successfully, meaning the theorem is true, when a contradiction occurs—that is, when an *empty clause* (generally represented by $\square$) is produced. Otherwise, if an empty clause cannot be produced, the theorem is false.

After step 1, our axiom set is $\neg$A $\lor$ B $\lor$ C, A $\lor$ C $\lor$ D, $\neg$A $\lor$ $\neg$B, $\neg$(C $\lor$ D). Note that the ", " symbol denotes a logical conjunction. Our first three axioms are already satisfying the form required by step 2 and the transformation of the last one results in $\neg$C $\land$ $\neg$D, (using de Morgan's laws) which amounts to two new axioms with our representation: $\neg$C and $\neg$D.

Our new axiom set is thus $\neg$A $\lor$ B $\lor$ C, A $\lor$ C $\lor$ D, $\neg$A $\lor$ $\neg$B, $\neg$C, $\neg$D. Applying step 3, after five deductions, we obtain the empty clause symbol ($\square$), which means that the theorem is proved (see Figure 8.4).

The resolution principle yields a sound and refutation complete inference algorithm for knowledge bases expressed in conjunctive normal form. Refutation completeness

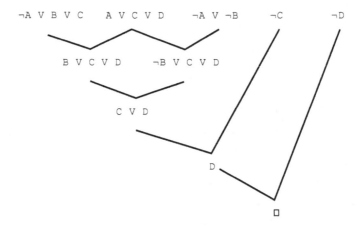

Figure 8.4 Resolution example in propositional logic.

implies that the inference rule is always able to confirm or refute a given axiom, but cannot be used to provide a list of true axioms.

The resolution principle can be adapted to first-order logic—that is, handling variables, quantifiers ($\forall, \exists$), and functions—via a series of formula transformations. We do not present the details of these transformations, but their main goal is to obtain some clausal forms without quantifiers. The inference rule is then also slightly modified to support two operations: *substitution*, which assigns terms like individuals to variables, and *unification*, which unifies some substitutions to obtain a resolvent. The last step of the method then remains unchanged.

We now propose an example where we represent the `Activity` concept subsumption relationships in first-order logic and try to deduce if `category(blog:Blog1, Activity)` holds. First, we state that the `blog:Blog1` entry is categorized as a `Running` blog entry:

```
category(blog:Blog1, Running)
```

Then we define the axioms representing the concept hierarchy:

```
∀x  category(x,Running)  → category(x,OutDoorActivity)
∀x  category(x,OutDoorActivity)  → category(x,PhysicalActivity)
∀x  category(x,PhysicalActivity)  → category(x,Activity)
```

We can drop the universal quantifier and replace the logical implication with a disjunction using the equivalence between $x \rightarrow y$ and $\neg x \lor y$. Our set of axioms, where each line represents a logical conjunction, thus becomes

```
category(blog:Blog1, Running)
¬ category(x,Running) ∨ category(x,OutDoorActivity)
¬ category(x,OutDoorActivity) ∨ category(x,PhysicalActivity)
¬ category(x,PhysicalActivity) ∨ category(x,Activity)
```

from which we would like to prove `category(blog:Blog1, Activity)`. Figure 8.5 presents the different deductions and unification (where X is substituted to `blog:Blog1`) that lead to the empty clause, satisfying the fact that `blog:Blog1` is categorized as a physical activity.

Demonstrations conducted by the resolution principle can take different forms. For instance, Figures 8.5 and 8.6 obtain the same result using two different approaches. The former is directed by data, i.e., the data are used first to deduce some resolvents, which are positive ones, before being able to obtain the empty clause using the goal. While the latter starts with the goal, producing negative resolvents, before obtaining the empty clause. Among the different possible approaches, some may permit to produce the empty clause much faster than other ones.

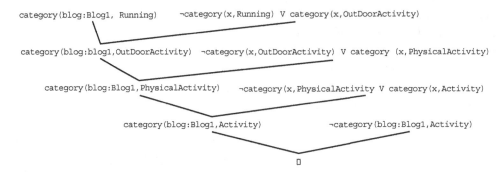

Figure 8.5 Bottom-up resolution example in first-order logic.

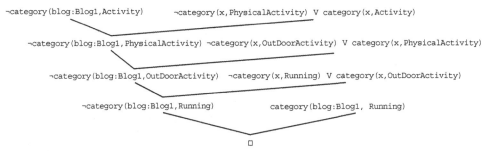

Figure 8.6 Top-down resolution example in first-order logic.

In practice, real-world knowledge bases contain clauses corresponding to *Horn clauses*, named after the researcher who first identified them in 1951, and have been extensively used in logic programming in general and the *Programming in Logic* (Prolog) language in particular. Horn clauses are characterized by having at most one positive literal and can therefore be represented as follows:

- X ∨ ¬Y1 ∨ ¬Y2 ∨ .. ∨ ¬Yn with n ≥ 0 and that can be transformed into:
- X ← Y1, Y2,.., Yn where the, symbol corresponds to a conjunction.

Horn clauses with exactly one positive literal are denoted as definite. Inferences over Horn clauses can be performed with forward and backward chaining algorithms. Forward chaining is a data–driven approach where known facts are used together with rules to produce new facts. This is largely used in the materialization solution of the previous section. Backward chaining works backward from the goal. It reformulates the problem of demonstrating the goal X into a conjunction of Ys and works recursively with each Y instance in the conjunction. It is the principal approach of the query rewriting solution of the previous section. Moreover, substituting the ← symbol to : - exactly yields a Prolog clause where X is called the head and the Ys are named the body of the rule.

Prolog was originally a strongly constrained resolution theorem prover and then turned into a more conventional programming language. This evolution implied the introduction of some extra logical features such as the built-in predicates `fail` (which automatically triggers a failure) and `cut` (which prevents an overuse of backtrackings during a search). Another limitation associated to this programming language is that the clauses of a program are tested strictly in the order of their appearance in the program. Therefore, programmers have to organize their goals' declaration in a more to less selective order. In practice, such an order can be rather hard to define for many application domains. The addition of these features to the backtracking-enabled depth-first search strategy of Prolog does not guarantee the termination of a recursive program, which is considered a big drawback for the adoption of this programming language in industry. Prolog is usually using the SLD (Selective Linear Definite) resolution algorithm, a refinement of resolution for definite Horn clauses, which adopts backward chaining.

Prolog has a tight relation with the Datalog language we presented earlier in this chapter when introducing deductive databases. With facts and rules represented as Horn clauses, Datalog can be considered a subset of general logic programming, and therefore a subset of Prolog. This enables Datalog programs to be parsed and executed by a Prolog engine. Nevertheless, they have some differences—for instance, the order of clauses in a Datalog program does not have any impact on the execution of the deduction process, and Datalog does not support the cut/fail predicates and does not allow functions.

From an operational point of view, this language has been designed to interact with large relational databases. A Datalog program consists of a finite set of clauses that are divided into two subsets: the *extensional database* (EDB) that contains the facts, and the *intentional database* (IDB) that contains the rules. We here recognize the distinction between the instance and knowledge components made in the context of a knowledge base. The predicates that occur in respectively the EDB and IDB are denoted as the EDB-predicates and the IDB-predicates. In a standard setting, EDB-predicates generally coincide with one or several relational tables, while the IDB-predicates correspond to views in the RDBMS.

These features provide Datalog with a nice set of properties but that has never gained attention from RDBMS vendors, be it commercial or open-source. The approach has rather been implemented through systems that can interact with a standard RDBMS. It is, for example, the case of the *XSB* system, which can transform a standard relational database into a deductive one. Anyhow, due to the emergence of Big Data and its need for parallel computation and distributed storage, Datalog is starting to gain more attention. This has motivated several Datalog 2.0 workshops emphasizing novel implementations and use cases for this language. This is also, for example, the case of the **Datomic** system (`http://www.datomic.com/`), which adopts a NoSQL-like approach for immutable data with queries expressed in Datalog. In the remainder of this chapter, we present an implementation of the Datalog language in the context of the Jena Semantic Web framework and highlight that several reasoners of the RDF stores are using either a Prolog or Datalog implementation.

8.3.3 Object-based approach

An object-based approach supports inference by inheritance. DLs and thus some members of the OWL family are particularly concerned by this approach. In the following, we present the structural subsumption–based, tableau-based, and consequence-based reasoning solutions.

8.3.3.1 Structural subsumption

The first DL systems were relying on structural algorithms to test for concept subsumption. That is, given two concepts C and D, one searches if C is subsumed by D (denoted C ⊑ D) in every model of the ontology. The main idea of the algorithm is to compare the syntactic structure of normalized concepts—that is, both concepts C and D have to be transformed into a normal form according to some rules that depend on the expressivity of the ontology language. The comparison is performed in regard to some conditions that try to unify some parts of both concepts.

As an example, considering the Activity concept hierarchy presented earlier in this chapter, given two concepts C and D defined, using a DL formalism, respectively as Blog ⊓ ∀category.Running and Blog ⊓ ∀category.Activity, we are trying to prove C ⊑ D — that is, a blog categorized in the Running category belongs to the set of blogs categorized in the Activity category. Both concepts are already in the expected normal form and we can proceed to the comparison. First, both concepts C and D contain the Blog concept, therefore we can concentrate on the subsumption of the rest of these concepts, which we name C′ and D′ : ∀category.Running ⊑ ∀category.Activity. Both of them consist of a universal quantifier over the same property (category), therefore, it's sufficient to check the subsumption of these quantifications' fillers (i.e., Running ⊑ Activity). According to our Activity subsumption hierarchy, this is valid and we can thus validate that C ⊑ D.

The goal of the algorithm was to provide a method to decide the subsumption in polynomial time. Although, this can be achieved for certain ontology languages in the absence of Tbox, this is generally not the case in the presence of a Tbox. This is due to the unfolding of concept definitions, which can cause an exponential blow-up. Moreover, this algorithm is sound and complete only for ontology languages with a low expressivity level. Whenever the DL integrates full negation, disjunction, and full existential restriction (∃R.C), the algorithm is not complete—that is, it's not able to detect all valid subsumption relationships. Considering the set on ontology languages of the Semantic Web, this does not leave a big space for this kind of inference mechanism. Nevertheless, the emergence of the OWL 2 profiles and in particular the OWL 2 EL rehabilitated the structural approach. In fact, the original classification inference proposed in the EL and EL++ DL, which underlies OWL 2 EL, is based on a form of structural subsumption.

8.3.3.2 Tableau

The limitation of the structural subsumption algorithm toward using expressive DLs was one of the motivations to switch to the tableau-based (a.k.a. semantic tableau) method. Since then it has been the most widely used reasoning technique in the context of expressive DLs. Due to the influence of expressive DLs on the design of OWL, it's not a surprise to encounter several reasoners implementing this approach for the OWL (2) DL languages, such as Fact++, DLP, Racer, Pellet, and Cerebra Engine.

Just like in the resolution inference, the tableau approach is based on a proof by contradiction. That is, in the typical case of subsumption checking, $C \sqsubseteq D$ is transformed into the equivalent contradiction checking (e.g., "Is $C \sqcap \neg D$ inconsistent?") where both concepts are transformed into a *negation normal form* (NNF)—that is, negation is applied only to concept names. Intuitively, this is performed by trying to construct a model that satisfies $C \sqcap \neg D$ using some so-called *expansion rules*. If a model is built out of this construction, then it means that C is not a subconcept of D, otherwise $C \sqsubseteq D$ is considered to hold. This method can be developed for the Tbox only and the conjunction of a Tbox and an Abox. It can also handle different ontology languages, mainly by adapting the set of expansion rules, consisting of a condition and action. Such expansion rules apply to each logical constructor some constraints that are applied to the construction (which takes the form of a graph).

Following is an example. We consider the following knowledge base:

- Abox = {Running(blog:Blog1)}, stating that the instance blog:Blog1 is of type Running
- Tbox = { Running $\sqsubseteq$ OutDoorActivity, OutDoorActivity $\sqsubseteq$ PhysicalActivity, PhysicalActivity $\sqsubseteq$ Activity }

We transform each concept inclusion of the form $C \sqsubseteq D$ of the Tbox into the following disjunction: $\neg C \sqcup D$. Therefore, we just need a single expansion rule for the disjunction ($\sqcup$), which is nondeterministic (i.e., it creates two branches). Its condition states that if the Abox (A) contains an axiom of the form $(C \sqcup D)(x)$ but it does not contain neither $C(x)$ nor $D(x)$, then the action consists in creating two Aboxes where $A' = A \cup \{C(x)\}$ and $A'' = A \cup \{D(x)\}$.

Our goal is to demonstrate that this knowledge base satisfies the assertion ActivityBlog(blog:Blog1) using both the Abox and the Tbox. Our first Abox is denoted A0 and uses the blog:Blog1 individual:

```
A0 = {Running(blog:Blog1),  (¬Running ⊔ OutDoorActivity)(blog:Blog1),
(¬OutDoorActivity   ⊔   PhysicalActivity)(blog:Blog1),   (¬PhysicalActivity
⊔  Activity)(blog:Blog1), ¬Activity(blog:Blog1)}.
```

We apply our expansion rule to obtain two new Aboxes A1' and A1":

```
A1' = A0 ∪ {¬Running(blog:Blog1)}
A1" = A0 ∪ {OutDoorActivity(blog:Blog1)}
```

The Abox A1′ presents a contradiction because we have `Running(blog:Blog1)` and `¬Running(blog:Blog1)` in the same branch tree. This is denoted as a *clash*, so we stop considering that branch.

The next application of the expansion rules generates the Abox A2′ and A2″ from A1″:

```
A2' = A1" ∪ {¬OutDoorActivity(blog:Blog1)}
A2" = A1" ∪ { PhysicalActivity(blog:Blog1)}
```

Again, A2′ presents a clash.

The last application of the rules produces the following Aboxes:

```
A3' = A2" ∪ {¬PhysicalActivity(blog:Blog1)}
A3" = A2" ∪ {Activity(blog:Blog1)}
```

Both these Aboxes contain a contradiction, on `PhysicalActivity(blog:Blog1)` for A3′ and on `Activity(blog:Blog1)` for A3″. That is, all branches of the tree are closed because of the presence of a clash on each of them. Because the tree cannot be expanded anymore, this ends our demonstration. We have proven that it cannot be satisfied by our knowledge to demonstrate the negation of `Activity(blog:Blog1)`, therefore this axiom is entailed by the knowledge base.

In the case of the classification service, the method iterates over all necessary pairs of classes and tries to build a model of the ontology that violates the subsumption relation between them. Moreover, modern tableau-based reasoners support optimization techniques that enable the reduction of the number of subsumption tests and allow the reusing of previously computed results.

8.3.3.3 Consequence

Consequence-based reasoning procedures are sometimes considered more practical than tableau-based ones for the following reasons: they never consider subsumption relationships that are not entailed and they can derive all of them with an algorithm running a single pass on the Tbox. Moreover, this method is also closely related to the resolution principle because they both derive new clauses that are consequences of the original or previously derived axioms. A limitation of the resolution approach is that it may produce a large number of unnecessary clauses, sometimes preventing existing reasoning tasks to terminate on practical large knowledge bases, such as the medical SNOMED CT ontology. The semantic aspect of the rules defined in the context of consequence-based reasoning supports more efficient derivations that prevent this to happen.

This method can be used for the classification, consistency-checking, and instance-retrieval reasoning tasks. It derives subsumption relationships by using a special set of inference rules. The four required steps are:

1. Normalize the Tbox.
2. Transform the TBox into a graph.

3. Complete the graph with completion rules.

4. Extract the subsumption relationships.

Such a procedure was first introduced for the EL and EL++ DL, which underlies the OWL 2 EL, and was later extended to Horn SHIQ and Horn SROIQ (corresponding to those OWL 2 DL ontologies that could be represented as Horn clauses). Several reasoners have been implemented using this procedure: CB, CEL, and ELK to name the main ones.

8.4 NONDISTRIBUTED SYSTEMS AND APPROACHES

In this section we concentrate on the description of reasoning services performed in the context of an RDF store running on a single machine.

8.4.1 RDF, RDFS, and some extensions

The semantics of RDF, RDFS, and close extensions are defined through a set of axiomatic triples and entailment rules. These rules enable us to determine a set of full inferences given an ontology and an RDF data set. Each rule consists of a body that is composed of a conjunction of RDF statements, possibly containing variables, and a head also composed of RDF statements. Applying the entailment rules to an RDF graph infers the triples present in the head of the activated rules. The inferred triples are usually denoted as the closure of a source graph. The only method to determine if a triples statement can be deduced from an RDF graph is to check if it's a member of the inferred closure.

Tables 8.3 and 8.4 present the entailment rules of respectively the RDF (minus the literal related rules) and RDFS vocabularies.

Clearly, in the context of an RDF store, `rdf1` is the most useful of the RDF entailment rules. This rule has a single antecedent. Note that some of the RDFS entailments also possess that single antecedent property, such as `rdfs1, rdfs4a, rdfs4b, rdfs6, rdfs8, rdfs10,` and `rdfs13`. Such rules can be computed easily in a single pass over the data. The computation of the two antecedent rules of the RDFS regime are more

Table 8.3 RDF Entailment Rules

Rule name	If the data set contains	Then add
rdf1	`uuu aaa yyy.`	`aaa rdf:type rdf:Property.`
rdf2	`uuu aaa lll.`	`_:nnn rdf:type`
	`where lll is a well-`	`rdf:XMLLiteral.`
	`typed XML literal.`	`where _:nnn identifies a`
		`blank node allocated to`
		`lll.`

Table 8.4 RDFS Entailment as Proposed in the RDF 1.1 Recommendation

Rule name	If the data set contains	Then add
rdfs1	any IRI aaa in D	aaa rdf:type rdfs:Datatype.
rdfs2	aaa rdfs:domain xxx. yyy aaa zzz.	yyy rdf:type xxx.
rdfs3	aaa rdfs:range xxx. yyy aaa zzz.	zzz rdf:type xxx.
rdfs4a	xxx aaa yyy.	xxx rdf:type rdfs:Resource.
rdfs4b	xxx aaa yyy.	yyy rdf:type rdfs:Resource.
rdfs5	xxx rdfs:subPropertyOf yyy. yyy rdfs:subPropertyOf zzz.	xxx rdfs:subPropertyOf zzz.
rdfs6	xxx rdf:type rdf:Property.	xxx rdfs:subPropertyOf xxx.
rdfs7	aaa rdfs:subPropertyOf bbb. xxx aaa yyy.	xxx bbb yyy.
rdfs8	xxx rdf:type rdfs:Class.	xxx rdfs:subClassOf rdfs:Resource.
rdfs9	xxx rdfs:subClassOf yyy. zzz rdf:type xxx.	zzz rdf:type yyy.
rdfs10	xxx rdf:type rdfs:Class.	xxx rdfs:subClassOf xxx.
rdfs11	xxx rdfs:subClassOf yyy. yyy rdfs:subClassOf zzz.	xxx rdfs:subClassOf zzz.
rdfs12	xxx rdf:type rdfs:Contain erMembershipProperty.	xxx rdfs:subPropertyOf rdfs:member.
rdfs13	xxx rdf:type rdfs:Datatype.	xxx rdfs:subClassOf rdfs:Literal

involved because they may require two passes. Another problem concerns the duplication of inferred triples. Figure 8.7 emphasizes this problem.

Consider the following ontology extract:

```
blog:isFollowing      rdfs:domain      blog:Person
blog:isFollowing      rdfs:range       blog:Person
```

And the following RDF assertions:

```
blog:JD       blog:isFollowing      blog:MS
blog:MS       blog:isFollowing      blog:JD
```

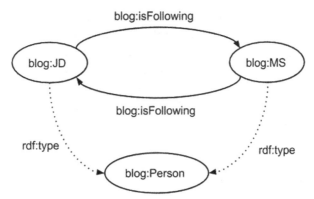

Figure 8.7 RDFS inference duplication where plain arrows are explicit relationships and dotted ones have been deduced, possibly several times.

Using rules `rdfs2` and `rdfs3` over the first assertion, one can deduce the following:

```
blog:JD        rdf:type       blog:Person
blog:MS        rdf:type       blog:Person
```

But these same assertions will be duplicated using the same two rules, using the second assertion of our source data set. Now imagine that the blog of John Doe is very popular, thousands or more followers, then the fact that `blog:JD` is of type `Person` will be deduced many times. The detection of these duplicates hampers performances of the reasoning system. Some systems aware of this problem try to detect and prevent this duplication behavior.

RDFS reasoning is quite popular among existing RDF stores. This is due to its interesting rule-based design and a relative trade-off between expressivity and computational complexity of reasoning services. But this may already be too cumbersome or not expressive enough, and some of these systems even consider subsets or extensions of RDFS. The subset approach is motivated by the fact that inconsistency can emerge from interpretations in the standard, so-called normative, RDFS semantics. For example, any triple (S, P, O) where P's domain is defined as an `rdf:Literal` would lead to an inconsistency because no edges can start from a literal in an RDF graph.

The cost of these checks is relatively high, and although it can be tolerated in a materialization approach (due to the cost of the overall task), it's not realistic in a query rewriting approach because it would slow the processing of each query. In the latter case, the choice is to rather select a so-called minimal RDFS, which is built on the ρdf fragment presented in Munoz et al. (2009). The ρdf vocabulary is defined as the subset of the RDFS vocabulary: `rdfs:subClassOf`, `rdfs:subPropertyOf`, `rdf:type`, `rdfs:domain`, and `rdfs:range`—that is, leaving out the likes of `rdfs:resource`, `rdfs:datatype`, and `rdfs:literal`. The deductive system for this fragment is adapted from the one defined for the RDF semantics but only considers its vocabulary, therefore a subset of the rules of Table 8.4.

All the other ontology languages (pD⋆, RDFS+, RDFS++, and OWL Prime) we present in this subsection are amenable to a rule-based reasoning approach.

pD⋆ (a.k.a. OWL Horst) was presented in Chapter 3 and its rule set corresponds to the one presented in Table 8.5. Note that an important portion of the rules involve two triples patterns in the body.

Table 8.5 Entailment Rules for pD*

ID	Body Terminological	Assertional	Head
rdfp1	*?p* a owl:FunctionalProperty.	*?x ?p ?y ,?z .*	*?y* owl:sameAs *?z* .
rdfP2	*?p* a owl:InverseFunctional Property.	*?x ?p ?z . ?y ?p ?z .*	*?x* owl:sameAs *?y* .
rdfp3	*?p* a owl:SymmetricProperty.	*?x ?p ?y .*	*?y ?p ?x* .
rdfp4	*?p* a owl:TransitiveProperty.	*?x ?p ?y . ?y ?p ?z .*	*?x ?p ?z* .
rdfp5a		*?x ?p ?y .*	*?x* owl:sameAs *?x* .
rdfp5b		*?x ?p ?y .*	*?y* owl:sameAs *?y* .
rdfp6		*?x* owl:sameAs *?y* .	*?y* owl:sameAs *?x* .
rdfp7		*?x* owl:sameAs *?y* . *?y* owl:sameAs *?z* .	*?x* owl:sameAs *?z* .
rdfp8a	*?p* owl:inverseOf *?q* .	*?x ?p ?y .*	*?y ?g ?x* .
rdfp8b	*?p* owl:inverseOf *?q* .	*?x ?q ?y .*	*?y ?p ?x* .
rdfp9	*?c* a owl:Class .	*?c* owl:sameAs *?d* .	*?c* rdfs:subClassOf *?d* .
rdfp10	*?p* a owl:Property.	*?p* owl:sameAs *?q* .	*?p* rdfs:subPropertyOf *?q* .
rdfp11		*?x* owl:sameAs *?x′* . *?y* owl:sameAs *?y′*. *?x ?p ?y* .	*?x′ ?p ?y′*.
rdfp12a	*?c* owl :equivalent Class *?d* .		*?c* rdfs:subClassOf *?d* .
rdfp12b	*?c* owl :equivalent Class *?d* .		*?d* rdfs:subClassOf *?c* .
rdfp12c	*?c* rdfs:subClassOf *?d* . *?d* rdfs:subClassOf *?c* .		*?c* owl:equivalentOf *?q* .
rdfp13a	*?p* owl:equivalent Property *?q* .		*?p* rdfs:subPropertyOf *?q* .
rdfp13b	*?p* owl:equivalent Property *?q* .		*?q* rdfs:subPropertyOf *?p* .
rdfp13c	*?p* rdfs:subPropertyOf *?q* . *?q* rdfs:subPropertyOf *?p* .		*?p* owl:equivalentProperty *?q* .
rdfp14a	*?c* owl: has Value *?y* ; owl:onProperty *?p* .	*?x ?p ?y .*	*?x* a *?c* .
rdfp14b	*?c* owl:hasValue *?y* ; owl:onProperty *?p* .	*?x* a *?c* .	*?x ?p ?y* .
rdfp15	*?c* owl: SomeValuesFrom *?d* ; owl:onProperty *?p* .	*?x ?p ?y . ?y* a *?d* .	*?x* a *?c* .
rdfp16	*?c* owl:allValuesFrom *?d* ; owl:onProperty *?p*.	*?x* a *?c; ?p ?y* .	*?y* a *?d* .

Includes RDFS entailment and P- axiomatic triples

Similarly, RDFS+, used in the Bigdata RDF store, extends RDFS with `owl:inverseOf`, `owl:SymmetricProperty`, `owl:TransitiveProperty`, `owl:equivalentClass`, `owl:sameAs`, `owl:equivalentProperty`, `owl:FunctionalProperty`, and `owl:InverseFunctionalProperty`.

Allegrograph uses RDFS++, which is defined as RDFS extended with `owl:inverseOf`, `owl:transitiveProperty`, and `owl:sameAs`. Therefore, it corresponds to a subset of RDFS+. Note that Allegrograph's reasoning engine maintains the ontological entailments in a dynamic manner—that is, no explicit materialization step is performed. The reasoning approach is based on a backward chaining approach.

Oracle 11g supports its own version of RDFS++, which extends RDFS with `owl:sameAs` and `owl:InverseFunctionalProperty`. IT also uses OWL Prime, a variant of pD*, which adds `owl:differentFrom` and `owl:disjointWith`.

Some interesting mechanisms have already been designed to handle updates together with reasoning services. The recent work of Goasdoué et al. (2013) presents an interesting strategy. In this system, a so-called *DB fragment* is defined as corresponding to nonrestricted RDF graphs together with an RDFS entailment. Such a fragment can be deployed over any non-native RDBMS or native single table via RDF-3X engines. Standard BGP queries, with blank nodes, are being used to query the DB fragment using the RDBMS engine query processor. This approach is supported by a correspondence between V-tables (Abiteboul et al., 1995) and RDF graphs.

V-tables are standard relations but allow variables in their tuples and are known to compute the exact answer set of any conjunctive query when variables are seen as constants. Thus, one can benefit from this perspective to answer BGP queries where blank nodes are replaced with nondistinguished variables. The work in Goasdoué et al. (2013) presents novel solutions for the materialization (called graph saturation in the paper) and query rewriting (denoted reformulation in the paper) of reasoning approaches.

Considering novel solutions, the main contribution consists in supporting update operations at both the instance (i.e., RDF triples) and the schema (i.e., modification of RDFS ontology) levels. The solution is based on an incremental algorithm that modifies the materialization according to some update operations. This is performed by qualifying each triple of the data set. This qualification consists of a pair of values. The first one takes the form of a Boolean value and specifies if the triple is the result that has been entailed (i.e., is it the result of the saturation) or if it's native to the database. The second maintains a counter on the triples appearance in the data set. Intuitively, triples insertion may increment the counter value of impacted triples. Similarly, deletion operations may decrease the counter values of many triples or even remove some impacted triples when these counter reach a value of 0. An evaluation conducted on real-world data sets emphasizes that schema-level updates are much more expensive than instance-level ones, which can be efficiently maintained.

The second reasoning approach tackled by this paper concerns query rewriting. It uses a set of rules to generate some queries that are forming the original query reformulation. A nonstandard handling of blank nodes is introduced to limit bindings for query variables and preventing them with blank nodes.

Finally, the paper highlights that their saturation and reformulation solutions perform differently. It comes at no surprise that the query rewriting approach is efficient when the reformulation is of medium size, while saturation is preferable for large reformulation queries. Obviously, to select between the two solutions, one would have to know in advance the kind of queries that will be performed over the database as well as the rate of update operations. Such metrics are rather hard to obtain in real-world scenarios.

8.4.2 OWL 2 profiles

This section considers the three profiles of the OWL 2 recommendation. In this setting, a profile corresponds to a sublanguage or fragment in the computational logic terminology. The main motivation of the design of these profiles is to trade some expressive power for the efficiency of reasoning. More precisely, these profiles are all tractable and have also been shown to be quite adapted to some precise use case. The main characteristics of these vocabularies have been described in Section 3.5. The following subsections concentrate on reasoning mechanisms and implemented systems.

8.4.2.1 OWL 2 RL

Systems supporting the OWL 2 RL profile are generally implemented using a rule-based reasoning engine (hence the RL acronym standing for Rule Language). This profile was inspired by the *Description Logic Program* (DLP)—that is, an attempt to specify the intersection of DL and logic programming, and pD⋆. The main inference services (i.e., ontology consistency, class expression satisfiability, class expression subsumption, instance checking, and conjunctive query answering) can be solved in polynomial time with respect to the size of the ontology.

Section 4.3 of the OWL 2 Web Ontology Language recommendation (`http://www.w3.org/TR/owl2-profiles/`) proposes a large set of "triples rules" where each body and head consist of an RDF-style triples pattern—that is, triples that can contain some variables. The head of some rules contain a `false` value that indicates that a ground instance of the body (i.e., containing constants only and no variables) is inconsistent. This is, for example, the case of the following rule, denoted `cax-dw` in the recommendation:

```
IF ?c1 owl;disjointWith ?c2 AND ?x rdf:type ?c1 AND ?x rdf:type ?c2 THEN
false
```

This rule states that if two classes are asserted to be disjoint then an individual cannot be an instance of both of these classes.

Because the vocabulary of OWL 2 RL is much larger than the one for RDFS, the number of rules is also increasing at around eighty rules. In an RDF context, a forward-chaining approach is most frequently used with OWL 2 RL to complete query answering. This is in part due to the large number of rules that would force a backward-chaining reasoning to perform very poorly. Two styles of query answering involving reasoning are possible. In a first one, the ontology is encoded in RDF triples and stored together with the instance data in a unique RDF graph. A Datalog program corresponding to OWL 2 RL rules can then operate this graph to reply to queries. This approach is known not to be efficient due to complex joins contained in these rules. In a second solution, the ontology is encoded into a Datalog program—that is, by following the DLP approach presented in Grosof et al. (2003)—that is kept separated from the RDF data set. The Datalog program is then executed to generate inferred triples. This approach is considered to be more efficient than the first one.

Some existing reasoners for OWL2RL are **Elly** (`http://elly.sourceforge.net/`), **Jena**, **OWLIM**, and **Oracle Database 11g OWL**. These systems are based on rule-extended triple stores and relational databases and adopt a materializing approach of the inferences.

8.4.2.2 OWL 2 QL

OWL 2 QL is underpinned by the DL-Lite description logic and has motivated the popular ontology-based database access (OBDA) approach. The main principle is to rewrite a given query into a complete set of queries that retrieve all valid answers. The most common approach involves an ontology and a set of mapping assertions as the input of the reasoner. The reasoner/ database coupling enables a direct communication. This solution benefits from the efficiency of the underlying query engine, in particular in the case of an RDBMS. The main issues concern the possibly exponential number of generated queries, sometimes with some redundancy and some unsatisfiable queries, and the performance associated to the generation of these reformulations. Next we present, in chronological order, the main systems existing in the ecosystem.

The **QuOnto** system (querying ontologies) (Acciarri et al., 2005) was the first implementation of a reasoning solution to answer complex queries over a DL-Lite ontology, which later motivated OWL 2 QL. QuOnto assumes that the Abox is stored in an RDBMS and handles the union of conjunctive queries that are composed of Abox assertions. The main idea of the query answering approach is to reformulate the query taking into account the Tbox using a set of mapping assertions. Such an assertion relates a SQL query to a union of conjunctive queries over the Tbox. That new version of the query is then evaluated over the RDBMS. Note that the reformulation of the query does not depend on the data. The main limitation of this system is the size of the rewritten query, which can be exponential with respect to the size of the original query and ontology. Thus, the reformulation can be costly to process and the evaluation of the reformulated query over the RDBMS can be costly or even unfeasible.

Requiem (Perez-Urbina et al., 2009) was one of the first systems to take this drawback into account and was aiming to produce small rewritings. The approach adopts a resolution-based query rewriting and is composed of three steps. First, a query Q and an ontology O are transformed into a set of clauses. The second step saturates the set of clauses by generating new clauses until none can be further produced. Finally in the last step, some clauses are filtered out by detecting peculiar properties of the remaining clauses, such as clauses that do not have the same head predicate as the original query are removed. This last filtering approach ensures that less queries will be evaluated, but it implies that unnecessary inferences are performed in the two previous steps, which degrades performance of the query reformulation.

The **Presto** system (Rosati and Almatelli, 2010) also addresses the limitation of QuOnto. This is performed by generating a nonrecursive Datalog program instead of a union of conjunctive queries. The resulting system has been demonstrated to be much more efficient than previous solutions and able to handle larger queries efficiently. Nevertheless, the approach tends to defer the main source of complexity to the database system.

The **Rapid** system (Chortaras et al., 2011) concentrates on the selectivity and stratification of resolution rules used to rewrite the original queries. The objective is to limit the number of unnecessary inferences and avoid redundant rewritings by taking advantage of the query structure and applying a restricted sequence of resolutions.

The **Quest** system (Rodriguez-Muro and Calvanese, 2012) is another approach that manipulates conjunctive queries to perform a complete and efficient reformulation. Note that we have already presented some of the advances of Quest in Chapter 5. More precisely, a semantic index technique is used to encode subsumption relationships of the Tbox using numerical indexes.

The last system we present here for OWL 2 QL is **Ontop** (Rodriguez-Muro et al., 2013). This system extends previous approaches with novel features that, for example, analyze database integrity constraints and SQL. This system is currently considered as the state of the art in OBDA.

Other implemented systems are **IQAROS**, **Clipper**, **Nyaya**, **Blackout** (which is the query rewriting–based reasoner of Stardog RDF Store), and Quill, which is a component of the Trowl reasoner presented later.

8.4.2.3 OWL 2 EL

The main reasoning task of OWL 2 EL is the classification of large ontologies that can be processed in polynomial time. Other services such as concept satisfiability, instance checking, and knowledge base consistency are reducible to classification. The classification algorithm requires the input ontology to be in special normal form, which can be computed in linear time and it may introduce some new concept names that are of course consistent with the former ontology. A set of completion rules is then used to derive new information. The algorithm is sound, complete, and guaranteed to terminate in polynomial time.

The nice properties of OWL 2 EL have motivated the design of several reasoners, some of which are **CEL**, **jCEL**, **ELK**, **CB**, and **Pellet** (which supports all OWL 2 systems but with optimization dedicated to EL). They all adopt a materialization approach in which the Tbox is extended to explicitly introduce all subsumption relationships holding between named concepts. The systems are in general quite efficient and the CB reasoner is, for example, known to classify the 400,000 concepts of the SNOMED-CT ontology in less than 60 seconds.

The CEL system (Baader et al., 2006a) is a free noncommercial reasoner that is based on the LISP programming language. It refines the original algorithm of the EL++ DL (Baad et al., 2006b) and supports new features like module extraction. The jCEL reasoner is a rewriting of CEL in the Java programming language.

The **Snorocket** (`https://github.com/aehrc/snorocket`) is another reasoner that implements the original classification algorithm of Baader et al. (2006a). Because the derivation of concept axioms is based on a set of completion rules, it's possible to use Datalog to perform this task efficiently. This corresponds to the direction adopted in Krotzsch (2011) and that requires a preprocessing of the input knowledge base. Intuitively, each axiom is translated in to a set of EDB Datalog facts. Then all derivations, referred to as consequences, can be computed in a bottom-up manner. This work later motivated the implementation of the ELK reasoner.

These reasoners do not integrate a database management system. This is motivated by the intrinsic characteristic of OWL 2 EL, which concentrates on very large Tboxes and rather small Aboxes compared to other ontology languages. Nevertheless, these systems can interact with an RDF store to deliver inferences. This is the case of the work presented in Lutz et al. (2009), which addresses reasoning with large Aboxes in the EL fragment by using a mix of materialization and query rewriting—that is, conjunctive query answering in the EL++ DL using a relational database. The method proposed supports sound and complete query answering using an off-the-shelf relational database. The approach states that both backward and forward chaining are not adapted to OWL 2 EL.

For backward chaining, the limitation is related to the data complexity of a conjunctive query, which is higher for EL than expected (polynomial time against log space). For forward chaining, due to the presence of existential quantifiers in the right-hand side of concept inclusions, an infinite number of new database entries may be generated. The approach of this system is based on preprocessing and query rewriting steps. Both these steps are different from their counterparts in OWL 2 QL and OWL 2 RL. For example, the query reformulation does not correspond to backward chaining and is independent of both the Abox and the Tbox. It aims to store auxiliary data that can be persisted in dedicated relational tables. The complexity of query rewriting is linear time, while it's

exponential in the general case for OWL 2 QL. The preprocessing phase also has its peculiarities. For instance, its complexity is quadratic time.

Like in any standard forward-chaining approach, the auxiliary data has to be updated
every time an insert or delete operation is performed on the Abox. To the best of our
knowledge this method has not been implemented.

8.4.3 Other reasoners

In this section, we present some interesting reasoners that cover several ontology languages, such as RDFS and some OWL 2 profiles, and approaches that tackle more expressive ontology languages, such as OWL 2 DL.

TrOWL (Thomas et al., 2010), which stands for tractable reasoning infrastructure for
OWL 2, is a free and open-source system that implements conjunctive query answering
for OWL 2 QL, EL, and RL, as well as approximate reasoning for Tbox and Abox reasoning. The system is based on language transformations and so-called lightweight reasoners. In the case of conjunctive query answering, a first form of transformation based
on a semantic approximation approach is used to obtain an OWL 2 QL ontology from
an OWL 2 DL one. Such an approximation uses a heavyweight reasoner, such as Pellet,
Hermit, Racer, and Fact++, to ensure that each axiom in the approximated ontology is
valid with respect to the original ontology.

Due to semantics compatibility between OWL 2 QL and OWL 2, this approach guarantees that all reasoning computed for the approximated ontology is sound. Moreover, for
a large class of practical queries, the results are also complete. If one needs to reason over
the Tbox, a syntactic approximation is used to transform an OWL 2 DL ontology into an
OWL 2 EL one. Additionally, TrOWL provides its own implementations of some reasoning
systems, which are denoted lightweight reasoners. **Quill** and **REL** respectively provide
reasoning services over OWL 2 QL and EL. Quill is involved in the semantic approximation process, while REL is considered a core component of the syntactic approximation.

The TrOWL reasoning system has recently been integrated with the **Oracle** Spatial and Graph inference interface, composing the **OWL–DBC** system. The connection
between the two systems provides an efficient and scalable ontology query answering
service for OWL 2, considering the different levels of expressivity of available ontologies. The two systems are complementary because for small Aboxes, OWL-DBC benefits
from the in-memory approach of REL, while for large Aboxes, Oracle Spatial and Graph
provides its machinery on persisted RDF data. The OWL-DBC system can adapt to
many situations (small knowledge bases fitting in main memory or large ones in need
of persistence in secondary memory) through a configuration approach that can be
handled by the end user.

Stardog is an RDF database produced by **Clark & Parsia**, a company best known
for its Pellet OWL 2 reasoner. Therefore, the support of all OWL 2 profiles as well
as OWL 2 DL is not a surprise. A lazy, late-binding, backward-chaining approach is

adopted. The system also comes with novel features such as the support for integrity constraint violations (a component denoted as ICV) and explanations of inferences.

Finally, **SHER** (Scalable Highly Expressive Reasoner) was developed by a team at **IBM** and obviously integrates easily with DB2, but it seems to be compatible with any RDBMS. The system supports a subset of OWL 2 DL and a complete version of OWL 2 EL ontologies. The system ensures a form of scalability by pruning parts of the ontology that are not relevant to the reasoning tasks, such as by removing some roles, and via summarizing the Abox by representing similar individuals (in terms of concepts and properties associated to them) by a single individual. The knowledge base is then persisted in an RDBMS from which relevant parts are extracted and stored in memory. The system can then reason efficiently over the in-memory version or the RDBMS representation if needed.

8.5 DISTRIBUTED REASONING

To address the volume and velocity aspects of Big Data, it has been shown in the Chapter 7 that several RDF stores are going for a distributed way to manage their data sets. In this chapter, we have emphasized that reasoning is an integral part of a KBMS. Thus, it's necessary to develop systems where the reasoning task is distributed over a cluster of machines. Some key requirements for these systems are to be efficient and scalable. In this context, scalability can be evaluated in terms of the input size—that is, being able to process increasing Abox and Tbox inputs—and of computational complexity—that is, the ability to support complex reasoning tasks associated with ontology languages of expanding expressivity.

The scale-out approach of reasoning raises the issue of data communication between machines. Most existing systems follow the requirement of Big Data, which considers that the programs should be placed where the data is, rather than moving the data to the program. This considerably limits the amount of data exchanged over the network, which can rapidly become a performance bottleneck. The data transfer issue also concerns the data exchanged between cluster nodes in order to generate the complete set of inferences. Dealing with a naive transfer approach can easily saturate the network bandwidth. Most available systems agree on this data-intensive reasoning aspect but differ on the manner the parallel processing is performed and/or the way the partitioning is handled.

Several systems are based on a partitioning of the workload, which in our context can be either the Abox and/or the Tbox. An earlier study of these possibilities is studied in Soma and Prasanna (2008) for OWL ontologies. Most of the systems adopt a data partitioning instead of an ontology one. That is, the set of rules enabling inference mechanisms as well as the complete ontology are copied on all machines of the cluster and it's the data that is partitioned over the different nodes. This particularly makes sense in the case of RDFS, or one of its subsets (minimal RDFS) or close extensions (OWL

Horst), due the small number of rules, such as less than 20 in the case of RDFS. We can also consider that the size of the Tbox is way smaller than the size of the Abox in practical cases.

In a first version, the **SAOR** system (Scalable Authoritative OWL Reasoning) (Hogan et al., 2010) was designed as a reasoner performing on a single machine for a subset of OWL Horst. The materialization of triples was performed using two passes over the data. Later, the system was transformed to support OWL 2 RL in a distributed setting. The system was one of the earliest solutions to distinguish between terminological and assertional flavors of triples in rules. In that regard, this work influenced some of the systems we present next.

In Weaver and Hendler (2009), such a rule-set partitioning is considered for a materialization of all inferences in the main memory. Particular attention is given on finding properties of RDFS reasoning to partition the data. The main goal is to enable the materialization on a single pass, even for rules that are containing two antecedents. This results in the definition of five classes of rules that are mainly motivated by the number of triples in rule antecedents as well as a qualification (i.e., assertional or terminological) of these triples. This approach enables us to design a single pass on which a parallel file I/O is performed using a C/MPI (Message Passing Interface) approach. This distributed reasoning solution has been experienced on the Billion Triple Challenge at the International Semantic Web Conference (ISWC) 2009 using the BitMat RDF store presented in Chapter 5. Note that only the derivation is performed in a distributed manner and that all triples are regrouped over a single, highly compressed BitMat instance.

A first set of propositions does not depend on a given programming framework and just considers that the ontology is copied on all machines of the cluster. This is the case of **4sr** (Salvadores et al., 2011), which extends the 4Store clustered system with minimal RDFS backward reasoning. Considering the architecture point of view, the approach relies on a decomposition consisting of one process node and several storage nodes (already presented in Chapter 5). A single new component, denoted *RDF sync*, takes care of the replication of the set of reasoning rules on each of the storage nodes. This set of minimal RDFS rules is taken care of at query answering time by the `bind` function. This function matches explicit and implicit quads and communicates with the process node to return the result set of a given query. Because the 4Store system distributes the data over segments in a nonoverlapping manner, no coordination is required concerning the inferences performed over each storage node. The original organization of 4Store is considered sufficient to handle the most practical queries.

The **MaRVIN** system (Oren et al., 2009) proposes a so-called *divide-conquer-swap* method for RDFS ontologies where each node of a P2P cluster infrastructure receives a (randomly) selected portion of the Abox and a complete copy of the Tbox. Each node then computes the closure of its partition and maintains a scoring solution to identify triples that may be the most useful for further inferencing. These triples are exchanged between nodes to produce new derivations on each node. This process is repeated until no new triples are derived. This scalable and load-balanced reasoning approach can be qualified as an eventually complete inference because after a number of steps, a complete materialization will be produced. The advantages of the approach are that the original partitions are of equal size and thus prevent data, the absence of a preprocessing phase, the ability to change the reasoner to support another ontology language, and the absence of a single point of failure because no central coordination is required. The main limitations are the slow performance compared to other solutions—an average of 450,000 triples generated per second while the most efficient solutions are in the range of a couple of million triples per second—and the lack of an update and duplicate detection policy.

QueryPie (Query Parallel Inference Engine) (Urbani et al., 2011) is a hybrid forward-/backward-chaining approach that does not rely on an existing programming framework. It requires a precomputation of the inference closure, which does not correspond to a full materialization and can be performed in parallel. The goal of this precalculation is to materialize only a set of predefined rule patterns that optimizes the step of backward chaining. The system handles RDFS as well as OWL Horst ontologies and later on OWL2 RL (but on a single machine).

WebPIE (Web-scale Parallel Inference Engine) (Urbani et al., 2010) is one of the first systems to consider the Hadoop MapReduce parallel framework to reason over Semantic Web knowledge bases. The solution considers a materialization approach for the RDFS and OWL Horst ontology languages. It demonstrates that a naive modelization of the `Map` and `Reduce` functions is not adapted for an efficient computation. The paper proposes a set of optimizations consisting in loading the schema triples in memory, preprocessing the triples in the `Map` function, and joining in the `Reduce` function to avoid inference duplications and an ordering of the RDFS rule set. A solution for OWL Horst based on some additional optimizations, such as smart handling of `sameAs` triples, extends the RDFS approach. Finally, the approach is extended with an incremental reasoning solution to handle updates. It still uses the MapReduce framework and identifies previously inferred triples using timestamps.

The system presented in Mutharaju et al. (2010) proposes to distribute reasoning using a MapReduce framework over OWL 2 EL ontologies. Just like in WebPIE, a naïve implementation of the `Map` and `Reduce` functions does not provide an efficient processing of inferences. One of the issues concerns the form of the original completion rules. While some of them are directly integrated in a MapReduce framework, others have to be split into multiple rules. This results in a new set of completion rules where some rules must be executed before others. This raises some important issues in this distributed context. Note that this system has not been tested over large data sets, which is the main forte of MapReduce.

Some of the most important commercial and production-ready RDF stores support distributed reasoning. This is the case for the Allegrograph, Bigdata, OWLIM, and Virtuoso systems.

The **Allegrograph** system proposes two forms of reasoning. A first one, denoted *RDFS++ reasoner*, generates derived triples at query runtime but does not store them in the triples stores. This approach is named *dynamic materialization* and is supposed to support fast access to inferred triples resulting from some updates. **Franc Inc.**, the company behind Allegrograph, does not provide many details on the implementation of this solution. The other one is based on the OWL 2 RL ontology language and adopts a materialization approach and is therefore not adapted to frequently changing domains. Allegrograph also proposes to derive new statements by using a Prolog engine. The goal of this approach is to ease the modeling of inference rules that would be complex to specify with RDFS and OWL.

Bigdata proposes a hybrid approach of forward reasoning over some RDFS+ inference rules and backward reasoning for some other entailments. The system enables the creation of custom inference engines by selecting the rules associated to a selected set of constructs from the RDFS+ vocabulary. The maintenance of materialized triples in situations of updates (i.e., truth maintenance) is only provided for the replication cluster (i.e., scale-up) and is absent for the parallel database (i.e., scale-out).

GraphDB (formerly OWLIM) uses Sesame's library for storing and querying but makes use of its own TRREE (Triple Reasoning and Rule Entailment Engine) for all inference aspects. TRREE is based on a forward-chaining strategy and therefore enables users to generate a total materialization of derivable inferences. The semantics handled by this component must coincide with Horn rules. This corresponds to the following set of supported ontology languages: RDFS, OWL Horst, OWL Lite, a subset of OWL 2 QL, and OWL 2 RL. But this characteristic limits the ability to consider more expressive ontologies. Nevertheless, it's possible to specify its own rule set, for example, by using one of the native defined ones. This may be quite useful if one requires a special set of inference rules. Some differences exist between the OWLIM editions. In the Lite version, derived statements are stored in the main memory, therefore it's very fast but limited in terms of the size of the data sets the system can handle. The Enterprise edition stores statements on disks and provides a set of reasoning optimizations, such as handling `owl:sameAs`. The truth maintenance solution of OWLIM is naive and inefficient because the idea is to recompute all inferences when updates occur. Of course, this strategy is insufficient with the workload of an RDF store handling a large number of transactions.

Virtuoso adopts a query-time inference strategy. The backward-reasoning approach supports the RDFS ontology language extended with `owl:sameAs`, `owl:equivalentClass`, `owl:equivalentProperty`, `owl:InverseFunctionalProperty`, `owl:inverseOf`, `owl:SymmetricalProperty`, and `owl:TransitiveProperty`. The system adopts a rule-based solution.

Table 8.6 Summary of Distributed Reasoning Systems

System	Chaining	Language	Distribution approach	Query processing	Size (triples) (M: million, B: billion, T: trillion , NC: Not Communicated)
4Store	Backward	Minimal RDFS	Partitioning	Yes	15 B
QueryPie	Hybrid	OWL Horst	Partitioning	No	1 B
WebPIE	Forward	RDFS, OWL Horst	MapReduce	No	100 B
SAOR	Forward	OWL 2 RL	Partitioning	No	1.1 B
MaRVIN	Forward	RDFS	Partitioning	No	1.12 B
(Weaver and Hendler, 2009)	Forward	Weak RDFS	Partitioning	No	NC
Bigdata	Hybrid	RDFS+		Yes	13 B
MapReduce EL+		OWL EL	MapReduce	No	NC
OWLim	Forward	RDFS, OWL Horst, OWL 2 QL and RL	Partitioning	Yes	20 B
Virtuoso	Backward	RDFS++	Partitioning	Yes	100 B
Allegrograph	Dynamic ma-terialization	RDFS++	Partitioning	Yes	1 T
RDFox	Forward	OWL 2 RL	Partitioning	Yes	250 M

RDFox (Motik et al., 2014) is tackling the OWL 2 RL profile by proposing a dynamic partitioning of rule instantiations to prevent data skews. Based on the partitioning, the materialization of implicit triples can be performed in parallel and stored in the main memory as the explicit triples. To be efficient, the store relies on a hash-based indexing solution.

Table 8.6 presents a summary of the distributed reasoning systems we have presented in this section.

8.6 SUMMARY

- The most advanced academic systems (RDF-3X, SW Store, Hexastore) do not implement any forms of reasoning services.
- Most commercial systems implement some form of reasoning.
- Two forms of rule-based reasoning are available: materialization (a.k.a. forward chaining) and query rewriting (a.k.a. backward chaining).
- Materialization requires a preprocessing step to persist all inferred statements, therefore it provides fast query answering. This approach can be considered when the data

rarely changes and the query workload is read intensive. In situations of high update rates, this approach suffers from the maintenance of inferred facts maintenance.

- Query rewriting does not require any preprocessing because it performs derivations at query time, which implies slow query answering. This solution is adapted when the data frequently changes or the size of the inference closure is too large to materialize. In the case of high read rates, this solution suffers from slow query performances.

- RDF stores with reasoning facilities usually adopt ontology languages ranging in the RDFS expressiveness with some systems tackling OWL2 fragments, e.g., RL. This is due to the associated complexity of reasoning with OWL 2 ontologies.

- Research conducted on distributed inference services is very active. Most production-ready systems provide such services.

CHAPTER NINE

Conclusion

The need to manage enormous quantities of data has never been greater. This fact is mainly due to the expansion of the Web and the load of information that can be harvested from our interactions with it, such as via personal computers, laptops, smartphones, and tablet devices. This data can be represented using various models and in the context of use cases thriving on the Web—that is, for social, geographical, recommendations, bioinformatics, network management, and fraud detection, to name a few, the graph data model is a particularly relevant choice.

RDF, with its W3C recommendation status and its set of companions like SPARQL, SKOS, RDFS, and OWL, plays a primordial role in the graph data model ecosystem. The quantity and quality of tools, such as parsers, editors, and APIs, implemented to ease the use of RDF data attests for the strong enthusiasm surrounding this standard, as well as the importance to manage this data appropriately. The number of academic, open-source and commercial RDF stores presented in this book emphasize the importance of this tool category, the diversity of possible approaches, as well as the complexity to design efficient systems. After all, we can consider that the potential of the Web of Data and the Semantic Web movements largely depends on the ability to address the storage, querying, and reasoning issues of RDF.

It's precisely this Web aspect that makes RDF stores so special compared to RDBMS and NoSQL systems. The Web-scale data integration, provided by the ability to follow URIs from one query answer to another, opens up new perspectives that cannot be tackled natively and easily by other database management systems. The heterogeneous distributed systems, and in particular federation query engines, presented in Chapter 7 exemplify this capacity. Nevertheless, to reach the Holy Grail of considering the World Wide Web a queryable database, a lot of efforts have to be conducted in dimensions that we have already unveiled. Next, we present the challenges that have to be overcome and then some features that are expected in future systems. Finally, we propose a vision on the use of RDF stores.

9.1 CHALLENGES

The management of update operations in RDF stores is currently not satisfactory in terms of performance. As a consequence, most of the big projects that we know of using production-ready RDF stores are taking a bulk-loading approach on the modifications they are performing on their databases. This is reminiscent of the OLAP systems where large transactions are periodically executed with usually the effect of blocking, for consistency reasons, the database access for a long period of time. This is to be opposed to the OLTP approach, which is characterized by a high rate of frequent short transactions. Although, we can argue that the typical use case of RDF stores corresponds to data discovery through data integration—that is, OLAP. This still makes the current poor update performances far from ideal.

In Chapter 8 we emphasized that this update limitation is exacerbated in the context of reasoning. Recall that the two main approaches to handle reasoning are materialization and query rewriting, which are respectively characterized by fast read/slow writes and slow read/fast writes.

We have emphasized that the schemaless property of RDF provides some flexiblility that can be an asset when designing a database management system. It can also be a limitation when one wants to express complex queries, i.e., requiring a rich navigation in a graph. This is even amplified when one writes queries in a query federation context where many graphs are being used. We consider that providing a simple and powerful interface for data integration in the Web of Data is one important challenge.

9.2 EXPECTED FEATURES

There are at least four features that seem to be needed in RDF stores. First is a feature that is already present in RDBMS but is missing in most RDF stores: support for integrity constraints. Several research projects have been conducted in this direction. In some of them, ontology assertions can be used for detecting integrity violations while others depend on end-user-defined rules. In general, the absence of such mechanisms disturbs users coming from a RDBMS background. This is the reason why we expect support for integrity constraints to appear more frequently in RDF stores. To the best of our knowledge, **Stardog** is the only system that integrates such a feature through an *integrity constraint validation* (ICV) component via the definition of rules.

With its flexible model, RDF is a great playground for data provenance, a feature that is attracting a lot of attention along all DBMSs. This aims at providing metadata on the lineage of data to qualify its quality, reliability, or trustworthiness. The PROV W3C recommendation (http://www.w3.org/TR/prov-overview/) aims at supporting an interoperable interchange of provenance information in environments such as the Web.

With the evolution of the Big Data phenomenon, streaming facilities in databases are needed. This feature enables the processing of a flow of fast-arriving information, e.g., think about sensors sending information every 10 s about the temperature and humidity rate of every room in a skyscraper. Due to a high throughput, it may not possible store all coming information. Hence, decision making over those streams is required to identify if a particular incoming information is worth persisting in the RDF stores. Such stream processing may require some data transformation or summarization. Several solutions have been proposed toward this direction, such as a query processing solution for SPARQL extensions like C-SPARQL (Barbieri et al., 2010) and CQELS (Le-Phuoc et al., 2011).

Finally, considering that RDF stores currently fit into an OLAP approach, we believe that query facilities, SPARQL extensions, or some other query language should be developed toward business analytics and intelligence, such as graph measures and clustering.

9.3 THE FUTURE OF RDF STORES

With the amount of RDF data being produced, the future seems bright for RDF stores. To accelerate their adoption, the overall picture of its ecosystem needs to be clearer. For instance, we know many projects where project leaders are having a hard time trying to decide which system to adopt. Note that the same can be said for the whole DBMS market because the standard row-oriented RDBMSs have several fierce competitors like NoSQL and NewSQL.

We agree with the vision of Martin Fowler (Sadalage and Fowler, 2013) that considers that "we are entering a world of Polyglot Persistence where enterprises, and even individual applications, use multiple technologies for data management" (p. 1). We are convinced that RDF stores, with their flexibility, data integration, and reasoning facilities, will find their place in the polyglot persistence landscape. A typical architecture may require a NoSQL key value store for serving a fast access to cached data, a standard RDBMS or NewSQL database to support high transaction rates, a RDF store to serve as a data warehouse and to enable data integration of Linked Open Data.

REFERENCES

Abadi, D.J., 2007. Column stores for wide and sparse data. CIDR, 292–297.

Abadi, D., Madden, S., Ferreira, M., 2006. Integrating compression and execution in column-oriented database systems. In: Proceedings of the 2006 ACM SIGMOD International Conference on Management of Data. ACM Press, New York, pp. 671–682.

Abadi, D.J., Marcus, A., Madden, S., Hollenbach, K.J., 2007a. Scalable semantic web data management using vertical partitioning. VLDB, 411–422.

Abadi, D.J., Myers, D.S., DeWitt, D.J., Madden, S.R., 2007b. Materialization strategies in a column-oriented DBMS. International Conference on Data Engineering, 466–475.

Abadi, D.J., Marcus, A., Madden, S., Hollenbach, K., 2009. Sw-store: a vertically partitioned DBMS for semantic web data management. VLDB 18 (2), 385–406.

Abiteboul, S., Hull, R., Vianu, V., 1995. Foundations of Databases. Addison-Wesley, Reading, MA.

Acciarri, A., Calvanese, D., De Giacomo, G., Lembo, D., Lenzerini, M., Palmieri, M., Rosati, R., 2005. Quonto: Querying ontologies. AAAI, 1670–1671.

Acosta, M., Vidal, M.-E., Lampo, T., Castillo, J., Ruckhaus, E., 2011. Anapsid: An adaptive query processing engine for SPARQL endpoints. International Semantic Web Conference 1, 18–34.

Adida, B., Birbeck, M., McCarron, S., Pemberton, S., 2008. RDFa in XHTML: syntax and processing—a collection of attributes and processing rules for extending XHTML to support RDF. W3C Recommendation.

Agrawal, R., Borgida, A., Jagadish, H.V., 1989. Efficient management of transitive relationships in large data and knowledge bases. In: Proc. of the ACM SIGMOD Int. Conf. on Management of Data, Portland, Oregon, pp. 253–262..

Akar, Z., Halaç, T.G., Ekinci, E.E., Dikenelli, O., 2012. Querying the web of interlinked datasets using void descriptions. LDOW, 10.

Alexaki, S., Christophides, V., Karvounarakis, G., Plexousakis, D., Tolle, K., 2001. The ICS-forth RDF suite: managing voluminous RDF description bases. In: 2nd International Workshop on the Semantic Web, Hong Kong, pp. 1–13.

Allemang, D., Hendler, J.A., 2011. Semantic Web for the Working Ontologist: Effective Modeling in RDFS and OWL, 2nd Edition Morgan Kaufmann, San Francisco.

Angles, R., Gutierrez, C., 2005. Querying RDF data from a graph database perspective. In: Proceedings of the Second European Semantic Web Conference, pp. 346–360.

Angles, R., Gutiérrez, C., 2008. Survey of graph database models. ACM Computing Survey 40 (1), 1–39.

Aranda, C.B., Hogan, A., Umbrich, J., Vandenbussche, P.-Y., 2013. Sparql web-querying infrastructure: Ready for action? International Semantic Web Conference 2, 277–293.

Arenas, M., Gutierrez, C., Perez, J., 2009. Foundations of RDF databases. In: Reasoning Web, 158–204. Available at: http://www.w3.org/2001/05/rdf-ds/DataStore

Atre, M., J, J.S., Hendler, J.A., 2009. Bitmat: a main memory RDF triple store. Technical report.

Atre, M., Chaoji, V., Zaki, M.J., Hendler, J.A., 2010. Matrix "bit" loaded: A scalable lightweight join query processor for RDF data. WWW, 41–50.

Baader, F., Calvanese, D., McGuinness, D.L., Nardi, D., Patel-Schneider, P.F. (Eds.), 2003. The Description Logic Handbook: Theory, Implementation, and Applications. Cambridge University Press, New York.

Baader, F., Lutz, C., Suntisrivaraporn, B., 2006a. Cel—A polynomial-time reasoner for life science ontologies. IJCAR, 287–291.

Baader, F., Lutz, C., Suntisrivaraporn, B., 2006. Efficient reasoning in EL+. Description Logics, 12.

Barbieri, D.F., Braga, D., Ceri, S., Valle, E.D., Grossniklaus, M., 2010. Querying RDF streams with C-SPARQL. SIGMOD Record 39 (1), 20–26.

Barstow, A., 2001. Survey of RDF/triple data stores. Technical report. available at http://www.w3.org/2001/05/rdf-ds/DataStore

Beckett, D., 2001. The design and implementation of the Redland RDF application framework. In: Proceedings of the 10th International Conference on World Wide Web. ACM Press, New York, pp. 449–456.

Beckett, D., 2002. Scalability and storage: survey of free software/open source RDF storage systems. Technical report 10.1, SWAD-Europe, http://www.w3.org/2001/sw/Europe/reports/rdf scalable storage report/.

Berners-Lee, T., 2006. Notation 3, http://www.w3.org/DesignIssues/Notation3.html/

Berners-Lee, T., Hendler, J., Lassila, O., 2001. The semantic web. Scientific American 284 (5), 34–43.

Bönström, V., Hinze, A., Schweppe, H., 2003. Storing RDF as a graph. In: Proceedings of the First Conference on Latin American Web Congress. IEEE Computer Society, Washington, DC, p. 27.

Bornea, M.A., Dolby, J., Kementsietsidis, A., Srinivas, K., Dantressangle, P., Udrea, O., Bhattacharjee, B., 2013. Building an efficient RDF store over a relational database. In: SIGMOD Conference, New York, NY, USA, pp. 121–132.

Bourgeois, N., Escoffier, B., Paschos, V.T., van Rooij, J.M.M., 2010. A bottom-up method and fast algorithms for max independent set. In: Kaplan, H. (Ed.), SWAT, Lecture Notes in Computer Science, vol. 6139, Springer Berlin Heidelberg, pp. 62–73.

Brachman, R.J., Levesque, H.J., 2004. Knowledge Representation and Reasoning. Elsevier, Boston.

Brewer, E.A., 2000. Towards robust distributed systems (abstract). In: Proceedings of the Nineteenth Annual ACM Symposium on Principles of Distributed Computing. ACM Press, New York, p. 7.

Brickley, D., Guha, R., 2004. RDF vocabulary description language 1.0: RDF schema. W3C Recommendation.

Bröcheler, M., Pugliese, A., Subrahmanian, V.S., 2009. DOGMA: a disk-oriented graph matching algorithm for RDF databases. In: The Semantic Web – ISWC 2009, Proceedings of 8th International Semantic Web Conference, ISWC 2009, Chantilly, VA, USA, October 25–29, 2009, 97–113.

Broekstra, J., Kampman, A., Harmelen, F.V., 2002. Sesame: a generic architecture for storing and querying RDF and RDF schema. In: ISWC, pp. 54–68.

Bshouty, N.H., Falk, G.T., 1992. Compression of dictionaries via extensions to front coding. In: Koczkodaj, W.W., Lauer, P.E., Toptsis, A.A. (Eds.), ICCI. IEEE Computer Society, pp. 361–364.

Burrows, M., Wheeler, D.J., Burrows, M., Wheeler, D.J., 1994. A block-sorting lossless data compression algorithm. Technical report.

Cai, M., Frank, M., Chen, J., Szekely, P., 2003. MAAN: A multi-attribute addressable network for grid information services. Journal of Grid Computing, IEEE Computer Society, p.184.

Cai, M., Frank, M., 2004. RDFPeers: A scalable distributed RDF repository based on a structured peer-to-peer network. In: Proceedings of the 13th International Conference on the World Wide Web. ACM Press, New York, pp. 650–657.

Carroll, J.J., Stickler, P., 2004. Trix: RDF triples in XML. Technical report HPL-2004-56, HP Labs.

Chang, F., Dean, J., Ghemawat, S., Hsieh, W.C., Wallach, D.A., Burrows, M., Chandra, T., Fikes, A., Gruber, R., 2006. Bigtable: A distributed storage system for structured data. OSDI, 205–218.

Chong, E.I., Das, S., Eadon, G., Srinivasan, J., 2005. An efficient SQL-based RDF querying scheme. In: Proceedings of the 31st International Conference on Very Large Databases. VLDB Endowment, pp. 1216–1227.

Chortaras, A., Trivela, D., Stamou, G.B., 2011. Optimized query rewriting for OWL 2 QL. CADE, 192–206.

Codd, E.F., 1970. A relational model of data for large shared data banks. Communication ACM 13 (6), 377–387.

Connolly, D., 2007. Gleaning resource descriptions from dialects of languages (GRDDL). Technical report.

Copeland, G.P., Khoshafian, S.N., 1985. A decomposition storage model. In: Proceedings of the 1985 ACM SIGMOD International Conference on Management of Data. ACM Press, New York, pp. 268–279.

Corbett, J.C., Dean, J., Epstein, M., Fikes, A., Frost, C., Furman, J.J., Ghemawat, S., Gubarev, A., Heiser, C., Hochschild, P., Hsieh, W.C., Kanthak, S., Kogan, E., Li, H., Lloyd, A., Melnik, S., Mwaura, D., Nagle, D., Quinlan, S., Rao, R., Rolig, L., Saito, Y., Szymaniak, M., Taylor, C., Wang, R., Woodford, D., 2013. Spanner: Google's globally distributed database. ACM Transactions on Computer Systems 31 (3), 8.

Cudré-Mauroux, P., Enchev, I., Fundatureanu, S., Groth, P.T., Haque, A., Harth, A., Keppmann, F.L., Miranker, D.P., Sequeda, J., Wylot, M., 2013. NoSQL databases for RDF: An empirical evaluation. International Semantic Web Conference 2, 310–325.

Dean, J., Ghemawat, S., 2004. MapReduce: Simplified data processing on large clusters. OSDI, 137–150.

DeCandia, G., Hastorun, D., Jampani, M., Kakulapati, G., Lakshman, A., Pilchin, A., Sivasubramanian, S., Vosshall, P., Vogels, W., 2007. Dynamo: Amazon's highly available key-value store. SOSP, 205–220.

DeHaan, D., Toman, D., Consens, M.P., Ozsu, M.T., 2003. A comprehensive XQuery to SQL translation using dynamic interval encoding. In: Proc. of the ACM SIGMOD Int. Conf. on Management of Data, San Diego, USA, pp. 623–634.

DeWitt, D., Gray, J., 1992. Parallel database systems: The future of high performance database systems. Communication ACM 35 (6), 85–98.

Ding, L., Wilkinson, K., Sayers, C., Kuno, H., 2003. Application-specific schema design for storing large RDF datasets. In: First International Workshop on Practical and Scalable Semantic Systems, pp. 1–14.

Dong, X., Halevy, A.Y., 2007. Indexing dataspaces. In: SIGMOD Conference, pp. 43–54.

Elmasri, R., Navathe, S., 2010. Fundamentals of Database Systems. Prentice Hall International, 6 edition.

Erling, O., Mikhailov, I., 2007. RDF support in the Virtuoso DBMS. In: Auer, S., Bizer, C., Mller, C., Zhdanova, A.V. (Eds.), Conference on Social Semantic Web, LNI, vol. 13, pp. 59–68.

Fernandez, J.D., Martinez-Prieto, M.A., Gutierrez, C., 2010. Compact representation of large RDF data sets for publishing and exchange. In: International Semantic Web Conference, vol. 1, pp. 193–208.

Ferragina, P., Manzini, G., 2000. Opportunistic data structures with applications. In: 41st Annual Symposium on Foundations of Computer Science, FOCS 2000, November 12–14, 2000, Redondo Beach, California, USA, pp. 390–398.

Fletcher, G.H., Beck, P.W., 2009. Scalable indexing of RDF graphs for efficient join processing. In: Proceeding of the 18th ACM Conference on Information and Knowledge Management. ACM Press, New York, pp. 1513–1516.

Franklin, M.J., Halevy, A.Y., Maier, D., 2005. From databases to dataspaces: A new abstraction for information management. SIGMOD Record 34 (4), 27–33.

Galarraga, L., Hose, K., Schenkel, R., 2012. Partout: a distributed engine for efficient RDF processing. CoRR, abs/1212.5636.

Gibbons, A., 1985. Algorithmic Graph Theory. Cambridge University Press, Cambridge.

Gilbert, S., Lynch, N.A., 2002. Brewer's conjecture and the feasibility of consistent, available, partition-tolerant web services. SIGACT News 33 (2), 51–59.

Goasdoué, F., Manolescu, I., Roatis, A., 2013. Efficient query answering against dynamic RDF databases. EDBT, 299–310.

Gospodnetic, O., Hatcher, E., McCandless, M., 2009. Lucene in Action, second ed. Manning Publications, New York, USA, p. 475. ISBN 1-9339-8817-7.

Görlitz, O., Staab, S., 2011. Splendid: SPARQL endpoint federation exploiting void descriptions. COLD, 12.

Grosof, B.N., Horrocks, I., Volz, R., Decker, S., 2003. Description logic programs: Combining logic programs with description logic. WWW, pp. 48–57.

Grossi, R., Gupta, A., Vitter, J.S., 2003. High-order entropy-compressed text indexes. SODA, 841–850.

Guha, R.V., 2000. RDFDB: an RDF database, http://www.guha.com/rdfdb/

Harizopoulos, S., Liang, V., Abadi, D.J., Madden, S., 2006. Performance tradeoffs in read-optimized databases. In: Proceedings of the 32nd International Conference on Very Large Databases. VLDB Endowment. pp. 487–498.

Harizopoulos, S., Abadi, D.J., Madden, S., Stonebraker, M., 2008. OLTP through the looking glass, and what we found there. In: SIGMOD Conference, Chantilly, VA, USA, pp. 981–992.

Harris, S., Gibbins, N., 2003. 3Store: efficient bulk RDF storage, http://ceur-ws.org/Vol-89/harris-et-al.pdf.

Harris, S., Lamb, N., Shadbol, N., 2009. 4Store: The design and implementation of a clustered RDF store. In: Proceedings of the 5th International Workshop on Scalable Semantic Web Knowledge Base Systems, 16.

Harth, A., Decker, S., 2005. Optimized index structures for querying RDF from the web. In: Proceedings of the Third Latin American Web Congress. IEEE Computer Society, Washington, DC, pp. 71–80.

Harth, A., Umbrich, J., Hogan, A., Decker, S., 2007. Yars2: A federated repository for querying graph structured data from the web. In: Proceedings of the 6th International Semantic Web Conference and 2nd Asian Semantic Web Conference, Busan, South Korea, LNCS, 3825. Springer, Berlin, pp. 211–224.

Hausenblas, M., Adida, B., 2007. RDFA in HTML overview.

Hayes, P., 2004. RDF semantics. Available at http://www.w3.org/TR/2004/REC-rdf-mt-20040210/

Hogan, A., Pan, J.Z., Polleres, A., Decker, S., 2010. SAOR: template rule optimizations for distributed reasoning over 1 billion linked data triples. In: International Semantic Web Conference, vol. 1, pp. 337–353.

Huang, J., Abadi, D.J., Ren, K., 2011. Scalable SPARQL querying of large RDF graphs. PVLDB 4 (11), 1123–1134.

Husain, M.F., Khan, L., Kantarcioglu, M., Thuraisingham, B.M., 2010. Data intensive query processing for large RDF graphs using cloud computing tools. IEEE CLOUD, 1–10.

Jacobson, G., 1989. Space-efficient static trees and graphs. FOCS, 549–554.

Janik, M., Kochut, K., 2005. Brahms: A workbench RDF store and high performance memory system for semantic association discovery. 4th International Semantic Web Conference. Springer, Berlin Heidelberg, pp. 431–445.

Kaoudi, Z., Koubarakis, M., Kyzirakos, K., Miliaraki, I., Magiridou, M., Papadakis-Pesaresi, A., 2010. Atlas: Storing, updating and querying RDF(s) data on top of DHTS. Journal of Web Semantics 8 (4), 271–277.

Karvounarakis, G., Alexaki, S., Christophides, V., Plexousakis, D., Scholl, M., 2002. RQL: A declarative query language for RDF. In: Proceedings of the 11th International Conference on World Wide Web. ACM Press, New York, pp. 592–603.

Kifer, M., Bernstein, A., Lewis, P.M., 2005. Database Systems: An Application Oriented Approach, Complete Version (2nd Edition). Addison-Wesley Longman Publishing Co., Inc., Boston, MA, USA.

Klyne, G., Carroll, J.J., 2004. Resource description framework (RDF): Concepts and abstract syntax. Technical report, W3C Recommendation 0, http://www.w3.org/TR/rdf-concepts/.

Kolas, D., Emmons, I., Dean, M., 2009. Efficient linked-list RDF indexing in parliament. In: Proceedings of the 5th International Workshop on Scalable Semantic Web Knowledge Base Systems. IEEE Computer Society, Washington, DC, pp. 17–32.

Krötzsch, M., 2011. Efficient rule-based inferencing for OWL EL. IJCAI, 2668–2673.

Ladwig, G., Harth, A., 2011. Cumulus RDF: Linked data management on nested key-value stores. In: Proceedings of the 7th International Workshop on Scalable Semantic Web Knowledge Base Systems at the 10th International Semantic Web Conference (ISWC2011), Springer Berlin Heidelberg, pp. 30-42.

Ladwig, G., Tran, T., 2010. Linked data query processing strategies. In: International Semantic Web Conference, vol. 1, pp. 453–469.

Larsson, N.J., Moffat, A., 1999. Offline dictionary-based compression. In: Data Compression Conference, DCC 1999, Snowbird, Utah, USA, March 29–31, 1999, pp. 296–305.

Le-Phuoc, D., Dao-Tran, M., Parreira, J.X., Hauswirth, M., 2011. A native and adaptive approach for unified processing of linked streams and linked data. In: Proceedings of the 10th International Conference on the Semantic Web. Springer, Berlin, pp. 370–388.

Levesque, H.J., 1984. Foundations of a functional approach to knowledge representation. Artificial Intelligence 23 (2), 155–212.

Lutz, C., Toman, D., Wolter, F., 2009. Conjunctive query answering in the description logic el using a relational database system. IJCAI, pp. 2070–2075.

Maduko, A., Anyanwu, K., Sheth, A.P., Schliekelman, P., 2008. Graph summaries for subgraph frequency estimation. ESWC, pp. 508–523.

Magkanaraki, A., Karvounarakis, G., Christophides, V., Plexousakis, P., Anh, T.T., 2002. Ontology storage and querying. Technical report 308, ICS-FORTH.

Martinez-Prieto, M.A., Gallego, M.A., Fernandez, J.D., 2012. Exchange and consumption of huge RDF data. ESWC, 437–452.

Matono, A., Pahlevi, S., Kojima, I., 2007. RDFCube: A P2P-based three-dimensional index for structural joins on distributed triple stores. Databases, Information Systems, and Peer-to-Peer Computing, 323–330.

McBride, B., 2002. Jena: A semantic web toolkit. IEEE Internet Computing 6 (6), 55–59.

McGlothlin, J., Khan, L.R., 2009a. RDFJoin: a scalable of data model for persistence and efficient querying of RDF datasets. Technical report UTDCS-08-09, UTDCS-08-09.

McGlothlin, J.P., Khan, L.R., 2009b. RDFKB: Efficient support for RDF inference queries and knowledge management. In: Proceedings of the 2009 International Database Engineering Applications Symposium. ACM Press, New York, pp. 259–266.

Morrison, D.R., 1968. Practical algorithm to retrieve information coded in alphanumeric. Journal of ACM 15 (4), 514–534.

Motik, B., Nenov, Y., Piro, R., Horrocks, I., Olteanu, D., 2014. Parallel materialization of Datalog programs in centralized, main-memory RDF systems. In: Brodley, C.E., Stone, P. (Eds.), In: Proceedings of the 28th AAAI Conference on Artificial Intelligence (AAAI 2014), pp. 129–137.

Muñoz, S., Pérez, J., Gutierrez, C., 2009. Simple and efficient minimal RDFS. Journal of Web Semantics 7 (3), 220–234.

Munro, J.I., 1996. Tables. FSTTCS, 37–42.

Mutharaju, R., Hitzler, P., Mateti, P., 2013a. Distel: A distributed EL+ ontology classiffier. SSWS@ISWC, 17–32.

Mutharaju, R., Sakr, S., Sala, A., Hitzler, P., 2013b. D-SPARQ: distributed, scalable and efficient RDF query engine. In: International Semantic Web Conference (Posters & Demos), Sydney, NWS, Australia, pp. 261–264.

Mutharaju, R., Maier, F., Hitzler, P., 2010. A mapreduce algorithm for el+. In: Description logics.

Myung, J., Yeon, J., Lee, S.-G., 2010. SPARQL basic graph pattern processing with iterative MapReduce. In: Proceedings of the 2010 Workshop on Massive Data Analytics on the Cloud. ACM Press, New York, pp. 6:1–16.

Nejdl, W., Wolf, B., Qu, C., Decker, S., Sintek, M., Naeve, A., Nilsson, M., Palmer, M., Risch, T., 2002. Edutella: a P2P networking infrastructure based on RDF. WWW, pp. 604–615.

Nejdl, W., Wolpers, M., Siberski, W., Schmitz, C., Schlosser, M., Brunkhorst, I., Löser, A., 2003. Super-peer-based routing and clustering strategies for RDF-based peer-to-peer networks. In: Proceedings of the 12th International Conference on World Wide Web. ACM Press, New York, pp. 536–543.

Neumann, T., Weikum, G., 2008. RDF-3X: a RISC-style engine for RDF. Proceedings of VLDB Endowment 1 (1), 647–659.

Neumann, T., Weikum, G., 2009. Scalable join processing on very large RDF graphs. In: SIGMOD Conference, Indianapolis, Indiana, USA, pp. 627–640.

Neumann, T., Weikum, G., 2010. X-RDF-3X: Fast querying, high update rates, and consistency for RDF databases. PVLDB 3 (1), 256–263.

NIST Big Data. Definitions and Taxonomies Version 1.0, p. 4. Available at bigdatawg.nist.gov/_uploadfiles/M0142_v1_3364795506.docx

Oren, E., Kotoulas, S., Anadiotis, G., Siebes, R., ten Teije, A., van Harmelen, F., 2009. Marvin: Distributed reasoning over large scale semantic web data. Journal of Web Semantics 7 (4), 305–316.

Pérez-Urbina, H., Horrocks, I., Motik, B., 2009. Efficient query answering for OWL 2. In: International Semantic Web Conference, Chantilly, VA, USA pp. 489–504.

Picalausa, F., Luo, Y., Fletcher G.H.L., Hidders, J., Vansaummeren, S., 2012. A Structural approach to indexing triples. In: ESWC, Heraklion, Crete, Greece, pp. 406–421.

Prasser, F., Kemper, A., Kuhn, K.A., 2012. Efficient distributed query processing for autonomous RDF databases. EDBT, 372–383.

Pritchett, D., 2008. Base: An acid alternative. ACM Queue 6 (3), 48–55.

Prud'hommeaux, E., Seaborne, A., 2007. SPARQL query language for RDF (working draft). Technical report, W3C.

Pu, X., Wang, J., Luo, P., Wang, M., 2011. Aweto: Efficient incremental update and querying in RDF storage system. In: Proceedings of the 20th ACM International Conference on Information and Knowledge Management. ACM Press, New York, pp. 2445–2448.

Quilitz, B., Leser, U., 2008. Querying distributed RDF data sources with SPARQL. ESWC, 524–538.

Robinson, J.A., 1965. A machine-oriented logic based on the resolution principle. Journal of ACM 12 (1), 23–41.

Rodriguez-Muro, M., Calvanese, D., 2012. High performance query answering over DL-lite ontologies. KR, Roma, Italy.

Rodriguez-Muro, M., Calvanese, D., 2012. High performance query answering over DL-Lite ontologies. In: Rodriguez-Muro, M., Kontchakov, R., Zakharyaschev, M. (Eds.), Ontology-based data access: ontop of databases. International Semantic Web Conference, vol. 1, pp. 558–573.

Rohloff, K., Schantz, R.E., 2010. High performance, massively scalable distributed systems using the MapReduce software framework: The shard triple-store. PSI EtA, 4.

Rosati, R., Almatelli, A., 2010. Improving query answering over DL-Lite ontologies. KR, pp. 290–300.

Sadalage, P.J., Fowler, M., 2013. NoSQL Distilled: A Brief Guide to the Emerging World of Polyglot Persistence, 2nd Edition Addison-Wesley, Reading, MA.

Saleem, M., Ngomo, A.-C.N., 2014. Hibiscus: Hypergraph-based source selection for SPARQL endpoint federation. ESWC, 176–191.

Saleem, M., Ngomo, A.-C. N., Parreira, J.X., Deus, H.F., Hauswirth, M., 2013. DAW: Duplicate-aware federated query processing over the web of data. In: International Semantic Web Conference, vol. 1, Sydney, NWS, Australia, pp. 574–590.

Salvadores, M., Correndo, G., Harris, S., Gibbins, N., Shadbolt, N., 2011. The design and implementation of minimal RDFS backward reasoning in 4Store. ESWC 2, 139–153.

Schätzle, A., Przyjaciel-Zablocki, M., Hornung, T., Lausen, G., 2013. PigSPARQL: a SPQRQL query processing baseline for big data. In: International Semantic Web Conference (Posters & Demos), Sydney, NWS, Australia, pp. 241–244.

Schwarte, A., Haase, P., Hose, K., Schenkel, R., Schmidt, M., 2011. FedX: A federation layer for distributed query processing on linked open data. ESWC 2, 481–486.

Seaborne, A., 2004. RDQL: a query language for RDF. Technical report, W3C (proposal).

Sidirourgos, L., Goncalves, R., Kersten, M., Nes, N., Manegold, S., 2008. Column-store support for RDF data management: not all swans are white. Proceedings of the VLDB Endowment 1 (2), 1553–1563.

Soma, R., Prasanna, V.K., 2008. Parallel inferencing for OWL knowledge bases. In: Proceedings of the 2008 37th International Conference on Parallel Processing. IEEE Computer Society, Washington, DC, pp. 75–82.

Stocker, M., Seaborne, A., Bernstein, A., Kiefer, C., Reynolds, D., 2008. SPARQL basic graph pattern optimization using selectivity estimation. WWW, 595–604.

Stoica, I., Morris, R., Karger, D., Kaashoek, M.F., Balakrishnan, H., 2001. Chord: a scalable peer-to-peer lookup service for internet applications. In: SIGCOMM'01, San Diego, CA, USA, pp. 149–160.

Stonebraker, M., 1986. The case for shared nothing. IEEE Database Engineering Bulletin 9 (1), 4–9.

Stonebraker, M., Abadi, D.J., Batkin, A., Chen, X., Cherniack, M., Ferreira, M., Lau, E., Lin, A., Madden, S., O'Neil, E., O'Neil, P., Rasin, A., Tran, N., Zdonik, S., 2005. C-store: A column-oriented DBMS. In: Proceedings of the 31st International Conference on Very Large Databases. VLDB Endowment. pp. 553–564.

Stonebraker, M., Abadi, D.J., DeWitt, D.J., Madden, S., Paulson, E., Pavlo, A., Rasin, A., 2010. MapReduce and parallel DBMSs: Friends or foes? Communication of ACM 53 (1), 64–71.

Stonebraker, M., Madden, S., Abadi, D.J., Harizopoulos, S., Hachem, N., Helland, P., 2007. The end of an architectural era (it's time for a complete rewrite). VLDB, 1150–1160.

ter Horst, H.J., 2005. Completeness, decidability and complexity of entailment for RDF schema and a semantic extension involving the OWL vocabulary. Journal of Web Semantics 3 (2–3), 79–115.

Thomas, E., Pan, J.Z., Ren, Y., 2010. TrOWL: tractable OWL 2 reasoning infrastructure. In: Proceedings of the Extended Semantic Web Conference, Heraklion, Crete, Greece, pp. 431–435.

Tran, T., Ladwig, G., Rudolph, S., 2009. Istore: efficient RDF data management using structure indexes for general graph structured data. Technical report, Institute AIFB, Karlsruhe Institute of Technology.

Tsatsanifos, G., Sacharidis, D., Sellis, T., 2011a. On enhancing scalability for distributed RDF/S stores. In: Proceedings of the 14th International Conference on Extending Database Technology. ACM Press, New York, pp. 141–152.

Tsatsanifos, G., Sacharidis, D., Sellis, T.K., 2011b. On enhancing scalability for distributed RDF/S stores. EDBT, 141–152.

Tsialiamanis, P., Sidirourgos, L., Fundulaki, I., Christophides, V., Boncz, P.A., 2012. Heuristics-based query optimization for SPARQL. EDBT, 324–335.

Udrea, O., Pugliese, A., Subrahmanian, V.S., 2007. GRIN: a graph based RDF index. In Proceedings of the Twenty-Second AAAI Conference on Artificial Intelligence, July 22–26, 2007, Vancouver, British Columbia, Canada, 1465–1470.

Urbani, J., Kotoulas, S., Maassen, J., van Harmelen, F., Bal, H.E., 2010. OWL reasoning with WebPIE: Calculating the closure of 100 billion triples. ESWC 1, 213–227.

Urbani, J., Maassen, J., Drost, N., Seinstra, F.J., Bal, H.E., 2013. Scalable RDF data compression with map reduce. Concurrency Comput. Practice Exp. 25 (1), 24–39.

Urbani, J., van Harmelen, F., Schlobach, S., Bal, H.E., 2011. QueryPIE: backward reasoning for OWL Horst over very large knowledge bases. In: International Semantic Web Conference, vol. 1, pp. 730–745.

Vogels, W., 2009. Eventually consistent. Communication of ACM 52 (1), 40–44.

W3C, 2004a. RDF vocabulary description language 1.0: RDF schema. http://www.w3.org/TR/rdf-schema/.

W3C, 2004b. RDF/XML syntax specification (revised). http://www.w3.org/TR/rdf-syntax-grammar/.

Weaver, J., Hendler, J.A., 2009. Parallel materialization of the finite RDFS closure for hundreds of millions of triples. In: International Semantic Web Conference, Chantilly, VA, USA, pp. 682–697.

Weiss, C., Bernstein, A., 2009. On-disk storage techniques for semantic web data: Are B-trees always the optimal solution? In: Proceedings of the 5th International Workshop on Scalable Semantic Web Knowledge Base Systems. IEEE Computer Society, Washington DC, pp. 49–64.

Weiss, C., Karras, P., Bernstein, A., 2008. Hexastore: Sextuple indexing for semantic web data management. Proceedings of the VLDB Endowment 1 (1), 1008–1019.

Wilkinson, K., 2006. Jena property table implementation. Technical Report HPL-2006-140, HP Labs.

Wilkinson, K., Sayers, C., Kuno, H.A., Reynolds, D., 2003. Efficient RDF storage and retrieval in Jena 2. SWDB, 131–150.

Williams, G.T., Weaver, J., Atre, M., Hendler, J.A., 2009. Scalable reduction of large datasets to interesting subsets. In: 8th International Semantic Web Conference (Billion Triples Challenge).

Wolff, J.G., 1975. An algorithm for the segmentation for an artificial language analogue. Br. J. Psychol. 66, 79–90.

Wood, D., Gearon, P., Adams, T., 2005. Kowari: A platform for semantic web storage and analysis. In: XTech 2005 Conference, pp. 5–13.

Yuan, P., Liu, P., Wu, B., Jin, H., Zhang, W., Liu, L., 2013. TripleBit: A fast and compact system for large scale RDF data. PVLDB 6 (7), 517–528.

Zeng, K., Yang, J., Wang, H., Shao, B., Wang, Z., 2013. A distributed graph engine for web scale RDF data. PVLDB 6 (4), 265–276.

Zou, L., Mo, J., Chen, L., Özsu, M.T., Zhao, D., 2011. GStore: Answering SPARQL queries via subgraph matching. PVLDB 4 (8), 482–493.

INDEX

Printed in the United States
By Bookmasters